1 MONTH OF
FREE
READING

at

www.ForgottenBooks.com

By purchasing this book you are eligible for one month membership to ForgottenBooks.com, giving you unlimited access to our entire collection of over 1,000,000 titles via our web site and mobile apps.

To claim your free month visit:
www.forgottenbooks.com/free212967

ISBN 978-0-260-52251-1
PIBN 10212967

THE

BENTLEY BALLADS:

𝔄 Selection

OF THE

CHOICE BALLADS, SONGS, &c., CONTRIBUTED TO
"BENTLEY'S MISCELLANY."

EDITED

By DR. DORAN,

Author of " Lives of the Queens of the House of Hanover," &c.

WITH FOUR BALLADS CONTRIBUTED BY THE EDITOR.

LONDON :

RICHARD BENTLEY, NEW BURLINGTON STREET.

1858.

LONDON:
BRADBURY AND EVANS, PRINTERS, WHITEFRIARS.

PREFACE.

In the reign of James I., there was a right merry Dean of Gloucester, who was addicted to the pleasant custom of entertaining many of his reverend brethren at dinner. On one of these occasions, the guests fell into talk as to how the Fathers might best be reconciled on certain points, whereon they differed. "Ah !" said the Dean, "if you will follow me, gentlemen, I will show you how the Fathers who differ may be made to agree." The company, therefore, followed their host to his library, where they saw a droll arrangement of the works of the Fathers in question; all the reverend authors being placed in a circle, with a quart of sack by the side of every one of them! In some such wise as the sack to the Fathers is the book of "Bentley Ballads" offered to the public. If the sack could make the Fathers agree, it is hoped that this volume may help to make their posterity laugh; and that there may be found in it something to gratify the taste, even of the more serious. The Ballads have been selected from a store that is far from being exhausted, and if this venture prove fortunate, the Editor may be tempted to dip again. Meanwhile, the bark freighted with its varied cargo, wooes a favouring gale. There is something in it for the scholar, something for the idler, something for those who love to think, something for those who love others to think for them. The grave, the gay, the lively, and the severe, may herein find something of what they lack. There is a trumpet tone for the heroic, and playfulness for gentler spirits, and mirth for those who care for it, and wit for those who admire it, and "delectable nonsense" for those who can stoop to pick up some trifles added by the Editor. As the Ballads are varied, so are the tones in which they are sung, extending from the roar and dash of the buccaneers, to the tremulous trill of the love-song, and the clashing of wine cups. In short, there is music of every measure : billows of sound to remind one of Beethoven, tones as awakening as a post-horn galop by König, or accents to dance off with the reader, gay and sparkling, like Miss Gilbert's Vandyke Polka. The reader is left to select, and after selection, it is hoped, to ask, like Oliver Twist, for "more ;"—if the request be made, ample means are at hand to provide for its prompt gratification.

J. DORAN.

November 25, 1857.

CONTENTS.

—◆—

THE
BENTLEY BALLADS.

OLD MORGAN AT PANAMA.

I.

IN the hostel-room we were seated in gloom, old Morgan's
    trustiest crew ;
No mirthful sound, no jest went round, as it erst was
    wont to do.
Wine we had none, and our girls were gone, for the last
    of our gold was spent ;
And some swore an oath, and all were wroth, and stern
    o'er the table bent ;
Till our chief on the board hurl'd down his sword, and
    spake with his stormy shout,
" Hell and the devil ! an' this be revel, we had better arm
    and out.
        Let us go and pillage old Panama,
           We, the mighty Buccaneers !"

II.

Straight at the word each girt on his sword, five hundred
    men and more ;
And we clove the sea in our shallops free, till we reach'd
    the mainland shore.
For many a day overland was our way, and our hearts
    grew weary and low,
And many would back on their trodden track, rather than
    farther go ;
But the wish was quell'd, though our hearts rebell'd, by
    old Morgan's stormy roar,—
"The way ye have sped is farther to tread, than the way
    which lies before."
           So on we march'd upon Panama,
              We, the mighty Buccaneers !

III.

'Twas just sunset when our eyes first met the sight of the
    town of gold ;
And down on the sod each knelt to his god, five hundred
    warriors bold ;
Each bared his blade, and we fervent pray'd (for it might
    be our latest prayer),
" Ransom from hell, if in fight we fell,—if we lived, for a
    booty rare !"
And each as he rose felt a deep repose, and a calm o'er all
    within ;
For he knew right well, whatever befell, his soul was
    assoil'd from sin.
           Then down we march'd on old Panama,
              We, the mighty Buccaneers !

IV.

The town arose to meet us as foes, and in order beheld us
      come ;—

They were three to one, but warriors none,—traders, and
      such like scum,

Unused to wield either sword or shield ; but they plied
      their new trade well.

I am not told how they bought and sold, but they fought
      like fiends of hell.

They fought in despair for their daughters fair, their
      wives, and their wealth, God wot !

And throughout the night made a gallant fight,—but it
      matter'd not a jot.

        For had we not sworn to take Panama,
          We, the mighty Buccaneers ?

V.

O'er dying and dead the morn rose red, and o'er streets of
      a redder dye ;

And in scatter'd spots stood men in knots, who would not
      yield or fly.

With souls of fire they bay'd our ire, and parried the hurl
      and thrust ;

But ere the sun its noon had won they were mingled with
      the dust.

Half of our host in that night we lost,—but we little for
      that had care ;

We knew right well that each that fell increased the
      survivor's share

        Of the plunder we found in old Panama,
          We, the mighty Buccaneers !

VI.

We found bars of gold, and coin untold, and gems which
      to count were vain ;
We had floods of wine, and girls divine, the dark-eyed
      girls of Spain.
They at first were coy, and baulk'd our joy, and seem'd
      with their fate downcast,
And wept and groan'd, and shriek'd and swoon'd ; but
      'twas all the same at last.
Our wooing was short, of the warrior's sort, and they
      thought it rough, no doubt ;
But, truth to tell, the end was as well as had it been
      longer about.
              And so we revell'd in Panama,
                  We, the mighty Buccaneers !

VII.

We lived in revel, sent care to the devil, for two or three
      weeks or so,
When a general thought within us wrought that 'twas
      getting time to go.
So we set to work with dagger and dirk to torture the
      burghers hoar,
And their gold conceal'd compell'd them to yield, and add
      to our common store.
And whenever a fool of the miser school declared he had
      ne'er a groat,
In charity due *we* melted a few, and pour'd them down
      his throat.
              This drink we invented at Panama,
                  We, the mighty Buccaneers !

VIII.

When the churls were eased, their bags well squeezed, we
    gave them our blessing full fain,
And we kiss'd our girls with the glossy curls, the dark-
    eyed girls of Spain;
Our booty we shared, and we all prepared for the way we
    had to roam,
When there rose a dispute as to taking our route by land
    or by water home.
So one half of the band chose to travel by land, the other
    to travel by sea:
Old Morgan's voice gave the sea the choice, and I follow'd
    his fortunes free,
        And hasten'd our leaving old Panama,
           We, the mighty Buccaneers!

IX.

A bark we equipp'd, and our gold we shipp'd, and gat us
    ready for sea;
Seventy men, and a score and ten, mariners bold were
    we.
Our mates had took leave, on the yester-eve, their way
    o'er the hills to find,
When, as morning's light pierced through the night, we
    shook her sails to the wind.
With a fresh'ning breeze we walk'd the seas, and the land
    sunk low and low'r;
A dreary dread o'er our hearts there sped we never should
    see land more—
        And away we departed from Panama,
           We, the mighty Buccaneers!

x.

For a day or two we were busy enow in setting ourselves
　　to rights,
In fixing each berth, our mess, and so forth, and the day's
　　watch and the night's;
But when these were done, over every one came the lack
　　of aught to do,
We listless talk'd, we listless walk'd, and we pined for
　　excitement new.
Oh! how we did hail any shift in the gale, for it gave us
　　a sail to trim!
We began to repent that we had not bent our steps with
　　our comrades grim.
　　　　　And thus we sail'd on from old Panama,
　　　　　　We, the mighty Buccaneers!

xi.

Day after day we had stagger'd away, with a steady breeze
　　abeam;
No shift in the gale; no trimming a sail; how dull we
　　were, ye may deem!
We sung old songs till we wearied our lungs; we push'd
　　the flagon about;
And told and re-told tales ever so old, till they fairly
　　tired us out.
There was a shark in the wake of our bark took us three
　　days to hook;
And when it was caught we wish'd it was not, for we
　　miss'd the trouble it took.
　　　　　And thus we sail'd on from old Panama,
　　　　　　We, the mighty Buccaneers!

XII.

At last it befell, some tempter of hell put gambling in
    some one's head ;
The devil's device, the cards and the dice, broke the
    stagnant life we led :
From morn till night, ay, till next morn's light, we plied
    the bones right well ;
Day after day the rattle of play clatter'd through the
    caravel.
How the winners laugh'd, how the losers quaff'd ! 'twas
    a madness, as it were.
It was a thing of shuddering to hark to the losers swear.
        And thus we sail'd on from old Panama,
           We, the mighty Buccaneers !

XIII.

From morn till night, ay, till next morn's light, for weeks
    the play kept on :
'Twas fearful to see the winners' glee, and the losers
    haggard and wan ;
You well might tell, by their features fell, they would ill
    brook to be crost ;
And one morn there was one, who all night had won
    jeer'd some who all night had lost.
He went to bed—at noon he was dead—I know not from
    what, nor reck ;
But they spake of a mark, livid and dark, about the dead
    man's neck !
        And thus we sail'd on from old Panama,
           We, the mighty Buccaneers !

XIV.

This but begun : and those who had won lived a life of
    anxious dread ;
Day after day there was bicker and fray ; and a man now
    and then struck dead.
Old Morgan stern was laugh'd to scorn, and it worried his
    heart, I trow ;
Five days of care, and his iron-grey hair was as white as
    the winter's snow :
The losers at last his patience o'erpast, for they drew
    their sword each one,
And cried, with a shout, "Hell take you ! come out, and
    fight for the gold ye have won—
        The gold that our blood bought at Panama :
          We, the mighty Buccaneers ! "

XV.

We never were slow at a word and a blow, so we cross'd
    our irons full fain ;
And for death and life had begun the strife, when old
    Morgan stopp'd it amain,
And thunder'd out with his stormy shout,—"Dogs, ye
    have had your day !
To your berths ! " he roar'd. "Who sheathes not his
    sword, Heaven grant him its grace, I pray !
For I swear, by God, I will cleave him like wood ! " There
    was one made an angry sign ;
Old Morgan heard, and he kept his word ; for he clove
    him to the chine.
        So ended *his* exploits at Panama :
          He, the mighty Buccaneer !

XVI.

At this we quail'd, and we henceforth sail'd, in a
    smouldering sort of truce;
But our dark brows gloom'd, and we inward fumed for a
    pretext to give us loose:
When early one morn—"A strange sail astern!" we heard
    the look-out-man hail;
And old Morgan shout, "Put the ship about, and crowd
    every stitch of sail!"
And around went we, surging through the sea at our island
    wild buck's pace;
In wonderment what old Morgan meant, we near'd to the
    fated chase—
        We, the pillagers of old Panama,
           We, the mighty Buccaneers!

XVII.

She went right fast, but we took her at last. 'Twas a
    little brigantine thing;
With some four men for crew, and a boy or two—a bark
    built for trafficking;
Besides this crew were three women, too: her freight was
    salt-fish and oil:
For the men on board, they were put to the sword; the
    women we spared awhile.
And all was surmise what to do with the prize, when old
    Morgan, calling us aft,
Roar'd, "Ye who have fool'd yourselves out of your gold
    take possession of yonder craft,
        And go pillage some other Panama,
           Ye, the mighty Buccaneers!

XVIII.

We were reckless and rude, we had been at feud till 'twas
     war to the very knife ;
But it clove each heart when we came to part from
     comrades in many a strife :
Over one and all a gloom seem'd to fall, and in silence
     they pack'd their gear,
Amid curses and sighs, and glistening eyes, and here and
     there a tear.
We gave brooches and things for keepsakes and rings ; and
     some truck'd the weapons they wore :
This Spanish gun was a token from one who had fought
     me a week before,
        While we diced for the spoils of old Panama,
          We, the mighty Buccaneers !

XIX.

Their traps all pack'd, there was nothing lack'd, but sharing
     the women three :
The odd one's choice was left to the dice, and she fell to
     the rich so free ;
When the losers 'gan swear the dice were unfair, and
     brawl'd till our chief gat wild,
And, without more ado, cut the woman in two, as Solomon
     shared the child.
Then each of each band shook each old mate's hand, and
     we parted with hearts full sore ;
We all that day watch'd them lessen away. They were
     never heard of more !
        We kept merrily on from old Panama,
          We, the mighty Buccaneers !

XX.

Their sufferings none know, but ours, I trow, were very,
    oh ! very sore ;
We had storm and gale till our hearts 'gan fail, and then
    calms, which harass'd us more ;
Then many fell sick ; and while all were weak, we rounded
    the fiery cape ;
As I hope for bliss in the life after this, 'twas a miracle
    our escape !
Then a leak we sprung, and to lighten us, flung all our
    gold to the element :
Our perils are past, and we're here at last, but as penniless
    as we went.
        And such was the pillage of Panama
           By the mighty Buccaneers !

                    G. E. INMAN.

Morgan, who was the son of a Welsh farmer, and who lived to be knighted, set out from Chagres with twelve hundred men, on the 18th of August, 1670. In ten days he reached Panama, which he at once attacked and destroyed. The Buccaneers left the ruins with a hundred and seventy-five beasts of burden, laden with silver, gold, and other precious articles; and with six hundred unhappy prisoners, men, women, children, and slaves.—ED.

MARS AND VENUS.

—◆—

One day upon that Trojan plain,
Where men in hecatombs were slain,
Th' immortal gods (no common sight)
Thought fit to mingle in the fight,
And found convincing proof that those
Who will in quarrels interpose
Are often doom'd to suffer harm—
Venus was wounded in the arm ;
Whilst Mars himself, the god of war,
Received an ignominious scar,
And, fairly beat by Diomed,
Fled back to heav'n and kept his bed.
That bed (the proof may still be seen)
Had long been shared with beauty's queen;
For, with th' adventure of the cage,
Vulcan had vented all his rage,*
And, like Italian husbands, he
Now wore his horns resignedly.

---

* Ovid thus speaks of the result of Vulcan's exposure of his wife's
infidelity :

"Hoc tibi profectum, Vulcane, quod ante tegebant,
    Liberius faciunt ut pudor omnis abest ;
Sæpe tamen demens stultè fecisse fateris,
    Teque ferunt iræ pœnituisse tuæ."

Ye modest critics ! spare my song :
If gods and goddesses did wrong,
And revell'd in illicit love,
As poets, sculptors, painters prove,
Is mine the fault ? and, if I tell
Some tales of scandal that befell
In heathen times, why need my lays
On ladies' cheeks more blushes raise,
When read (if such my envied lot)
In secret boudoir, bower, or grot,
Than scenes which, in the blaze of light,
They throng to witness ev'ry night ?
Ere you condemn my humble page,
Glance for a moment at the stage,
Where twirling gods to view expose
Their pliant limbs in tighten'd hose,
And goddesses of doubtful fame
   Are by lord chamberlains allow'd,
With practised postures, to inflame
   The passions of a gazing crowd :
And if great camels, such as these,
Are swallow'd with apparent ease,
Oh ! strain not at a gnat like me,
Nor deem me lost to decency,
When I now venture to declare
That Mars and Venus—guilty pair—
On the same couch extended lay,
And cursed the fortunes of the day.
The little Loves, who round them flew,
Could only sob to show their feeling,
Since they, of course, much better knew

The art of wounding than of healing,
And Cupid's self essay'd in vain
To ease his lovely mother's pain :
The chaplet that his locks confined
He tore indeed her wound to bind ;
But from her sympathetic fever
He had no nostrum to relieve her,
And, thinking that she might assuage
That fever, as she did her rage,
By talking loud,—her usual fashion
Whenever she was in a passion,—
He stóod, with looks resign'd and grave,
Prepared to hear his mother rave,
Who thus began : "Ah ! Cupid, why
Was I so silly as to try
My fortune in the battle-field,
Or seek a pond'rous spear to wield,
Which only Pallas (hated name !)
    Of all her sex can wield aright ?
What need had I of martial fame,
    Sought 'midst the dangers of the fight,
When beauty's prize, a trophy far
More precious than the spoils of war,
Was mine already, won from those
Whom rivalry has made my foes,
And who on Trojan plains would sate
E'en with my blood that ranc'rous hate
Which Ida's neighb'ring heights inflame,
And not this wound itself can tame ?
Ah ! why did I not bear in mind
That Beauty, like th' inconstant wind,

. Is always privileged to raise
The rage of others to a blaze,
Then, lull'd to rest, look calmly on,
And see the work of havoc done ?
'Twas well to urge your father, Mars,
To mingle in those hated wars ;
'Twas well—"   But piteous cries of pain,
From him she named, here broke the chain
Of her discourse, and seem'd to say,
"What want of feeling you display !"
So, turning to her wounded lover,
She kindly urged him to discover
By whom and where the wound was given,
That sent him writhing back to heaven.
The god, thus question'd, hung his head,
A burning blush of shame o'erspread
With sudden flush his pallid cheek,
As thus he answer'd : "Dost thou seek
To hear a tale of dire disgrace,
Which all those honours must efface,
That, hitherto, have made my name
Pre-eminent in warlike fame ?
Yet—since 'twas thou who bad'st me go
To fight with mortals there below—
'Tis fitting, too, that thou shouldst learn
What laurels 'twas my fate to earn.
At first, in my resistless car,
I seem'd indeed the god of war ;
The Trojans rallied at my side ;
Changed in its hue, the Xanthus' tide
Its waters to the ocean bore,

Empurpled deep in Grecian gore ;
And o'er the corpse-impeded field
The cry was still, 'They yield !—they yield !'
But soon, the flying ranks to stay,
Thy hated rivals join'd the fray :
They nerved, with some accursed charm,
Each Greek's, but most Tydides' arm,
And, Venus, thou first felt the smart
Of his Minerva-guided dart.
I saw thee wounded, saw thee fly,—
I saw the chief triumphantly
Tow'rds me his ardent coursers turn,
As though from gods alone to earn
The highest honours of the fight ;
I know not why, but, at the sight—
Eternal shame upon my head !—
A panic seized me, and I fled—
I fled, like chaff before the wind,
And, ah ! my wounds are all—behind ! "
When thus at length the truth was told,
    (The shameful truth of his disgrace,)
Again, within his mantle's fold,
    The wounded coward hid his face ; *
Whilst Venus, springing from his side,
With looks of scornful anger, cried,

---

* The ancients were seldom guilty of making the actions of their gods inconsistent with their general character and attributes; but there seems to have been much of the Captain Bobadil in the mighty god of war, and the instance of cowardice here alluded to is not the only one recorded of him by the poets. In the wars with the Titans he showed a decided "white feather," and suffered himself to be made prisoner.

"And didst thou fly from mortal foe,
Nor stay to strike one vengeful blow
For her who fondly has believed,
By all thy valorous boasts deceived,
That in the god of war she press'd
The first of heroes to her breast?
Cupid, my swans and car prepare—
To Cyprus we will hasten, where
Some youth, as yet unknown to fame,
May haply raise another flame;
For Mars may take his leave of Venus,
   No coward shall enjoy my love;
And nothing more shall pass between us,—
   I swear it by my favourite dove."
She spake; and through the realms of air,
Before the humbled god could dare
Upraise his head to urge her stay,
Already she had ta'en her way;
And in her Cyprian bower that night,
(If ancient scandal tell aright,)
Forgetful of her recent wound,
In place of Mars another found,
And to a mortal's close embraces
Surrender'd her celestial graces.
'Tis said that Venus, wont to range
Both heav'n and earth in search of change,
Was not unwilling to discover
Some pretext to desert her lover;
Nor do I combat the assertion,
But from the *cause* of her desertion,

Whilst you, fair readers, justly rail
 Against *her morals,* I will dare
To draw *this moral* for my tale—
 " None but the brave deserve the fair !"

THE "ORIGINAL" DRAGON.

A LEGEND OF THE CELESTIAL EMPIRE.

Freely translated from an undeciphered MS. of Con-fuse-us,* and dedicated to
Colonel Bolsover (of the Horse Marines), by C. J. Davids, Esq.

I.

A DESPERATE dragon, of singular size,—
  (His name was *Wing-Fang-Scratch-Claw-Fum,*)—
Flew up one day to the top of the skies,
  While all the spectators with terror were dumb.
The vagabond vow'd as he sported his tail,
  He'd have a *sky lark,* and some glorious fun :
For he'd nonplus the natives that day without fail,
  By causing a *total eclipse of the sun !* †
He collected a crowd by his impudent boast,
  (Some decently dress'd—some with hardly a rag on,)
Who said that the country was ruin'd and lost, .
  Unless they could compass the death of the *dragon.*

---

* "Better known to illiterate people as *Confucius.*"—WASHINGTON
IRVING.

† In *China* (whatever European astronomers may assert to the
contrary) an *eclipse* is caused by a *great dragon eating up the sun.*
To avert so shocking an outrage, the natives frighten away the
monster from his intended *hot* dinner, by giving a morning concert, *al
fresco ;* consisting of drums, trumpets, cymbals, gongs, tin-kettles, &c.

II.

The emperor came with the whole of his court,—
  (His majesty's name was *Ding-Dong-Junk*)—
And he said—to delight in such profligate sport,
  The monster was mad, or disgracefully drunk.
He call'd on the army : the troops to a man
  Declared—though they didn't feel frighten'd the least—
They never could think it a sensible plan
  To go within reach of so ugly a beast.
So he offer'd his daughter, the lovely *Nan-Keen*,
  And a painted pavilion, with many a flag on,
To any brave knight who could step in between
  The *solar eclipse* and the dare-devil *dragon*.

III.

Presently came a reverend bonze,—
  (His name, I'm told, was *Long-Chin Joss*,)—
With a phiz very like the complexion of bronze ;
  And for suitable words he was quite at a loss.
But, he humbly submitted, the orthodox way
  To succour the *sun*, and to bother the foe,
Was to make a new church-rate without more delay,
  As the clerical funds were deplorably low.
Though he coveted nothing at all for himself,
  (A virtue he always delighted to brag on,)
He thought, if the priesthood could pocket some pelf,
  It might hasten the doom of this impious *dragon*.

IV.

The next that spoke was the court buffoon,—
  (The name of this buffer was *Whim-Wham-Fun*,)—

Who carried a salt-box and large wooden spoon,
   With which, he suggested, the job might be done.
Said the jester, " I'll wager my rattle and bells,
   Your pride, my fine fellow, shall soon have a fall :
If you make many more of your horrible yells,
   I know a good method to make you sing small ! "
And when he had set all the place in a roar,
   As his merry conceits led the whimsical wag on,
He hinted a plan to get rid of the bore,
   By putting some *salt* on the *tail* of the *dragon !*

v.

At length appear'd a brisk young knight,—
   (The far-famed warrior, *Bam-Boo-Gong,*)—
Who threaten'd to burke the big blackguard outright,
   And have the deed blazon'd in story and song.
With an excellent shot from a very *long bow*
   He damaged the dragon by cracking his crown ;
When he fell to the ground (as my documents show)
   With a smash that was heard many miles out of town.
His death was the signal for frolic and spree—
   They carried the corpse, in a common stage-waggon ;
And the hero was crown'd with the leaves of green tea,
   For saving the *sun* from the jaws of the *dragon.*

vi.

A poet, whose works were all the rage,—
   (This gentleman's name was *Sing-Song-Strum,*)—
Told the terrible tale on his popular page :
   (Compared with *his* verses, *my* rhymes are but rum !)

The Royal Society claim'd as their right
   The spoils of the vanquish'd—his wings, tail, and claws;
And a brilliant bravura, describing the fight,
   Was sung on the stage with unbounded applause.
"The valiant *Bam-Boo*" was a favourite toast,
   And a topic for future historians to fag on,
Which, when it had reach'd to the Middlesex coast,
   Gave rise to the legend of "*George and the Dragon.*"

RATHER HARD TO TAKE.

AN artist—'tis not fair to tell his name ;
   But one whom Fortune, in her freakish tricks,
   Saluted with less smiles than kicks,
More to the painter's honour, and her shame,—
Was one day deep engaged on his *chef d'œuvre,*
(A painting worthy of the Louvre,)
Dives and Lazarus the theme,—
The subject was his earliest boyish dream !
And, with an eye to colour, breadth, and tone,
   He painted, skilfully as he was able,
   The good things on the rich man's table,—
Wishing they were, no doubt, upon his own ;
When suddenly his hostess—best of creatures !—
Made visible her features,
And to this world our artist did awaken :
   " A gentleman," she said, " from the next street,
   Had sent a special message in a heat,
Wanting a likeness taken."
The artist, with a calmness oft the effect
Of tidings which we don't expect,
Wiped all his brushes carefully and clean,
Button'd his coat—a coat which once had been,—

Put on his hat, and with uncommon stress
On the address,
Went forth, revolving in his nob
How his kind hostess, when he'd got the job,—
Even before they paid him for his skill,—
Would let him add a little to the bill.

He found a family of six or seven,
　　All grown-up people, seated in a row ;
There might be seen upon each face a leaven
　　Of recent, and of decent woe,
But that the artist, whose chief cares
Were fix'd upon his own affairs,
Gazed, with a business eye, to be acquainted
Which of the seven wanted to be painted.

But a young lady soon our artist greeted,
Saying, in words of gentlest music, " Ah !—
Pray, Mr. Thingo'me, be seated,—
We want a likeness of our grandpapa."

Such chances Fortune seldom deigns to bring :
The very thing !
How he should like
To emulate Vandyke !
Or, rather—still more glorious ambition—
To paint the head like Titian,
A fine old head, with silver sprinkled :
A face all seam'd and wrinkled :—
The painter's heart 'gan inwardly rejoice ;
　　But, as he ponder'd on that "fine old head,"

Another utter'd, in a mournful voice,
 "But, sir, he's dead!"

The artist was perplex'd—the case was alter'd :
 Distrust, stirr'd up by doubt, his bosom warps ;
"Dead is the gentleman!" he falter'd ;
 "But surely, you can let me see the corpse ?
An artist but requires a hint :
There are the features—give the cheeks a tint—
Paint in the eyes—and, though the task's a hard 'un,
 You'll find the thing, I'll swear,
As like as he can,—no, I beg your pardon,—
 As like as he *could* stare !"

"Alas ! alas !" the eldest sister sigh'd,
And then she sobb'd and cried,
So that 'twas long ere she again could speak,—
"We buried him last week !"

The painter heaved a groan : "But, surely, madam,
 You have a likeness of the dear deceased ;
 Some youthful face, whose age might be increased ?"
"No, no,—we haven't, sir, no more than Adam ;
 Not in the least !"

This was the strangest thing that e'er occurr'd ;—
 "You'll pardon me," the baffled painter cried ;
"But, really, I must say, upon my word,
 You might have sent for me before he died."
And then he turn'd to the surviving tribe,—
"Can you describe

But a few items, features, shape, and hue?
I'll warrant, I'll still paint the likeness true!"

"Why, yes, we could do that," said one : "let's see ;
He had a rather longish nose, like me."
"No," said a second ; "there you're wrong,
His nose was not so very long."
"Well, well," pursued the first ; "his eyes
Were rather smaller than the common size."
"How?" cried a third, "how?—not at all ;
Not small—not small !"
"Well, then, an oval face, extremely fine."
"Yes," said the eldest son, "like mine."
The painter gazed upon him in despair,—
The fellow's face was square !

"I have it," cried another, and arose ;
"But wait a moment, sir," and out she goes.
With curiosity the artist burn'd—
"What was she gone for?" but she soon return'd.
"I knew from what *they* said, to expect to gain
A likeness of grandpa was quite in vain ;
But, not upon that point to dwell,
I have got something here will do as well
As though alive he for his portrait sat !"
    So, saying, with a curtsey low,
She from behind, with much parade and show,
    Presented an old hat !

                                        C. W.

THE TWO WREATHS.

IT was eve ; and the Bulbul had just begun
His favourite song to the setting sun,
And the Rose, the Bulbul's own bright flower,
Had waited long for the happy hour
When daylight dies in mystic shade,
And the Bulbul trills his serenade,
While every gentle Rose that's nigh
Flutters her leaves in ecstacy,
And thinks, as the love-notes flutter along,
That there's nothing on earth like her Bulbul's song.

It was eve, and the rising Queen of night
Threw a silvery hue o'er the soft twilight,
And o'er heaven's deep sea of blue above,
Like a vessel of light did gently move ;
And on her course o'er that sea afar,
There twinkled the rays of the single star
That shines but for lovers.   Its softest smile
Fell that night on the loveliest isle
That ever mortal eye did see,—
Kiss'd by the waters of Araby.

It was eve ;—but eve fast fading away ;—
The sea round that island as placid lay
As one vast mirror of steel so bright,
Reflecting the charms of our eastern night,
Soft as the slumber of childhood ;—while
No breeze fann'd the palms of that spicy isle,
Nor shook the sweets from each laden bough,
Nor sigh'd o'er beds where wild flowers grow ;—
There wanted but some bright eyes, to bless
My summer-night's dream of loveliness.

The wish I had fondly breathed, scarce fell
From my lips, when a voice from th' acacia dell
Call'd aloud on the name of Abdulzyde,
And I flew to the gentle Leela's side.
She smiled—such smiles are to houris giv'n !—
She look'd like a Peri just lit from heav'n :
Her Saba-silk girdle was studded with pearls,
Her foot was more light than a dancing girl's
From sunny Egypt.   No Caubulee
Ever sang with such voice of harmony.

"See," said the blushing girl, "I've got
    Two wreaths to deck my own love's brow ;
They're not from fragrant Yezd ;—they're not
    From groves where Shiraz roses grow.
This one, look, Abdulzyde, is made
    Of flowers of golden hue, that never
Are known, whate'er their age, to fade,—
    A type of Love that lives for ever.*

* A sempiternal flower, common to the East.

"While this,—and 'tis the fairest one
 To look at, but 'twill never last,
Springs into life with the bright sun,
 But, with his rays at eve, so fast
Doth all its brightness fade away,
 And die beneath the rising moon,
That all *my* care could scarcely stay
Its beauty since the parting day,—
 This type of Love that dies too soon!" *

She ceased for a while, but again her sweet voice
Woke in music once more ; and she ask'd that the choice
I should make of a wreath, (here that sweet voice trembled,)
Might be one which most nearly my love resembled.
She blush'd while speaking, her head sunk low,
And as graceful as water-lilies bow,
At eve, their tops beneath the stream
On whose surface their day has been one glad dream,
And who hide all their blushes at coming night,
'Neath their wat'ry veils, from the pale moonlight.†

* The Gum Cistus, profuse in blossoming, "exhibits," says Curtis, "a remarkable instance of quickly fading beauty, opening and expanding to the morning sun, and, before night, strewing the ground with elegant remains of its blossoms. As each succeeding day produces new blossoms, this deciduous disposition of the petals, common to the genus, is the less to be regretted." The younger Tradescant brought this flower to England in 1656. He introduced it from Spain and Portugal, and they had it from the East.

† Pliny mentions this of the Nymphea Lotus, affirming that it retires under water during the night, so far as to be out of reach of the hand. The purple-flowered Hydropeltis of the North American lakes sinks at night to the surface of the water, and sleeps there, expanding its flowers and diverging its anthers at the approach of morning.

And thus I answer'd, while the maid
With either wreath at moments play'd,
And look'd, so lovely was she there,
Like those bright spirits, the all fair
And young Devatas who of yore[*]
Have lived upon the earth before,
Then dwelt awhile among those eyes
That light our Prophet's paradise,
Whence, chasten'd from each earthly stain,
They're sent to bless this world again.

 "The wreath, the bright wreath
  I select for my brow,
 Is this light Cistus crown
  With its leaflets of snow.
Though frail, though it fade,
  Though at night it be shorn
Of all its sweet flowers,
  Yet each sunny morn,
The stem where they flourish'd
  And laugh'd in the breeze,
Will put forth even fairer
  And brighter than these.
'Tis, my Leela, a type,
  Not of Love that has in it
A million of sweets

* "The Devatas are believed to be spirits which have formerly animated mortal frames, and when the periods during which they have been judged worthy to enjoy bliss in heaven, on account of their virtues, have respectively drawn to a close, they must again return to the earth, to undergo probation in new states of existence."—*Capt. Low, Transactions R. As. Soc.*

That all die in a minute,
But of the one heart,
With its feelings that flower
Still brighter and purer
For thee every hour—
While this sullen wreath,
Though its colours still keep
Some few tints they once had,
All its scent is asleep;
No sooner its odour
O'er morning was shed,
Than its sweets, like the love
That fades soonest, were fled.
'Tis a type, that chill wreath
Of a life without fame,
Of a heart that knows little
Of Love but the name."

"Ah hold! this wreath be thine!" she cried,
" I twined it for my Abdulzyde;
And happily has he reveal'd
The meaning that its leaves conceal'd.
But oh! this other wreath has, too,
Its virtues, though despised by thee.
To me it speaks of service true,
Of firm unshaken constancy,
Of feelings deathless, and of faith
Pledged never, throughout life, to falter,
Of Love worth living for, that breath
Of this cold world could never alter."

"And I here swear, this happy night,"
   I said, "to love through good, through ill,
And be our fortunes dark or bright,
   In joy, in woe, to love on still.
Through brightness, still with truth ; and when
   Such nights as this shine out, what pride
To roam at eve through sweet Yemen
   With my own Leela at my side!"   .

"And if our lives are doom'd to be
   Not all of sunny, golden hues,
Then, like the lovely tamarind tree,
   That sheathes its fruit from noxious dews
Which fall at night, (her careful leaves
   Around the buds are gently twining,
While, in the damp of summer eves,
   Sickly and faint they lie reclining),*
Then like that tree, should sorrow wield
   Her withering arm, or show her form,
The arms of Abdulzyde will shield
   His Leela from the coming storm.
He only asks, should clouds arise
   To darken views that now lie fair
And smiling under sunny skies,
He need but look in Leela's eyes,
   To always find a summer there!"

      " 'Tis the cool evening hour ;
         The Tamarind, from the dew,
         Sheathes its young fruit, yet green."—*Thalaba.*

This fact was first recorded by the old traveller, Mondelslo.
                          J. D.

THE LEGEND OF MANOR HALL.

BY THE AUTHOR OF "HEADLONG HALL."

—•—

OLD Farmer Wall, of Manor Hall,
　　To market drove his wain :
Along the road it went well stowed
　　With sacks of golden grain.

His station he took, but in vain did he look
　　For a customer all the morn ;
Though the farmers all, save Farmer Wall,
　　They sold off all their corn.

Then home he went, sore discontent,
　　And many an oath he swore,
And he kicked up rows with his children and spouse,
　　When they met him at the door.

Next market-day he drove away
　　To the town his loaded wain :
The farmers all, save Farmer Wall,
　　They sold off all their grain.

D

No bidder he found, and he stood astound
   At the close of the market-day,
When the market was done, and the chapmen were gone
   Each man his several way.

He stalked by his load along the road ;
   His face with wrath was red :
His arms he tossed, like a good man crossed
   In seeking his daily bread.

His face was red, and fierce was his tread,
   And with lusty voice cried he,
" My corn I'll sell to the devil of hell,
   If he'll my chapman be."

These words he spoke just under an oak
   Seven hundred winters old ;
And he straight was aware of a man sitting there
   On the roots and grassy mould.

The roots rose high, o'er the green-sward dry,
   And the grass around was green,
Save just the space of the stranger's place,
   Where it seemed as fire had been.

All scorched was the spot, as gipsy-pot
   Had swung and bubbled there :
The grass was marred, the roots were charred,
   And the ivy stems were bare.

The stranger up-sprung : to the farmer he flung
    A loud and friendly hail,
And he said, " I see well, thou hast corn to sell,
    And I'll buy it on the nail."

The twain in a trice agreed on the price ;
    The stranger his earnest paid,
And with horses and wain to come for the grain
    His own appointment made.

The farmer cracked his whip, and tracked
    His way right merrily on :
He struck up a song as he trudged along,
    For joy that his job was done.

His children fair he danced in the air ;
    His heart with joy was big ;
He kissed his wife ; he seized a knife,
    He slew a sucking pig.

The faggots burned, the porkling turned
    And crackled before the fire ;
And an odour arose that was sweet in the nose
    Of a passing ghostly friar.

He twirled at the pin, he entered in,
    He sate down at the board ;
The pig he blessed, when he saw it well dressed,
    And the humming ale out-poured.

The friar laughed, the friar quaffed,
  He chirped like a bird in May;
The farmer told how his corn he had sold
  As he journeyed home that day.

The friar he quaffed, but no longer he laughed,
  He changed from red to pale:
"Oh, helpless elf! 'tis the fiend himself
  To whom thou hast made thy sale!"

The friar he quaffed, he took a deep draught;
  He crossed himself amain:
"Oh, slave of pelf! 'tis the devil himself
  To whom thou hast sold thy grain!

"And sure as the day, he'll fetch thee away,
  With the corn which thou hast sold,
If thou let him pay o'er one tester more
  Than thy settled price in gold."

The farmer gave vent to a loud lament,
  The wife to a long outcry;
Their relish for pig and ale was flown;
The friar alone picked every bone,
  And drained the flagon dry.

The friar was gone: the morning dawn
  Appeared, and the stranger's wain
Came to the hour, with six-horse power,
  To fetch the purchased grain.

The horses were black : on their dewy track
    Light steam from the ground up-curled ;
Long wreaths of smoke from their nostrils broke,
    And their tails like torches whirled.

More dark and grim, in face and limb,
    Seemed the stranger than before,
As his empty wain, with steeds thrice twain,
    Drew up to the farmer's door.

On the stranger's face was a sly grimace,
    As he seized the sacks of grain ;
And, one by one, till left were none,
    He tossed them on the wain.

And slily he leered as his hand up-reared
    A purse of costly mould,
Where, bright and fresh, through a silver mesh,
    Shone forth the glistering gold.

The farmer held out his right hand stout,
    And drew it back with dread ;
For in fancy he heard each warning word
    The supping friar had said.

His eye was set on the silver net ;
    His thoughts were in fearful strife ;
When, sudden as fate, the glittering bait
    Was snatched by his loving wife.

And, swift as thought, the stranger caught
    The farmer his waist around,
And at once the twain and the loaded wain
    Sank through the rifted ground.

The gable-end wall of Manor Hall
    Fell in ruins on the place :
That stone-heap old the tale has told
    To each succeeding race.

The wife gave a cry that rent the sky
    At her goodman's downward flight :
But she held the purse fast, and a glance she cast
    To see that all was right.

'Twas the fiend's full pay for her goodman gray,
    And the gold was good and true ;
Which made her declare, that "his dealings were fair,
    To give the devil his due."

She wore the black pall for Farmer Wall,
    From her fond embraces riven :
But she won the vows of a younger spouse
    With the gold which the fiend had given..

Now, farmers, beware what oaths you swear
    When you cannot sell your corn ;
Lest, to bid and buy, a stranger be nigh,
    With hidden tail and horn.

And, with good heed, the moral a-read,
   Which is of this tale the pith,—
If your corn you sell to the fiend of hell,
   You may sell yourself therewith.

And if by mishap you fall in the trap,
   Would you bring the fiend to shame,
Lest the tempting prize should dazzle her eyes,
   Lock up your frugal dame.

THERE'S NO MISTAKE IN THAT!

" Errors excepted."—Bill of Costs.

—•—

In public life it is most true
 That men are wide awake ;
In private matters, doubtless, too,
 There now is no mistake.
Whate'er is thought of, said, or done,
 Whate'er we would be at,
We all take care of Number One,—
 There's no mistake in that !

The Outs, now long deprived of place,
 Of course the Ins oppose :
The Ins rejoice, while, face to face,
 Their " ayes " can beat the " noes."
" Voluntas " (this their daily song)
 " Pro ratione stat ; "
Which means, "We'll go it, right or wrong!"—
 There's no mistake in that !

Good Louis Philippe feels, 'tis said,
 In very doleful plight,
Since Frenchmen practise at his head
 With bullets day and night.

For diadems, some play odd tricks ;
    They're safer in a hat :
Few crowns are now worth two-and-six,—
    There's no mistake in that !

" No man," (erst said Sir Boyle,) "'tis plain,
    Unless a bird were he,
Can be at once in places twain ; "
    Of course, much less in three.
But, what with railway and balloon,
    It would surprise the Pat
In ten at once to see us soon,—
    There's no mistake in that !

But what have I with home affairs,
    Or foreign news, to do ?
I've got enough of private cares,
    And woes of deepest hue ;
My landlord just has called to say
    (That odious Peter Platt !)
That Friday last was quarter day,—
    There's no mistake in that !

My banker, too, in language bland,
    Presents his kind respects,
And gives me plain to understand
    That I have " no effects ; "
And then, the matter short to cut,
    Proceeds to tell me flat,
My bill is due,—most sorry, but—
    There's no mistake in that !

Last month my friends at Rottingness
  (That borough pure and bright)
Requested I'd resign, unless
  I voted black was white.
To take the Chiltern Hundreds let,
  Again I never sat,—
The only hundreds I shall get !—
  There's no mistake in that !

My health of late has suffered much ;
  So in came Dr. Grains,
My pulse and fees alike to touch,
  And banish all my pains.
Quoth he, returning watch to fob,
  "We must reduce this fat ;
And then, methinks, we'll do your job,"—
  There's no mistake in that !

My tailor, too, his small account
  Has thrice for payment sent ;
I promised him the full amount
  When I received my rent.
In anger to and fro he stalked,
  And changed his civil chat,
And soon of Doe and Roe he talked,—
  There's no mistake in that !

'Twas then I wooed the Widow Stokes,
  Who did not say me "nay ;"
And, though I've found her wealth's a hoax,
  Still I must wed to-day !

Ah ! would that I had never popped !
  But Lawyer Latitat
Some hints of " breach of promise " dropped,—
  There's no mistake in that !

                TRISTRAM MERRYTHOUGHT.

THE TEMPTATIONS OF ST. ANTHONY.

—◆—

"He would have passed a pleasant life of it, in despite of the devil and all his works, if his path had not been crossed by a being that causes more perplexity to mortal man than ghosts, goblins, and the whole race of witches put together, and that was—a woman."—*Sketch-Book.*

ST. ANTHONY sat on a lowly stool,
   And a book was in his hand ;
Never his eye from its page he took,
Either to right or left to look,
But with steadfast soul, as was his rule,
   The holy page he scanned.

"We will woo," said the imp, "St. Anthony's eyes
   Off from his holy book :
We will go to him all in strange disguise,
And tease him with laughter, whoops, and cries,
   That he upon us may look."

The Devil was in the best humour that day
   That ever his highness was in :
And that's why he sent out his imps to play,
And he furnished them torches to light their way,
Nor stinted them incense to burn as they may,—
   Sulphur, and pitch, and rosin.

So they came to the Saint in a motley crew,
    A heterogeneous rout:
There were imps of every shape and hue,
And some looked black, and some looked blue,
And they passed and varied before the view,
    And twisted themselves about:
And had they exhibited thus to you,
I think you'd have felt in a bit of a stew,—
    Or so should myself, I doubt.

There were some with feathers, and some with scales,
    And some with warty skins;
Some had not heads, and some had tails,
And some had claws like iron nails;
And some had combs and beaks like birds,
And yet, like jays, could utter words;
    And some had gills and fins.

Some rode on skeleton beasts, arrayed
    In gold and velvet stuff,
With rich tiaras on the head,
Like kings and queens among the dead;
While face and bridle-hand, displayed,
In hue and substance seemed to cope
With maggots in a microscope,
And their thin lips, as white as soap,
    Were colder than enough.

And spiders big from the ceiling hung,
    From every creek and nook:

They had a crafty, ugly guise,
And looked at the Saint with their eight eyes ;
And all that malice could devise
Of evil to the good and wise
   Seemed welling from their look.

Beetles and slow-worms crawled about,
   And toads did squat demure ;
From holes in the wainscoting mice peeped out,
Or a sly old rat with his whiskered snout ;
And forty-feets, a full span long,
Danced in and out in an endless throng :
There ne'er has been seen such extravagant rout
   From that time to this, I'm sure.

But the good St. Anthony kept his eyes
   Fixed on the holy book ;—
From it they did not sink nor rise ;
Nor sights nor laughter, shouts nor cries,
   Could win away his look.

A quaint imp sat in an earthen pot,
   In a big-bellied earthen pot sat he :
Through holes in the bottom his legs outshot,
And holes in the sides his arms had got,
And his head came out through the mouth, God wot!
   A comical sight to see.

And he drummed on his belly so fair and round,
   On his belly so round and fair ;

And it gave forth a rumbling, mingled sound,
'Twixt a muffled bell and a growling hound,
   A comical sound to hear :
And he sat on the edge of a table-desk,
   And drummed it with his heels ;
And he looked as strange and as picturesque
As the figures we see in an arabesque,
Half hidden in flowers, all painted in fresque,
   In Gothic vaulted ceils.

Then he whooped and hawed, and winked and grinned,
   And his eyes stood out with glee ;
And he said these words, and he sung this song,
And his legs and his arms, with their double prong,
Keeping time with his tune as it galloped along,
Still on the pot and the table dinned
   As birth to his song gave he.

" Old Tony, my boy ! shut up your book,
   And learn to be merry and gay :
You sit like a bat in his cloistered nook,
Like a round-shoulder'd fool of an owl you look ;
But straighten your back from its booby crook,
   And more sociable be, I pray.

" Let us see you laugh, let us hear you sing ;
   Take a lesson from me, old boy !
Remember that life has a fleeting wing,
And then comes Death, that stern old king,
   So we'd better make sure of joy."

But the good St. Anthony bent his eyes
   Upon the holy book :
He heard that song with a laugh arise,
But he knew that the imp had a naughty guise,
   And he did not care to look.

Another imp came in a masquerade,
   Most like to a monk's attire :
But of living bats his cowl was made,
Their wings stitched together with spider thread ;
And round and about him they fluttered and played ;
And his eyes shot out from their misty shade
   Long parallel bars of fire.

And his loose teeth chattered like clanking bones,
   When the gibbet-tree sways in the blast :
And with gurgling shakes, and stifled groans,
He mocked the good St. Anthony's tones
   As he muttered his prayer full fast.

A rosary of beads was hung by his side,—
   Oh, gaunt-looking beads were they !
And still, when the good Saint dropped a bead,
He dropped a tooth, and he took good heed
To rattle his string, and the bones replied,
   Like a rattle-snake's tail at play.

But the good St. Anthony bent his eyes
   Upon the holy book ;
He heard that mock of groans and sighs,

And he knew that the thing had an evil guise,
 And he did not dare to look.

Another imp came with a trumpet-snout,
 That was mouth and nose in one :
It had stops like a flute, as you never may doubt,
Where his long lean fingers capered about,
As he twanged his nasal melodies out,
 In quaver, and shake, and run.

And his head moved forward and backward still
 On his long and snaky neck ;
As he bent his energies all to fill
His nosey tube with wind and skill,
And he sneezed his octaves out, until
 'Twas well-nigh ready to break.

And close to St. Anthony's ear he came,
 And piped his music in :
And the shrill sound went through the good Saint's
    frame,
With a smart and a sting, like a shred of flame,
Or a bee in the ear,—which is much the same,—
 And he shivered with the din.

But the good St. Anthony bent his eyes
 Upon the holy book ;
He heard that snout with its gimlet cries,
And he knew that the imp had an evil guise,
 And he did not dare to look.

A thing with horny eyes was there,
  With horny eyes like the dead :
And its long sharp nose was all of horn,
And its bony cheeks of flesh were shorn,
And its ears were like thin cases torn
From feet of kine, and its jaws were bare ;
And fish-bones grew, instead of hair,
  Upon its skinless head.

Its body was of thin birdy bones,
  Bound round with a parchment skin ;
And when 'twas struck, the hollow tones
That circled round like drum-dull groans,
  Bespoke a void within.

Its arm was like a peacock's leg,
  And the claws were like a bird's :
But the creep that went, like a blast of plague,
To loose the live flesh from the bones,
And wake the good Saint's inward groans,
As it clawed his cheek, and pulled his hair,
And pressed on his eyes in their beating lair,
  Cannot be told in words.

But the good St. Anthony kept his eyes
  Still on the holy book ;
He felt the clam on his brow arise,
And he knew that the thing had a horrid guise,
  And he did not dare to look.

An imp came then like a skeleton form
   Out of a charnel vault :
Some clingings of meat had been left by the worm,
Some tendons and strings on his legs and arm,
And his jaws with gristle were black and deform,
   But his teeth were as white as salt.

And he grinned full many a lifeless grin,
   And he rattled his bony tail ;
His skull was decked with gill and fin,
And a spike of bone was on his chin,
And his bat-like ears were large and thin,
   And his eyes were the eyes of a snail.

He took his stand at the good Saint's back,
   And on tiptoe stood a space :
Forward he bent, all rotten-black,
And he sunk again on his heel, good lack !
And the good Saint uttered some ghostly groans,
For the head was caged in the gaunt rib-bones,—
   A horrible embrace !
And the skull hung o'er with an elvish pry,
And cocked down its India-rubber eye
   To gaze upon his face.

Yet the good St. Anthony sunk his eyes
   Deep in the holy book :
He felt the bones, and so was wise
To know that the thing had a ghastly guise,
   And he did not dare to look.

Last came an imp,—how unlike the rest !—
  A beautiful female form :
And her voice was like music, that sleep-oppress'd
Sinks on some cradling zephyr's breast ;
And whilst with a whisper his cheek she press'd,
  Her cheek felt soft and warm.

When over his shoulder she bent the light
  Of her soft eyes on to his page,
It came like a moonbeam silver bright,
And relieved him then with a mild delight,
For the yellow lamp-lustre scorched his sight,
  That was weak with the mists of age.

Hey ! the good St. Anthony boggled his eyes
  Over the holy book :
Ho ho ! at the corners they 'gan to rise,
For he knew that the thing had a lovely guise,
  And he could not choose but look.

There are many devils that walk this world,—
  Devils large, and devils small ;
Devils so meagre, and devils so stout ;
Devils with horns, and devils without ;
Sly devils that go with their tails upcurled,
Bold devils that carry them quite unfurled ;
  Meek devils, and devils that brawl ;
Serious devils, and laughing devils ;
Imps for churches, and imps for revels ;

Devils uncouth, and devils polite ;
Devils black, and devils white ;
Devils foolish, and devils wise ;
But a laughing woman, with two bright eyes,
    Is the worsest devil of all.

T. H. S.

A TALE OF GRAMMARYE.

The Baron came home in his fury and rage,
He blew up his Henchman, he blew up his Page;
The Seneschal trembled, the Cook looked pale,
As he ordered for supper grilled kidneys and ale,
Vain thought! that grill'd kidneys can give relief,
When one's own are inflamed by anger and grief.

What was the cause of the Baron's distress?
   Why sank his spirits so low?—
The fair Isabel, when she should have said "Yes,"
   Had given the Baron a "No."
He ate, and he drank, and he grumbled between:
First on the viands he vented his spleen,—
The ale was sour,—the kidneys were tough,
And tasted of nothing but pepper and snuff!
—The longer he ate, the worse grew affairs,
Till he ended by kicking the butler down stairs.

All was hushed—'twas the dead of the night—
   The tapers were dying away,
And the armour bright
Glanced in the light
   Of the pale moon's trembling ray;

Yet his Lordship sat still, digesting his ire,
With his nose on his knees, and his knees in the fire,—
All at once he jump'd up, resolved to consult his
Cornelius Agrippa de rebus occultis.

He seized by the handle
A bed-room flat candle,
And went to a secret nook,
Where a chest lay hid
With so massive a lid,
His knees, as he raised it, shook,
Partly, perhaps, from the wine he had drunk,
Partly from fury, and partly from funk;
For never before had he ventured to look
In his Great-Great-Grandfather's conjuring-book.

Now Lord Ranulph Fitz-Hugh,
As lords frequently do,
Thought reading a bore,—but his case is quite new;
So he quickly ran through
A chapter or two,
For without Satan's aid he knew not what to do,—
When poking the fire, as the evening grew colder,
He saw with alarm,
As he raised up his arm,
An odd-looking countenance over his shoulder.

Firmest rock will sometimes quake,
Trustiest blade will sometimes break,
Sturdiest heart will sometimes fail,
Proudest eye will sometimes quail;—

No wonder Fitz-Hugh felt uncommonly queer
Upon suddenly seeing the Devil so near,
Leaning over his chair, peeping into his ear.

      The stranger first
      The silence burst,
And replied to the Baron's look :—
      "I would not intrude,
      But don't think me rude
If I sniff at that musty old book.
      Charms were all very well
      Ere Reform came to Hell ;
But now not an imp cares a fig for a spell.
      Still I see what you want,
      And am willing to grant
The person and purse of the fair Isabel.
Upon certain conditions the maiden is won ;—
You may have her at once, if you choose to say 'Done!'

      "The lady so rare,
      Her manors so fair,
Lord Baron, I give to thee :
      But when once the sun
      Five years has run,
Lord Baron, thy soul's my fee !"

Oh ! where wert thou, ethereal Sprite ?
  Protecting Angel, where ?
Sure never before had noble or knight
  Such need of thy guardian care !
No aid is nigh—'twas so decreed ;—

The recreant Baron at once agreed,
And prepared with his blood to sign the deed.

    With the point of his sword
    His arm he scored,
And mended his pen with his Misericorde ;
    From his black silk breeches
    The stranger reaches
A lawyer's leathern case,
    Selects a paper,
    And snuffing the taper,
The Baron these words mote trace :—
"Five years after date, I promise to pay
My soul to Old Nick, without let or delay,
For value received."—"There, my Lord, on my life,
Put your name to the bill, and the lady's your wife."

      *   *   *   *

    All look'd bright in earth and heaven,
      And far through the morning skies
    Had Sol his fiery coursers driven,—
    That is, it was striking half-past éleven
      As Isabel opened her eyes.

All wondered what made the lady so late,
    For she came not down till noon,
Though she usually rose at a quarter to eight,
    And went to bed equally soon.
But her rest had been broken by troublesome dreams :—
She had thought that, in spite of her cries and her screams,
Old Nick had borne off, in a chariot of flame,
The gallant young Howard of Effinghame.

Her eye was so dim, and her cheek so chill,
The family doctor declared she was ill,
And muttered dark hints of a draught and a pill.

All during breakfast to brood doth she seem
   O'er some secret woes or wrongs ;
For she empties the salt-cellar into the cream,
   And stirs up her tea with the tongs.
But scarce hath she finished her third round of toast,
   When a knocking is heard by all—
" What may that be ?—'tis too late for the post,—
   Too soon for a morning call."
   After a moment of silence and dread,
       The court-yard rang
       With the joyful clang
    Of an armed warrior's tread.
Now away and away with fears and alarms,—
The lady lies clasped in young Effinghame's arms.

She hangs on his neck, and she tells him true,
How that troublesome creature, Lord Ranulph Fitz-Hugh,
Hath vowed and hath sworn with a terrible curse,
That, unless she will take him for better for worse,
   He will work her mickle rue !

" Now, lady love, dismiss thy fear,
Should that grim old Baron presume to come here,
We'll soon send him home with a flea in his ear ;—
   And, to cut short the strife,
    My love ! my life !
Let me send for a parson, and make you my wife !"

No banns did they need, no licence require,—
  They were married that day before dark :
The Clergyman came,—a fat little friar,
  The doctor acted as Clerk.

    But the nuptial rites were hardly o'er,
    Scarce had they reached the vestry door,
      When a knight rushed headlong in ;
        From his shoes to his shirt
        He was all over dirt,
      From his toes to the tip of his chin ;
  But high on his travel-stained helmet tower'd
  The lion-crest of the noble Howard.

By horrible doubts and fears possest,
The bride turned and gaz'd on the bridegroom's breast—
  No Argent Bend was there ;
      No Lion bright
      Of her own true knight,
  But his rival's Sable Bear !
The Lady Isabel instantly knew
'Twas a regular hoax of the false Fitz-Hugh ;
And loudly the Baron exultingly cried,
" Thou art wooed, thou art won, my bonny gay bride !
Nor heaven nor hell can our loves divide ! ''

This pithy remark was scarcely made,
When the Baron beheld, upon turning his head,
  His Friend in black close by ;
He advanced with a smile all placid and bland,
Popp'd a small piece of parchment into his hand,
  And knowingly winked his eye.

As the Baron perused,
His cheek was suffused
With a flush between brick-dust and brown;
While the fair Isabel
Fainted, and fell
In a still and death-like swoon.
Lord Howard roar'd out, till the chapel and vaults
Rang with cries for burnt feathers and volatile salts.

"Look at the date!" quoth the queer-looking man,
In his own peculiar tone;
My word hath been kept,—deny it who can,—
And now I am come for mine own."
Might he trust his eyes?—Alas! and alack!
'Twas a bill ante-dated full five years back!
'Twas all too true—
It was over due—
The term had expired!—he wouldn't "renew,"—
And the Devil looked black as the Baron looked blue.

The Lord Fitz-Hugh
Made a great to-do,
And especially blew up Old Nick,—
"'Twas a stain," he swore,
"On the name he bore
To play such a rascally trick!"—
"A trick?" quoth Nick, in a tone rather quick,
'It's one often played upon people who 'tick.'"
Blue flames now broke
From his mouth as he spoke,
They went out, and left an uncommon thick smoke,

Which enveloping quite
Himself and the Knight,
The pair in a moment were clean out of sight.
When it wafted away,
Where the dickens were they?
Oh! no one might guess—Oh! no one might say,—
But never, I wis,
From that time to this,
In hall or in bower, on mountain or plain,
Has the Baron been seen, or been heard of again.

As for fair Isabel, after two or three sighs,
She finally opened her beautiful eyes.
She coughed, and she sneezed,
And was very well pleased,
After being so rumpled, and towzled, and teased,
To find when restored from her panic and pain,
My Lord Howard had married her over again.

MORAL.

Be warned by our story, ye Nobles and Knights,
Who're so much in the habit of "flying of kites;" .
And beware how ye meddle again with such Flights:
At least, if your energies Creditors cramp,
Remember a Usurer's always a Scamp,
And look well at the Bill, and the Date, and the Stamp:
Don't sign in a hurry, whatever you do,
Or you'll go to the Devil, like Baron Fitz-Hugh.

DALTON.

THE RELICS OF ST. PIUS.

—·◆—

Saint Pius was a holy man,
   And held in detestation
The wicked course that others ran,
   So lived upon starvation.

He thought the world so bad a place
   That decent folks should fly it ;
And, dreaming of a life of grace,
   Determin'd straight to try it.

A cavern was his only house,
   Of limited expansion,
And not a solitary mouse
   Durst venture near his mansion.

He told his beads from morn to night,
   Nor gave a thought to dinner ;
And, while his faith absorb'd him quite,
   He ev'ry day grew thinner.

Vain ev'ry hint by Nature given,
  His saintship would not mind her ;
At length his soul flew back to heaven,
  And left her bones behind her.

Some centuries were gone and past,
  And all forgot his story,
Until a sisterhood at last
  Reviv'd his fame and glory.

To Rome was sent a handsome fee,
  And pious letter fitted,
Requesting that his bones might be
  Without delay transmitted.

The holy see with sacred zeal
  Their relic hoards turn'd over,
The skeleton, from head to heel,
  Of Pius to discover ;

And having sought with caution deep,
  To pious tears affected,
They recognised the blessed heap
  So anxiously expected.

And now the town, that would be made
  Illustrious beyond measure,
Was all alive with gay parade
  To welcome such a treasure.

The bishop, in his robes of state,
  Each monk and priest attending,
Stood rev'rently within the gate
  To view the train descending;

The holy train that far had gone
  To meet the sacred relic,
And now with joyous hymns came on.
  Most like a band angelic.

The nuns the splendid robes prepare,
  Each chain, and flower, and feather;
And now they claim the surgeon's care
  To join the bones together.

The head, the arms, the trunk, he found,
  And placed in due rotation;
But, when the legs he reach'd, around
  He stared in consternation!

In vain he twirl'd them both about,
  Took one and then took t'other,
For one turn'd in, and one turn'd out,
  Still following his brother.

Two odd left legs alone he saw.
  Two left legs! tis amazing!
"Two left legs!" cried the nuns, with awe
  And anxious wonder gazing.

The wonder reach'd the list'ning crowd,
  And all the cry repeated ;
While some press'd on with laughter loud,
  And some in fear retreated.

The bishop scarce a smile repress'd,
  The pilgrims stood astounded ;
The mob, with many a gibe and jest,
  The holy bones surrounded.

The abbess and her vestal train,
  The blest Annunciation,
With horror saw the threaten'd stain
  On Pius' reputation.

" Cease, cease ! ungrateful race ! " cried she,
  " This tumult and derision,
And know the truth has been to me
  Revealèd in a vision !

" The saint who now, enthron'd in heav'n,
  Bestows on us such glory,
Had *two* left legs by Nature given,*
  And, lo ! they are before ye !

" Then let us hope he will no more
  His blessed prayers deny us,
While we, with zeal elate, adore
  The left legs of St. Pius."

C. S. L.

* As was the case with Jacob Tonson, the publisher.—ED.

F

COQUETRY AND INNOCENCE.

Two nymphs, one day, a compact made
(Each from her home had idly stray'd)
That both united would, henceforth,
Roam over east, south, west, and north.
The one bright as a summer-rose
When with the sun's warm kiss it glows ;
The other like the fragrant flow'r
Of what men call the " virgin's bow'r,"—
Her name was Innocence.   The free
And tender beauty's—Coquetry.
And 'tis my task to tell you whether
These fair ones travell'd long together.

When first these maidens sallied out
Upon their long and unknown rout,
Coquetry swore ('twas to herself)
    That nothing ever should divide,
Though she were offer'd endless pelf,
    The maiden with her, from her side.
While Innocence,—she did not swear,
    ·But vainly, foolishly, she thought,
That, for herself, no force could tear
    Her from the compact she had sought.

Thus, ev'n nymphs of fabled birth
Are very like our nymphs on earth.

I need not tell you, ladies, sure,
That Coquetry was always poor :
While Innocence possess'd the merit
Of being rich,—for, to inherit
Riches from one's very birth
Is no slight merit, upon earth.
You see, then, ev'n from the first,
Th' assortment was about the worst
That simple Innocence could make,
Rich, and with ev'rything at stake.
Coquetry's wealth was in the friend
   With whom to journey through all climes
She had engag'd ;—there did it end :
   Nought could be poorer—save these rhymes.

Coquetry, too, was full as wild
As the first-born and fav'rite child
Of Ignorance is known to be,—
That parentage of misery !
While Innocence wore on her face
That inborn charm, that silent grace,
Simplicity, her mother wore,
Gain'd from her mother long before,
Sweet Purity ; her father's state
Was soften'd in her gentler gait ;
Yet none, e'en there, could fail to see
Much of her father, Dignity.

At first, so well the pair agreed,
That Innocence had little need
Ev'n to blush, much less to pay
Any of her wealth away.
So long as Coquetry confin'd
    Herself to changing simple smiles,
Innocence kept close behind,
    And fear'd no danger from such wiles.
E'en when a sigh fell on her ear,
She thought there was not much to fear ;
And only for the first time trembled
    When Coquetry, from youthful Bliss,
Stole, as he slumber'd, what resembled
    Something,—very like a kiss.
Here was for her pure soul a grief,—
Coquetry known to be a thief !

A little ruffled in her mind,
    Still Innocence kept on her way,
Hoping yet better things to find,
    While things look'd graver ev'ry-day.
Thus, Coquetry would sometimes run,
    With wanton step and eager haste,
Where flowers rose blooming in the sun,
    And laid the sweetest *parterres* waste.
But most she seem'd to take delight
(Less like a nymph than evil sprite)
In tearing up those pretty flowers,
    Whose names are most to lovers known
Forget-me-nots she'd crush for hours,
    And trample hosts of hearts-ease down.

And Innocence, who had to pay
For ev'ry whim and foolish *trait*,
Discover'd that she had to rue
That Coquetry was cruel too.

Thus matters went, till came the day
   When Coquetry no more could call
Upon her gentle friend, to pay
   For ev'ry chance that could befall.
She had, one starry night, sought rest,
Her head reclin'd on Passion's breast ;
And when with blushing morn she rose,
   And went to greet the youthful maid,
She miss'd her friend,—nor could suppose
   Where the pretty loit'rer stay'd.
"She's gone !" cried an angelic youth,—
Coquetry knew that he was Truth ;
Who, looking at some maidens shy
That timidly were standing by,
While Coquetry dissolv'd in tears,—
" Lend me," he said, " attentive ears :
Oh ! maids who scarce have yet begun
Your race upon the world to run,
Learn that when Coquetry doth please
   To gratify her ev'ry sense,
The penalty,—each maiden sees,—
   Is at the cost of Innocence."

                               J. D.

THE HANDSOME CLEAR-STARCHER.

A LEGEND OF THE DAYS OF QUEEN ELIZABETH.

WE talk of the Goddess of Fashion ; but where
   Has her Goddessship deigned to be seen ?
Though her taste is consulted each day by the fair,
While men of all ages admiringly stare ?—
   She can be no one else than The Queen.

So, at least, it was erst, when Eliza the Great
   Of our isle was the pride and the pet ;
For though dress form'd small part of her right royal state,
And she valued alike her proud foes' love and hate,
   She was once pleased a fashion to set.

Her sole reason for choosing was what ladies give,—
   'Twas her pleasure, and that was enough.
But, when once it was seen, none without it could live,
'Twould have been all the same if 'twere coarse as a sieve,
   But the " set " was a fine stiffen'd ruff.

'Twas a sort of a " *chevaux-de-frise* "-looking thing,
   Such as still in her portraits is drawn,
Encircling her neck in an odd zig-zag ring ;
And the model, perhaps, was a church-cherub's wing,
   Though 'twas formed of crape, muslin, or lawn.

Or of gossamer, gauze, tissue, leno, blonde, lace,—
   If such elegant names were then known
For those air-woven textures that aye find a place
In the toilet of beauty, and still add a grace
   When, with taste, they o'er beauties are thrown.

But in those days no throwing was ever allow'd,
   " *Négligées* " wer'nt admitted at court ;
Where, stately and formal, the fair, well-drest crowd
Moved rustling like peacocks or turkeys so proud,
   And look'd even demure at their sport.

Some wore gowns thickly 'broider'd like garlands of May ;
   All wore stomachers hard as a shield,
Standing upright and stiff, as in martial array,
(Of the march of clear-starching it then was the day,)
   And all else but the face was conceal'd.

But the ruff ! the white, well-stiffen'd, well clear-starch'd
      ruff
   More than lace, silk, or velvet was prized.
"Its edges," they said, "like a saw should be rough ;"
And slanderers declare they their handmaids would cuff
   If it was not well starch'd, gumm'd, or sized.

'Tis a pity when ladies so pretty allow
   Themselves to fall into a pet,
And, in their own boudoirs to "kick up a row,"
About things they're to wear, with the what, where, or how.
   Anger ne'er made a maid pretty yet.

But, alas! in those days some few fair ones were frail,
    And their tempers would sometimes rebel :
Though perhaps the great breakfasts of beef-steaks and
        ale*
Might have heated the blood of the maid of our tale,
    And caused what we've now got to tell.

Her name we don't mention, because it may chance
    That she yet hath relations at court :
Suffice it, her beauty was such as romance
For all heroines claims,—she could sing, play, and dance
    À merveille,—but to dress was her forte,

Or, say, rather her foible ; so when ruffs came in,
    And good starch rose uncommonly high,
She assured her clear-starcher she cared not a pin
For the price, but her ruffs must be stiff as block-tin ;
    And the clear-starcher said she would try.

* The following is an extract from an order of King Henry the
Eighth for a daily allowance to a maid of honour in 1522.

"*First.* Every morning at brekefast oon chyne of beyf at our kechyn,
oon chete loff and oon maunchet at our panatrye barr, and a galone of
ale at our buttrye barr.

"*Item.* At dyner a pese of beyf, a stroke of roste, and a reward at
our said kechyn, a caste of chete brede at our panatrye barr, and a
galone of ale at our buttrye barr.

"*Item.* At afternoone a maunchet of brede at our panatrye barr,
and half a galone of ale at our buttrye barr.

"*Item.* At supper a messe of potage, a pese of mutten, and a reward
at our said kechyn, a cast of chete brede at our panatrye, and a galone
of ale at our buttrye.

"*Item.* At after supper a chete loff, and a maunchet at our panatrye
barr, and half a galone of ale at our seller barr."

So her ruffs were well-starch'd, dried, and starch'd o'er
    again,
    And both cold and hot-ironed, and prest,
And plaited, et cetera ;—but all was in vain,
For she spake naughty words, and declared it was plain
    Her "artiste" was a fool like the rest.

Then she tried many others ; but all fail'd alike
    This most whimsical fair one to please.
Some pleaded their work-folks had "struck up a strike ;"
Some swore that the ruffs' points were stiff as a pike :
    She declared they were soft as boil'd peas.

She was sadly provok'd, and yet dared not rebel
    Against fashion's imperious decree ;
So, when next her handmaiden desired her to tell
Where her ruffs should be sent, she cried, "Send them
    to h—,
    And the d—l may starch them for me."

These were very bad words to escape from the lips
    Of a lady so handsome and young.
But, when passion's our tyrant, morality trips,
While the tempter keeps watch for such sad naughty slips
    As our maiden had made with her tongue.

And scarce had she spoken, when suddenly came
    An odd sort of "Rat ! tat !" at her door.
'Twas not loud enough quite for a lord or a dame,
Nor yet for her tradesfolk sufficiently tame.
    She had ne'er heard such knocking before.

And of course she felt curious to know what it meant,
　So her handmaid immediately ran
To the window ; and, when o'er the casement she leant,
Exclaim'd, with an air of exceeding content,
　" A remarkably handsome young man ! "

The young man, when shown up, bow'd and smil'd with
　　　　much grace,
　And soon, whispering, ventured to say,
" Gentle lady, excuse me, but such is my case
That indeed we must be quite alone face to face.
　Do, pray, send your handmaiden away ! "

Some signal, no doubt often practised before,
　Caused her maid through the doorway to glide,
While the lady, embarrass'd, look'd down on the floor,
And blush'd (perhaps) for a moment, and when that was
　　　　o'er,
　Found the handsome young man at her side.

The fine figure and face of that singular beau
　All comparisons seem'd to defy ;
And his dress at all points was completely "the go,"
Yet there still was a something not quite "*comme il faut*"
　In the sly wicked glance of his eye.

But his manner was humble, and silvery the tone
　Of his voice, as, in euphonic strain,
He said, " Pride of the palace ! well worthy the throne !
If legitimate claim were with beauty a̶l̶o̶n̶e,
　All your rivals' pretensions were vain ! "

Then (as then was the mode) he the lady compared
  To the sun, moon, and stars, and their light ;
Nor the heathen mythology's goddesses spared.
Any maiden of our modest days would have stared,
  And some, perhaps, have run off in a fright.

But she listen'd, and aye as the flatterer spake
  Smiled, and gracefully flirted her fan,
And, much wondering what end to his speech he would
      make,
Sigh'd, and thought, " Though I fear he's a bit of a rake,
  He is really a charming young man ! "

The gallant's peroration at length took a turn
  That appear'd a most singular whim ;
He found fault with her ruff, and declared he could earn
Her applause (since he'd travelled clear-starching to learn)
  If she would but entrust one with him.

The request was a strange one.   Yet wherefore refuse ?
  " Well,—pray take one ! " she said with a laugh.
" Do your best.   It may serve your waste time to amuse.
But it's really so odd !   Have you learnt to black shoes
  In your travels ? or dye an old scarf ? "

" I have learnt many things," was the stranger's reply,
  " And you'll soon find I know quite enough
To fulfil your commission, for certainly I
Can hotpre̶s̶ ̶c̶o̶l̶l̶a̶ra ; and so, now, good-bye,
  Till I come back again with your ruff."

The next drawing-room day our fair maiden began
    Her court toilet ; but all went so-so.
"Ugh !" she cried, " I'm quite frightful, do all that I can!
There's nothing so fickle and faithless as man !
    What's become of my clear-starching beau ? "

" Ah ! my lady !" said Abigail, plastering her hair,
    That young fellow has play'd you a trick,
And stole——"   But her mistress cried, "Phoo ! I don't
      care !
If I could get but only *one* ruff fit to wear,
    I would don it, though brought by Old Nick."

There's a proverb that says, " If you speak of some folks
    They are sure very soon to appear."
And, while Abigail call'd the beau's visit a hoax,
And his clear-starching one of young gentlemen's jokes,
· His odd "Rat ! tat !" proclaim'd he was near.

" Then he has not deceived me !" the lady exclaim'd,
    " Why don't some of 'em answer the door ?
To doubt of his honour you're much to be blamed.
But I can't see him thus ! I should feel quite ashamed.
    He must wait till I'm drest.   What a bore !"

"Take this box to your mistress, and make my respects,"
    Said the starcher as fierce as a Don,
While he strode down the hall, "and observe she neglects
Not to put on the ruff as my paper d■■■ ■
    And I'll settle the plaits when 'tis on."

What that paper contain'd is a mystery still,
   Since the chronicles only disclose
That she said his request she would strictly fulfil,
And then smiling, exclaim'd, " What a moderate bill !
   Well, he must see all right, I suppose."

Then—her toilet completed—her pride was immense.
   'Twas " a love of a ruff !" she declared,
As it compass'd her neck with its firm triple fence.
Her sole feeling was self-admiration intense,
   While her handmaid admiringly stared,

And then cried, " La ! I never saw nothing so nice :
   What a clever young man that must be !
I suppose, though, he'll charge an extravagant price ? "
" No," her lady replied, " 'twas a cunning device !
   And he's no common tradesman, you'll see.

" The fact is, that he mention'd his charge, and you know
   That I've now no engagement on hand.
At least nothing—quite serious—or likely—and so—
After all—what's a kiss from a handsome young beau ?
   Well—be silent—you now understand.

" When he comes to inspect that my ruff sets all well,
   Just step out for a minute or two ;
Not much longer, because there's a proverb folks tell,
' Give some people an inch, and they'll soon take an
     ell.' "
   " I wish, Miss," said her maid, " I was you."

Then with looks so demure as might Cerberus bilk,
　The young gentleman bow'd himself in.
His dress was embroider'd rich velvet and silk,
His point-lace and kid-gloves were as white as new milk,
　And jet-black was the tuft on his chin.

"Fairest lady!" he said, "may I venture to hope
　That you deign to approve of my work?
This I'll venture to say, that such clear-starch and soap
Never stiffen'd a collar for queen, king, or pope,
　Nor his most sublime-porte-ship the Turk."

"And I've got" (here he smiled) "a particular way,
　Which I'll show you, of finishing off.
Just allow me! Phoo—nonsense! You promised to pay—"
But the lady drew back, frown'd, and said, "Not now,
　　pray!"
　And sent Abigail out by a cough.

All that afterwards happen'd is dingy as night,
　Though her maiden, as maids would of old,
Peeep'd and listen'd, at first with a curious delight,
Then grew anxious,—and then was thrown into a fright.
　And this was the story she told.

She declared the beau boasted his wonderful knack
　Of full-dressing for banquet and ball;
And that, presently after, she heard a loud smack,
And, immediately after, a much louder crack;
　Then a shriek that was louder than all.

To her mistress's aid she accordingly ran,
    Wondering much what the matter could be ;
Since a simple salute from a handsome young man
Never caused such an uproar since kissing began.
    But no mistress nor beau could she see !

Both were gone ! where and how it was fearful to guess,
    As a sulphureous odour remain'd,
While thick smoke still obscured the bay-window's recess,
And, with burnt hoof-like marks, and a cindery mess,
    The best carpet was shockingly stain'd.

What occurr'd at the window the smoke might conceal,
    Though the maid often vow'd that she saw
What was horrid enough all her blood to congeal,
A long black thing that twisted about like an eel,
    And the tips of two horns, and a claw.

But, more certain it is, from that day ne'er again
    Did that lady at court reappear,
Nor amid the *beau monde.* All inquiries were vain.
So, though how they eloped must a mystery remain,
    What the clear-starcher was, seem'd too clear.

Now, ye ladies of England ! young, charming, and fair !
    Pray, be warn'd by this maiden's sad fate !
And, whenever strange beaux, gay and handsome, may
      dare
To approach you with flattering speeches, beware
    Lest their falsehood you rue when too late.

Above all, while your hearts are warm, tender, and young,
   Let no art of the tempter prevail
To extort a rash promise ; since slips of the tongue
O'er fair prospects have often a gloomy veil flung,
And caused ladies' disasters in rhymes to be strung,
   As hath chanced to the maid of our tale.

SARDANAPALUS.

—◆—

SARDANAPALUS was Nineveh's king ;
And, if all be quite true that the chroniclers sing,
    Loved his song and his glass,
    And was given, alas !
    Not only to bigamy,
    Nor even to trigamy,
But (I shudder to think on 't) to rankest polygamy :
For his sweethearts and wives were so vast in amount,
They 'd take you a week or two *only* to count !

One morning his Majesty jumped out of bed,
And hitting his valet a rap on the head,
By way of a joke, "Salamenes," he said,
    "Go, proclaim to the court,
    " 'Tis our will to resort,
    " By way of a lark,
    " To our palace and park
"On the banks of Euphrates, and there, with our wives,
" Sing, dance, and get fuddled, for once in our lives ;
" So bid our state-rulers and nobles, d 'ye see,
" Hie all to our banquet not later than three,
" And prepare for a long night of jollity."—

" Very good," said the valet ; then eager and hot
On his errand, ducked thrice, and was off like a shot.

When the court heard these orders, with rapture elate,
They adjourned all the business of church, and of state,
      And hurried off, drest
      Each man in his best ;
      While the women, sweet souls,
      Went with them by shoals,
Some in gigs, some in cabs, some on horseback so gay,
And some in an omnibus hired for the day.—
(If busses in those days were not to be seen,
All I can say is, they *ought* to have been.) —
      Like a torrent, the throng
      Roll'd briskly along,
Cheering the way with jest, laughter, and song,
To the Banquetting Hall, where the last of the group
Arrived, by good luck, just in time for the soup.

The guests set to work in superlative style,
And his Majesty, equally busy the while,
Encouraged their efforts with many a smile.
      The High Priest was the first,
      Who seemed ready to burst ;
      (For the ladies so shy,
      They swigged on the sly !)
But proud of his prowess he scorn'd to give o'er,
'Till at length with a hiccup he fell on the floor,
      Shouting out, mid his qualms,
      That verse in the Psalms,

Which saith (but it surely can't mean a whole can!)
That "Wine maketh merry the heart of a man."

While thus they sate tippling, peers, prelates, and all,
And music's sweet voice echoed light through the Hall;
     His Majesty rose,
     Blew his eloquent nose,
And exclaiming, by way of exordium, "Here goes!"
Made a speech which produced a prodigious sensation,
Greatly, of course, to the King's delectation:
One courtier, o'erpower'd by its humour and wit,
Held both his fat sides, as if fearing a fit;
While another kept crying, "Oh dear, I shall split!"
(So when a great Publisher cracks a small joke,
His authors at table are ready to choke.)
And all, with the lungs of a hurricane, swore
They had ne'er heard so droll an oration before,
With the single exception of one silly fellow,
Who not being, doubtless, sufficiently mellow,
Refused to applaud, or to join in the laughter,
And was hang'd for a traitor just ten minutes after.

By this time Dan Phœbus in ocean had sunk,
And the guests were all getting exceedingly drunk,
     When, behold! at the door
     There was heard a loud roar,
And in rush'd a messenger covered with gore,
Who bawl'd out, addressing the Head of the State,
"If your Majesty pleases, the Foe's at the gate,
"And threaten to kick up the Devil's own din,
"If you do not surrender, and bid them come in;

"The mob, too, has risen,
"And let out of prison,
"With the jailor's own keys (but it's no fault of *his'n*),
"Some hundreds of burglars, and fences, and prigs,
"Who are playing all sorts of queer antics and rigs;
"Already they've fired up one church for a beacon,—
"Hocussed a bishop, and burked an archdeacon,
"And swear, if you don't give them plenty of grog,
"They'll all become Chartists, and go the whole hog!"

Scarce had he ended, when hark! with a squall,
A second grim herald pops into the Hall,
        And, "Woe upon woe!
        "The desperate foe,"
Quoth he, "Have forced open the gates of the town,
"And are knocking by scores the rich citizens down;
        "As I pass'd with bent brow,
        "By the Law Courts just now,
"Lo, sixty attorneys lay smash'd in a row,
"Having just taken wing for the regions below,
"(When lawyers are dead, none can doubt where they go,)
"'Mid the cheers of each snob, who sung out, as he past,
"'So the scamps have gone home to their father at
        last!'"

Oh! long grew the face of each guest at this tale,
The men they turn'd red, and the women turn'd pale;
But redder and paler they turn'd when they heard
The more terrible tidings of herald the third!—
In he bounced with a visage as black as a crow's,
And a mulberry tinge on the tip of his nose;

He'd a rent in his breeches,
    A tergo, the which is
(As Smollett has taught us long since to believe *)
Not the pleasantest sight for the daughters of Eve ;
And he shook like a leaf, as thus hoarsely he spake
In the gruff and cacophonous tones of a drake, —
    " The town's all on fire,
    " Hut, palace, and spire
" Are blazing as fast as the foe can desire :
    " Such crashing and smashing,
    " And sparkling and darkling !
" Such squalling, and bawling, and sprawling,
" And jobbing, and robbing, and mobbing !
" Such kicking and licking, and racing and chasing,
" Blood-spilling and killing, and slaughtering and quar-
    tering !
" You'd swear that Old Nick, with Belphegor his clerk,
" And Moloch his cad, were abroad on a lark ! "

" Here's a go ! " said the King, staring wild like a bogle
At these tidings, and wiping his eyes with his fogle ;
    " 'Tis vain now to run for
    " Our lives, for we're done for ;
" So, away with base thoughts of submission or flight,
" Let's all, my brave boys, die like heroes to-night ;
" Raise high in this Hall a grand funeral pile,
" Then fire it, and meet our death-doom with a smile ! "
He ceased, when a courtier replied in low tone,
" If your Majesty pleases, I'd rather live on ;

* Vide Miss Tabitha Bramble, in Smollett's "Humphrey Clinker."

" For, although you may think me as dull as a post,
" Yet I can't say I've any great taste for a roast ;
" 'Tis apt to disorder one's system ; and so,
" Good-night to your Majesty—D. I. O. !"
So saying, he made for the door and rush'd out,
While quick at his heels rush'd the rest of the rout,
  Leaving all alone,
  The King on his throne,
With a torch in one hand which he waved all abroad,
And a glass in the other, as drunk as a Lord !

That night, from the Hall, late so joyous, there broke,
Spreading wild in 'mid air, a vast column of smoke ;
  While, higher and higher,
  Blazed up the red fire,
As it blazed from Queen Dido's funeral pyre !—
Hark to the crash, as roof, pillar, and wall
Bend—rock—and down in thunder fall !
Hark to the roar of the flames, as they show
Heaven and earth alike in a glow !
The hollow wind sobs through the ruins, as though
'Twere hymning his dirge who, an hour ago,
Was a King in all a King's array ;
But now lies, a blackened clod of clay,
In that Hall whose splendours have past away,
Save in old tradition, for ever and aye !

RICHELIEU; OR, THE CONSPIRACY.

CARDINAL RICHELIEU was Premier of France ;
He was keen as a fox, and you read at a glance,
In his phiz so expressive of malice and trick,
That he'd much of the nature ascribed to Old Nick ;
If a noble e'er dared to oppose him, instead
Of confuting his lordship, he whipped off his head :
  He fixed his grim paw,
  Upon church, state, and law,
With as much cool assurance as ever you saw ;
  With his satire's sharp sting
  He badgered the King,
   Bullied his brother,
   Transported his mother,
And (what is a far more astonishing case)
Not only pronounced him an ass to his face,
But made love to his Queen, and because she declined
His advances, gave out she was wrong in her mind !

Now the nobles of France, and still more the poor King,
Disliked, as was natural, this sort of thing ;
The former felt shocked that plebeian beholders
Should see a peer's head fly so oft from his shoulders,

And the latter was constantly kept upon thorns
By the Cardinal's wish to endow him with horns ;
      Thus rankling with spite,
      A party one night
Of noblemen met, and determined outright
      (So enraged were the crew)
      First, to murder Richelieu,
And, if needful, despatch all his partisans too :
      Next to league with the foes
      Of the King, and depose
The fat-pated monarch himself, for a fool
Rebellion ne'er uses, except as a tool.

On the night that Richelieu was thus marked out for
    slaughter,
He chanced to be tippling cold brandy and water
With one Joseph, a Capuchin priest—a sly dog,
And by no means averse to the comforts of grog,
As you saw by his paunch, which seemed proud to reveal
How exactly it looked like a fillet of veal.
They laughed and they quaffed, 'till the Capuchin's
    nose
('Twas a thorough-bred snub) grew as red as a rose ;
And, whenever it chanced that his patron, Richelieu,
Cracked a joke, even though it was not very new ;
And pointed his smart conversational squibs,
By a slap on Joe's back, or a peg in his ribs ;
The priest, who was wonderfully shrewd as a schemer,
Would bellow with ecstacy, "'Gad, that's a *screamer !* "
Thus they chatted away, a rare couple well met,
And were just tuning up for a pious duet,

When in rushed a spy,
With his wig all awry,
And a very equivocal drop in his eye,
Who cried (looking blue
As he turned to Richelieu)
"Oh, my lord, lack-a-day !
Here 's the devil to pay,
For a dozen fierce nobles are coming this way ;
One of whom, an old stager, as sharp as a lizard,
Has threatened to stick a long knife in your gizzard ;
While the rest of the traitors, I say it with pain,
Have already sent off a despatch to Spain,
To state that his Majesty's ceased to reign,
And order the troops all home again."

When his Eminence heard these tidings, "Go,"
He said, in the blandest of tones, to Joe,
"And if you can catch
The traitors' despatch,
I swear—no matter how rich it be—
You shall have, dear Joe, the very next see !"—
(*Nota bene*, whenever Old Nick is wishing
To enjoy the prime sport of parson-fishing,
He always, like Richelieu, cunning and quick,
Baits with a good fat bishoprick !)

No sooner had Joe turned his sanctified back—
I hardly need add he was off in a crack—
Than up the grand stairs rushed the murderous pack,
Whereon the sly Cardinal, tipping the wink
To the spy, who was helping himself to some drink

At a side-table, said,
"Tell 'em I'm dead ! "
Then flew to his chamber, and popped into bed.
"What, dead ?" roared the traitors. "I stuck him myself,
With a knife which I snatched from the back-kitchen
    shelf,"
    Was the ready reply
    Of the quick-witted spy,—
Who in matters of business ne'er stuck at a lie.
"Huzza, then, for office ! " cried one, and cried all,
"The government's ours by the Cardinal's fall,"
    And, so saying, the crew
    Cut a caper or two,
Gave the spy a new four-penny piece and withdrew.

Next day all the papers were full of the news,
Little dreaming the Cardinal's death was a *ruse ;*
In parliament, too, lots of speeches were made,
And poetical tropes by the bushel displayed ;
The deceased was compared to Ulysses and Plato,
To a star, to a cherub, an eagle, and Cato ;
And 'twas gravely proposed by some gents in committee
To erect him a statue of gold in the city ;
But when an economist, caustic and witty,
    Asked, "Gentlemen, pray,
    Who is to pay ? "
The committee, as if by galvanic shock jolted,
Looked horrified, put on their castors, and bolted !

Meanwhile the shrewd traitors repaired in a bevy,
All buoyant with hope, to his Majesty's levee,

When, lo ! as the King with anxiety feigned,
Was beginning to speak of the loss he'd sustained,
  In strutted Richelieu,
  And the Capuchin too,
Which made each conspirator shake in his shoe ;
One whispered a by-stander, looking him through,
"By Jove, I can scarcely believe it ! can you ?"
Another cried, "Hang it, I thought 'twas a *do !*"
And a third muttered faintly, o'ercome by his fear,
"Talk of the devil, and he's sure to appear !"

When the King, who at first hardly trusted his eyes,
Had somewhat recovered the shock of surprise,
  He shook his thick head
  At the Cardinal, and said,
In tones in which something of anger still lurked,
"How's this ?   Why, good gracious, I thought you were
  burked ?"
"Had such been my fate," quickly answered Richelieu,
"Had they made me a *subject*, the rascally crew,
My liege, they'd have soon made another of you.
Look here !" and he pulled out the nobles' despatch,
Who felt that for once they had met their match,
  And exclaiming, "'Od rot 'em,
  The scoundrels, I've got 'em !"
Read it out to the King from the top to the bottom.

Next morning twelve scaffolds, with axes of steel,
Adorned the fore-court of the sprightly Bastile ;
And at midnight twelve nobles, by way of a bed,

Lay snug in twelve coffins, each *minus* a head—
A thing not uncommon with nobles, 'tis said.
  Priest Joe got his see,
  And delighted was he,
For the bishoprick suited his taste to a T ;
And Richelieu, the stern, unforgiving, and clever,
Bullied king, church, and people, more fiercely than ever !

  Such the theme which Sir Lytton
  Has recently hit on,
To expand his rare fancy, and feeling, and wit on ;
And the moral is this—if, conspiring in flocks,
Silly geese will presume to play tricks with a fox,
And strive by finesse to get rid of the pest,
They must always expect to come off second best !

THE ABBOT'S OAK.

A LEGEND OF MONEY-HUTCH LANE.

———

"In the parish of Redgrave, skirting the park, is a narrow bye-road, which has from time immemorial borne the name of 'Money-Hutch Lane.' Tradition says that it derived its appellation from a treasure buried in its immediate neighbourhood, at the time of the suppression of the monasteries, one of which, a small offshoot from the great parent stem of St. Edmondsbury, stood in its vicinity. It is added, that though deposited under the guardianship of spell and sigil, it may yet be recovered by any one who bides the happy minute."—*Collect. for Hist. of Suffolk.*

THE Abbot sat by his glimmering lamp,
 His brow was wrinkled with care,
And his anxious look, was fixed on his book,
 With a sad and a mournful air,
  And ever anon,
  As the night wore on,
He would slowly sink back in his oaken chair,
While his visage betrayed from the aspect it bore,
That his studies perplexed him more and more.

On that Abbot's brow the furrows were deep,
 His hair was scant, and white,
And his glassy eyes had known no sleep
 For many a live-long night.

His lips so thin had let nothing in
Save brown bread, and water untempered by gin,
 During his sojourn there ;
His hopes of succeeding at all with his reading
Seemed to rest on his firmly abstaining from feeding,
 And sticking like wax to his chair.
One would think, from the pains which he took with his
   diet, he
Meant to establish a Temperance Society.
His fasting, in short, equalled that of those mighties,
St. Ronald, Dun Scotus, and Simon Stylites—
  No wonder his look
  On that black-letter book
Had a sad and a mournful air.

 But oh ! what pleasure now gleams from his eyes,
  As he gazes around his cell !
The Abbot springs up in delight and surprise,
 " I have it, I have it, I have it ! " he cries,
  " I have found out the mystic spell ! "—
'Twas a wonderful thing for so aged a man
To hop, skip, and jump, and to run as he ran,
 But something had tickled him sore.
  He just stayed to sing
  Out, for some one to bring
His best suit of robes, and his crosier and ring,
While his mitre, which hung by a peg on the door,
 In his hurry he popped on the hind side before,
 And then, though 'twas barely dawn of day,
He summoned a council without delay,

With a hint that he'd something important to say,
And commenced his address in the following way :—

" Unaccustom'd, my brethren, as I am to speaking,
  To keep you long waiting is not my intention ;
I'll merely observe, that the charm I've been seeking
  I've found out at length in a book I won't mention.—
    Yes, my brethren, I have found
      Where to hide our riches vast,
    Buried deep in holy ground,
      I've found the spell that binds them fast.
        The proud, the profane,
        Will search all in vain,
    If they hunt for them over and over again.
        One day in the year
        Was tarnish'd, I fear,
By some trifling *faux pas* in our Patron's career ;
    That's the time, and that's the hour,
    When fails our Saint's protecting power,
    Gallant hearts and steady hands
    Then, and then only, may burst the bands,
Our treasures may win, if their patience but let's them ;
As for Harry the Eighth, I'm—"—he cough'd—"if he
      gets them.
    And now, my brethren, all to bed ;
    We'll consider our early matins as said ;
    And if by good luck into any one's head
    A better device or more feasible plan
    To bother that corpulent horrid old man,
And that rascally renegade Cromwell, than this come ;

The morning will show it,
Then let me know it.

I'm sleepy just now—so good night—*Pax vobiscum !*"

It's pretty well known in what way the Eighth Harry,
When wearied of Catherine, he wanted to marry
Miss Boleyn,—he'd other points also to carry,—
Applied to the Pope for his aid ;

Which not being granted
As soon as he wanted,

The hot-headed monarch right solemnly said,
For bulls and anathemas feeling no dread,

That the Pope might go
To Jericho,—

And, instead of saluting his Holiness' toes,
He'd pull without scruple his Holiness' nose ;—
That way he brought the affair to a close.

Things being thus,
Without any fuss

He kicks out the monks from their pleasant locations ;

To their broad lands he sends
His most intimate friends,

And bestows their domains on his needy relations ;

And, sad to relate,
As we are bound to confess it is,
Pockets their plate

For his private necessities :
And whenever his Majesty finds a fresh dun arise,
Gives him a cheque on the abbeys and nunneries.
So you'll not be surprised that the very next morning,
As the Abbot his person was gravely adorning,

A note by express
Put all notions of dress
Instanter to flight by its terrible warning.
I say by express,
Though you'll probably guess
That no gentlemen deck'd in gold, scarlet, and blue,
Walked round in those days, as at present they do,
Charging eightpence for billets which shouldn't cost two—
(The reason they say for folks writing so few).
But a change, we are told, will be made in a trice,
And epistles of all sorts be brought to one price,
Despite the predictions of Mr. Spring Rice.
We shall not for any
Pay more than a penny,
No matter how great the dimensions or distance.
An excellent plan for the public; for then 'tis his
Own fault if any one spurns such assistance,
Nor writes every day to his fellow-apprentices
All laud to 'Hill
For this levelling bill,
Which will make, by the aid of the Whigs, its abettors,
The General Post a Republic of Letters.*

As it's everywhere voted remarkably rude
Into other folks' secrets to peep and intrude,
My Muse, for the present, shall so play the prude,
As not to let out
What this note was about,
Or what it was stagger'd an Abbot so stout.

* The change alluded to took place on January 10, 1840.—ED.

H

The result's all we care to make public in this story,
And to that we've a right, as mere matter of history.
 On the night of that ill-omen'd day
 A band of Monks pursued their way
 From the postern-gate of that Abbey grey,
  To the churchyard damp and drear,
   They bore three "hutches,"—
   In Suffolk such is
The word they use, as lately I've read
In Johnson, for boxes in which folks make bread.
The aged men totter'd with toil and with pain,
As to carry their burthen they strove might and main.
The Abbot marched first in that slow-going train,
  The Sexton brought up the rear.
   Near a newly-made vault
   They came to a halt,
With no unequivocal symptoms of pleasure,
   Then each ponderous box,
   With its three patent locks,
They buried, and filled up the hole at their leisure.
They planted above in a magical figure
Five acorns as big as five walnuts, or bigger.
 Then the torches' fitful glare
 Fell on the Abbot's silvery hair,
(I allude to his beard—his head was bare,)
As he read from a book, what perhaps was a prayer ;
But whether 'twas Sanscrit, Chinese or Hindoo,
I believe not a soul of his auditors knew,
And it matters but little to me or to you,
   But you'll find in swarms,
   Similar forms,

If you read Sandivogis',
A learn'd old fogie's
Dissertation " De Goblinis, Ghostis, et Bogis."

" 'Tis done—'tis done,"
Cried the Abbot ; "now run—
We need some refection.   And, hark ! it strikes one !
Our treasure here placed beyond human reach is,
And safe as if stored in St. Benedict's breeches.
King Harry may come ; but he 'll ne'er, in good sooth,
    pick
Up enough plate for a decent-sized toothpick."

'Tis said the course of true love never
Yet ran smooth ; in fact, if ever
        It does so run,
        It's very soon done,
        Like ladies, they say,
        Who have their own way,
It dwindles as snow on a very warm day ;
And, although unromantic may seem the admission,
Dies from the want of well-timed opposition.

        But so mournful a fate
        Seems not to await
The lovers whose griefs I 'm about to relate.
        A noble pair,
        One wondrous fair,
    One manly, tall, and debonair,
    Are whispering their vows in the evening air.

H 2

Vain, vain,
Hapless twain !
The Lady of Bottesdale ne'er may be
Mate to a squire of low degree !
Ralph of Redgrave is stout and true,
Ralph of Redgrave is six feet two
As he stands in his stockings without a shoe ;
But, like Tully, his family's rather new,—
And, what is far worse,
Ralph's private purse
By no means is heavy, but quite the reverse,—
Two failings which make an indifferent catch
For a lady of title in want of a match.
That lady's papa is stingy and close ;
As for his features—one look is a dose.
He is ugly and old,
Unfeeling and cold,
With a *penchant* for nothing but bank-notes or gold.
His estates, too, are mortgaged or sold ; for the fact is, his
Youth had been spent in most dissolute practices,
Gaming, and drinking,
Cockfighting, and winking
At ladies, without ever dreaming or thinking
His means were all gone, and his credit fast sinking ;
While he'd now to " come down " with a pretty smart
fine
For sundry exploits in the Jacobite line ;—
A mode by which Tories in those days were pepper'd,
As you'll find if you read Mr. Ainsworth's "Jack Sheppard :"
All these things induced him to aid the advances
(Not being the person to throw away chances)

Of a wealthy old lord to his fair daughter Frances,
Which he thought no bad spec. to recruit his finances.

Slowly and sadly the lovers were walking,
On their hardships, and some other odd matters talking ;
   The lady had said
   That rather than wed
An old noodle just ready to take to his bed,
   She 'd perish outright,
   Were it only to spite
Her father for taking such things in his head.
   Ralph then swore he
   Would die before he
Allowed any man, Baron, Viscount, or Earl,
To walk off to church with his own darling girl.
But, meanwhile, as dying was rather a bore, he
Would first tell the lady a singular story.

  He said,—" At Preston's bloody fray,
  As night closed o'er the well-fought day,
  An aged man sore wounded lay,
  And just as two troopers were ready to twist,
  The old gentleman's neck, with one blow of his fist
 He, Ralph, strongly hinted they'd better desist.
  Then the old man smiled a remarkable smile.
  And clasping that same stout fist the while,
Acknowledged his kindness, and swore, too, that '*dem it*' he
Would serve him in turn at his direst extremity.
That, last night, which must still more remarkable seem,
That remarkable man had appeared in a dream,
And had bid him, without any nonsense or joke,

Wrap himself up snug and warm in his cloak,
And meet him at twelve by the " Abbot's old oak."

Meanwhile the clouds were collecting on high,
Darker and darker grew the sky,
And a rain-drop moistened that lady's eye
  As big as a half-crown piece.
The lady she sighed, perchance for a coach,
Threw on her lover one glance of reproach,
  And one on her satin pelisse.
At this moment, when what to do neither could tell, a
Page appeared, bearing a brown silk umbrella.
   I don't mean a page
   Of this civilized age,
In a very tight jacket, with very short tails,
Studded all over with brass-headed nails ;
But an orthodox page, who, on bended knee,
Said, " Miss, be so good as to come and make tea."

   Ralph instantly rose ;
   One kiss ere he goes—
The page most discreetly is blowing his nose,—
And, before you can thrice on John Robinson call,
Ralph has cleared with a bound that garden wall.
  With no less speed
  He has mounted his steed,—
  A noble beast of bone and breed,
   Of sinewy limb,
   Compact, yet slim,
"Warranted free from vice and from whim."
Meanwhile the rain was beginning to soak

Through a very bad shift for a MacIntosh cloak,
    Which—a regular *do*,—
    When only half new,
Ralph had bought some time back from a parrot-nosed
    Jew,
Trusting his word, with no further thought or proof,
For it's being a patent-wove, London-made waterproof,—
A fact, by the way, which most forcibly shows men
How sharp they must look when they deal with old clothes-
    men.

Little reck'd Ralph of the wind and the rain,
. On his inmost heart was preying that pain
Which man may know once, but can ne'er know again ;
    That bitterest throe
    Of deepest woe,
To feel he was loved, and was loved in vain.

Now fiercer grew the tempest's force,
And the whirlwind eddied round rider and horse,
As onward they urged their headlong course.
    O'er bank, brook, and briar,
    O'er streamlet and brake,
    By the red lightning's fire
    Their wild way they take.
A country so awkward to go such a pace on
Might have pozed Captain Beecher, Dan Seffert, or Mason.

    At once a flash, livid and clear,
    Shows a moss-grown ruin mouldering near ;
    The horseman stays his steed's career,

And slowly breasts the steep.
As slowly climbs that ancient mound,
His courser spurns the holy ground,
Where the dead of other days around
   Lie clasped in stony sleep.
And mark against the lurid sky
An oak uprears its form on high,
   And flings its branches free ;
A thousand storms have o'er it broke,
But well hath it stood the tempest stroke,—
It is, it is the Abbot's oak,
   It is the trysting-tree.
An hour hath passed, an hour hath flown,
Ralph stands by the tree, but he stands alone.
Till, surmising his dream is a regular hoax,
He " confounds," with much energy " Abbots and oaks,
And old gentlemen dying from Highlanders' strokes,"
Then enters a shed, which, though rather a cool house,
     Might serve at less need ·
     To hold him and his steed,—
As it formerly served the old monks for a tool-house.

   Another hour was past and gone,
   Another day was stealing on,
   When Ralph, who was shaking
   With cold, thought of taking
A nap, and was just between sleeping and waking,
Was roused by his horse, who stood trembling and shaking.
     He opens his eyes,
     To raise himself tries,
But a weight seems to press on his arms, chest, and thighs,

Like a lifeless log he helplessly lies—
Then conceive his amazement, alarm, and surprise,
      When, on every side,
      In its ancient pride,
He sees an old monastery slowly arise ;
      Chapel and hall,
      Buttress and wall,
    Ivied spire, and turret tall,
  Grow on his vision one and all.
      Airy and thin,
      At first they begin
To fall into outline, and slowly fill in ;
At length in their proper proportions they fix,
And assume an appearance exactly " like bricks."

From the postern-gate of that Abbey grey
A band of monks pursue their way
Till they come to the Abbot's oak.
Ralph sees an eye he before has known,—
'Tis the eye of their leader,—fixed on his own !
      It is, it is,
      The identical phiz
Of his friend, or one precisely like his !
These words from his thin lips broke :—
" This the time, and this the hour,
Fails the Saint's protecting power,
Gallant heart and steady hand,
Now may burst the charmed band—
    Now—" Here the knell
    Of an Abbey bell,
On the ear of the wondering listener fell ;

As if the sound,
His limbs unbound,
His strength, so strangely lost, is found !

Howling fled the wild Nightmare,
As Ralph leaped forth from his secret lair,
And gained at a bound the open air ;—
He gazed around, but nothing was there !
Nothing save the roofless aisle,
Nothing save the mouldering pile,
Which looked, in the deepening shade half hid,
As old and as ugly as ever it did.
The storm had passed by,
And the moon on high
Beamed steadily forth from the deep-blue sky.
One single ray through the branches broke,
It fell at the foot of the " Abbot's old oak."

Still in Ralph's ear the words were ringing
The words he had heard the old gentleman singing,
" This the time, and this the hour,"
He felt that the tide at last was come, now or
Never, to lead him to fortune and power.
Of his trusty blade
He very soon made
An apology—poor one I grant—for a spade,
And proceeded to work, though new at the trade,
With hearty good will, where the roots seemed decayed.
With labour and toil
He turned up the soil,
While he thought—

As he ought—
On that adage which taught
"Perseverance, and patience, and plenty of oil;"
　　Till, wearied grown,
　　Muscle and bone,
His sword broke short on a broad flag stone.

　　-　　　　-　　　　*　　　　-

In Redgrave church the bells are ringing;
To Redgrave church a youth is bringing
His bride, preceded by little boys singing,—
A custom considered the regular thing in
Times past, but gone out in these latter days,
When a pair may get married in fifty queer ways.

In Redgrave church blush bridesmaids seven,
One had turned faint, or they would have blushed
　　even;
In Redgrave church a bride is given
In face of man, in face of Heaven.
In her sunshine of youth, in her beauty's pride
The lady of Bottesdale stands that bride;
And Ralph of Redgrave stands by her side;
　　But no longer drest
　　In homely vest,
Coat, waistcoat and breeches, are all of the best;
　　His look so noble, his air so free,
　　Proclaim a squire of high degree;
　　The lace on his garments is richly gilt,
　　His elegant sword has a golden hilt,
　　His "tile" in the very last fashion is built,

His Ramillie wig
Is burly and big,
And a ring with a sparkling diamond his hand is on,
Exactly as Richardson paints Sir Charles Grandison.

Nobody knows
Or can even suppose,
How Ralph of Redgrave got such fine clothes ;
For little Ned Snip, the tailor's boy said,—
And a 'cuter blade was not in the trade,—
That his master's bill had been long ago paid.
Ah ! little, I ween, deem these simple folks,
Who on Ralph's appearance are cracking their jokes,
How much may be gained by a person who pokes,
At the right hour, under the right sort of oaks.

DALTON.

HAROUN ALRASCHID.

O'ER the gorgeous room a luxurious gloom,
　　Like the glow of a summer's eve, hung;
From its basin of stone, with rose-leaves bestrown,
　　The fountain its coolness flung;
Perfumes wondrously rare fill'd the eunuch-fann'd air,
　　And on gem-studded carpets around
The poets sung forth tales of glory or mirth
　　To their instruments' eloquent sound;
On a throne framed of gold sat their monarch the bold,
　　With coffers of coin by his side,
And to each, as he sung, lavish handfuls he flung,
　　Till each in his gratitude cried,
"Long, long live great Haroun Alraschid, the Caliph of
　　Babylon old!"

Disturbing the feast, from the Rome of the East
　　An embassage audience craves;
And Haroun, smiling bland, cries, dismissing the band,
　　"We will look on the face of our slaves!"
Then the eunuchs who wait on their Caliph in state
　　Lead the messenger Lords of the Greek.

Proud and martial their mien, proud and martial
  their sheen,
  But they bow to the Arab right meek ;
And with heads bending down, though their brows
  wear a frown,
  They ask if he audience bestow.
" Yea, dogs of the Greek, we await ye, so speak !—
  Have ye brought us the tribute you owe ?
Or what lack ye of Haroun Alraschid, the Caliph of
  Babylon old ?"

Then the Greek spake loud, " To Alraschid the
  Proud
  This message our monarch doth send :
While ye play'd 'gainst a Queen, ye could mate her,
  I ween—
  She could ill with thy pieces contend ;
But Irene is dead, and a Pawn in her stead
  Holds her power and place on the board :
By Nicephorus stern is the purple now worn,
  And no longer he owns thee for lord.
If tribute ye claim, I am bade in his name
  This to tell thee, O King of the World,
With these, not with gold, pays Nicephorus bold !"—
  And a bundle of sword-blades he hurl'd
At the feet of stern Haroun Alraschid, the Caliph of
  Babylon old.

Dark as death was his look, and his every limb
  shook,
  As the Caliph glared round on the foe—

" View my answer !" he roar'd, and unsheathing his
    sword,
    Clove the bundle of falchions right through.
" Tell my slave, the Greek hound, that Haroun the
    Renown'd,
    Ere the sun that now sets rise again,
Will be far on the road to his wretched abode,
    With many a myriad of men.
No reply will he send, either spoken or penn'd ;
    . But by Allah, and Abram our sire,
He shall read a reply on the earth, in the sky,
    Writ in bloodshed, and famine, and fire !
Now begone !" thundered Haroun Alraschid, the Caliph
    of Babylon old.

As the sun dropt in night by the murky torch-
    light,
    There was gathering of horse and of man :
Tartar, Courd, Bishareen, Persian, swart Bedoween,
    And the mighty of far Khorasan—
Of all tongues, of all lands, and in numberless bands,
    Round the Prophet's green banner they crowd,
They are form'd in array, they are up and away,
    Like the locusts' calamitous cloud ;
But rapine or spoil, till they reach the Greek soil,
    . Is forbidden, however assail'd.
A poor widow, whose fold a Courd robb'd, her tale
    told,
    And he was that instant impaled
By the stern wrath of Haroun Alraschid, the Caliph of
    Babylon old !

On o'er valley and hill, river, plain, onwards still,
 Fleet and fell as the desert-wind, on !
Where was green grass before, when that host had
  pass'd o'er,
 Every vestige of verdure was gone !
On o'er valley and hill, desert, river, on still,
 With the speed of the wild ass or deer,
The dust of their tread, o'er the atmosphere spread,
 Hung for miles like a cloud in their rear.
On o'er valley and hill, desert, river, on still,
 Till afar booms the ocean's hoarse roar,
And amid the night's gloom are seen tower, temple,
  dome—
 Heraclea, that sits by the shore !
The doom'd city of Haroun Alraschid, the Caliph of
 Babylon old.

There was mirth at its height in thy mansions that
  night,
 Heraclea, that sits by the sea !
Thy damsels' soft smiles breathed their loveliest wiles,
 And the banquet was wild in its glee !
For Zoe the fair, proud Nicephorus' heir,
 That night was betrothed to her mate,
To Theseus the Bold, of Illyria old,
 And the blood of the Island-kings great.
When lo ! wild and lorn, and with robes travel-torn,
 And with features that pallidly glared,
They the Arab had spurn'd from Damascus return'd,
 Rush'd in, and the coming declared
Of the armies of Haroun Alraschid, the Caliph of Babylon
 old.

A faint tumult afar, the first breathing of war,
    Multitudinous floats on the gale ;
The lelie shout shrill, and the toss'd cymbals peal,
    And the trumpet's long desolate wail,
The horse-tramp of swarms, and the clangour of
    arms,
    And the murmur of nations of men.
Oh woe, woe, and woe, Heraclea shall know—
    She shall fall, and shall rise not again ;
The spiders' dusk looms shall alone hang her rooms,
    The green grass shall grow in her ways,
Her daughters shall wail, and her warriors shall quail,
    And herself be a sign of amaze,
Through the vengeance of Haroun Alraschid, the Caliph
    of Babylon old.

'Tis the dawn of the sun, and the morn-prayer is
    done,
    And the murderous onset is made ;
The Christian and foe they are at it, I trow,
    Fearfully plying the blade.
Each after each rolls on to the breach,
    Like the slumberless roll of the sea.
Rank rolling on rank rush the foe on the Frank,
    Breathless, in desperate glee ;
The Greek's quenchless fire, the Mussulman's ire
    Has hurled over rampart and wall.
And 'tis all one wild hell of blades slaughtering fell,
    Where fiercest and fellest o'er all
Work'd the falchion of Haroun Alraschid, the Caliph of
    Babylon old.

But day rose on day, yet Nicephorus grey,
    And Theseus, his daughter's betrothed,
With warrior-like sleight kept the town in despite,
    Of the Moslem insulted and loathed.
Morn rose after morn on the leaguers outworn,
    Till the Caliph with rage tore his beard ;
And, terribly wroth, sware a terrible oath—
    An oath which the boldest ev'n fear'd.
So his mighty Emirs gat around their compeers,
    And picked for the onslaught a few.
Oh! that onslaught was dread,—every Moslem struck
    dead !
    But, however, young Theseus they slew,
And that gladdened fierce Haroun Alraschid, the Caliph
    of Babylon old.

Heraclea, that night in thy palaces bright
    There was anguish and bitterest grief.
"He is gone! he is dead!" were the words that they
    said,
    Though the stunn'd heart refused its belief;
Wild and far spreads the moan, from the hut, from
    the throne,
    Striking every one breathless with fear.
"Oh! Theseus the bold, thou art stark,—thou art
    cold,—
    Thou art young to be laid on the bier."
One alone makes no moan, but with features like
    stone,
    In an ecstacy haggard of woe,
Sits tearless and lorn, with dry eyeballs that burn,

And fitful her lips mutter low
Dread threatenings against Haroun Alraschid, the Caliph
of Babylon old.

The next morn on the wall, first and fiercest of all,
The distraction of grief cast aside,
In her lord's arms arrayed, Zoe plies the death-
blade,—
Ay, and, marry, right terribly plied.
Her lovely arm fair, to the shoulder is bare,
And nerved with a giant-like power
Where her deadly sword sweeps fall the mighty in
heaps ;
Where she does but appear the foe cower.
Rank on rank they rush on,—rank on rank are
struck down,
Till the ditch is choked up with the dead.
The vulture and crow, and the wild dog, I trow,
Made a dreadful repast that night as they fed
On the liegemen of Haroun Alraschid, the Caliph of
Babylon old.

This was not to last.—The stern Moslem, downcast,
Retrieved the next morning their might ;
For Alraschid the bold, and the Barmecide old,
Had proclaimed through the camp in the night,
That whoso should win the first footing within
The city that bearded their power,
Should have for his prize the fierce girl with black
eyes,
And ten thousand zecchines as her dower.

It spurred them right well; and they battled and fell,
    Like lions, with long hunger wild.
Ere that day set the sun Heraclea was won,
    And Nicephorus bold, and his child,
Were captives to Haroun Alraschid, the Caliph of
    Babylon old.

To his slave, the Greek hound, roared Haroun the
    Renowned,
    When before him Nicephorus came,
"Though the pawn went to queen, 'tis checkmated,
    I ween.
    Thou'rt as bold as unskilled in the game.
Now, Infidel, say, wherefore should I not slay
    The wretch that my vengeance hath sought?"—
"I am faint,—I am weak,—and I thirst," quoth
    the Greek,
    "Give me drink." At his bidding 'tis brought;
He took it; but shrank, lest 'twere poison he drank.
    "Thou art safe till the goblet be quaffed!"
Cried Haroun. The Greek heard, took the foe at
    his word,
    Dashed down on the pavement the draught,
And claimed mercy of Haroun Alraschid, the Caliph of
    Babylon old.

Haroun never broke word or oath that he spoke,
    So he granted the captive his life,
And then bade his slaves bear stately Zoe the fair,
    To the warrior who won her in strife;
But the royal maid cried in the wrath of her pride,

She would die ere her hand should be given,
Or the nuptial caress should be lavished to bless
Such a foe to her house and to Heaven.
Her entreaties they spurned, and her menace they
scorned ;
But, resolute, spite of their power,
All food she denied, and by self-famine died ;
And her father went mad from that hour.
Thus triumph'd stern Haroun Alraschid, the Caliph of
Babylon old !

G. E. INMAN.

A TALE OF A CALF;

OR, "DOING" A GENSD'ARME.

—◆—

MOST folks with virtuous indignation
Would "flare-up" at the imputation,
(However well-deserved the same,)
Upon their fair and honest fame,
Of trickery, and double-dealing,
And such-like covert acts of stealing,
Which don't amount to downright robbery,
At which you could "kick up a bobbery,"
But just sail near enough the wind
To leave the impression on your mind
That you've been regularly "done,"
Of which few persons see the fun.
Yet, somehow, these same honest people
Their principle in practice keep ill;
For, though they'd talk of hostile meeting,
And mayhap treat you to a beating,
If you but hinted they were cheating,
And, rather than defraud their neighbour,
Would undergo twelve months' hard labour:
They think it quite a different thing
To *chouse* our Sovereign Lord the King;

Or rather, now-a-days, I mean
Her Gracious Majesty the Queen.
That is, in fact, they reckon smuggling
A very clever kind of juggling;
And, that they may the better do it, aye
Exert their utmost ingenuity.
And, certes, 'tis some consolation
To soften down one's indignation
At being hurried to that *bore*
Of travellers, the custom-house,
And there watched as by cat a mouse,
While they your luggage are unpacking,
And every trunk and bag ransacking,
Turning your chattels topsy-turvy,
And treating them in way most scurvy,
To search if 'midst the various particles
There lie hid any smuggled articles.
I say you feel a satisfaction,
As if you'd done a worthy action,
To know that, spite of all their prying,
They've missed, in some snug corner lying,
No end of gloves, or Brussels lace,
Or satins, as may be the case,
Things which you've fetched across the Channel,
(Whose billows often make a man ill!)
With sundry other odds and ends,
As presents to your lady friends;
All specimens of foreign finery,
That ne'er were wrought by home machinery,
And should, in consequence, pay duty
'Ere they adorn a native beauty.

Well, I was going to tell a story
To illustrate the case before ye,
That somehow men are all inclined,
If but occasion they can find,
To cheat the royal revenue,
Nor, as they are enjoined to do,
Give custom to whom custom's due;
No matter whence those customs rise,
From tolls, or taxes, or excise.
"Be't known to all men by these presents,"
That, to raise money from the peasants,
And other traders, who bring down
Their country wares to sell in town,
There stands in every road in France
A *bureau d'octroi*, in advance
Of each town's suburbs, where they levy
A toll proportionally heavy
On every article that passes;
On pigs, and sheep, and fowls, and asses,
On *vin du pays*, corn, and brandy,
And other things which they command ye:
And deuced sharp those gensd'armes look
That none escape, by hook or crook,
·From "forking out" the full amount,
For every item of the account;
And they must sure be "artful dodgers"
Who can evade such prying codgers;
Though many "try it on," and so
A few succeed, as I shall show.
It happened that (no matter where
It might be, Dieppe or St. Omer,)

An honest butcher went one day
A call *professional* to pay
To some old farmer near the town,
Whose grazing-stock held high renown,
And purchase for his week's supply,
Unless he found the price too high,
A well-fed calf, or some such beast,
On which his customers to feast.
One was selected from the lot,
Which Jean said was the best he'd got,
And asked, of course, a longish price,
Which Pierre refused him in a trice,
Saying, he asked too much by half
For such a "*morceau*" of a calf.
On this they set to work, and grumbled,
And haggled, "sacré'd," swore, and stumbled
Upon some rather awkward names,
Which added fuel to the flames,
And might perchance have led to *murther*,
Had they proceeded any further.
But luckily a Frenchman's quarrel,
As *Johnny Crapaud* does but *spar* ill,
After a wordy contest ends,
In general in making friends—
"Eh bien," the former says at last,
After this little *breeze* was past,
"Though on the price we can't agree,
You're a good customer to me,
And so for once, to make things pleasant,
I'll make you of the calf a present ;
But, mind you, Pierre, on one condition,

Which is, despite the prohibition,
That, while to town the beast conveying,
You pass the *octroi* without paying."
"Done!" cries the butcher; "come, I'll take it,
Since you are willing thus to stake it;
And that gensd'arme, or any such man,
If I don't chouse him, I'm a Dutchman!
But will you be so good as lend me
That dog of yours there to attend me?"
His willingness did Jean express,
Though Pierre's intent he could not guess;
So, without asking his permission,
After some growls and opposition,
He cramm'd the dog into a sack,
And trudg'd off with him on his back,
Giving him now and then a licking,
To stop his howling and his kicking,
Until at last the brute lay quiet,
And didn't dare to make a riot.
The *octroi* reach'd, he never stay'd,
But look'd as if he wish'd to evade
The keeper's eye, and hasten'd onward,
Directing still his progress townward.
Old *Cerberus*, as he expected,
A *something* from his look suspected,
Which made him think all was not right;
So, in a manner most polite,
He forthwith called the *gemman* back,
And ask'd him what was in his sack.
"Je vous assure, Monsieur, ce n'est rien,"
Says Pierre, " qu'une pauvre bête de chien,

Dont un de mes amis m'a fait
Le cadeau—voilà tout ce que c'est ! "
" Tell that to the marines," says t'other ;
" So, come, let's see, without more bother,
What you've got in that sack.   I'll wager
It's no dog.   I'm too old a stager
To humbug thus, you may depend on't ;
And I *must* know,—so there's an end on't ! "
Pierre made a well-feign'd opposition
Before he deign'd to make submission,
Grumbling that, if he oped the sack,
The dog would *cut* him, and run back,
And he should have his toil and trouble,
By running after him, made double.
Finding, at length, remonstrance vain,
(Just what he wish'd, his end to gain,)
He quietly untied the string,
And so contrived that one good spring
Set free the dog, who, not admiring
His narrow berth, with speed untiring,
And Pierre's loud voice his terror heightening,
Bolted off home like " butter'd lightning."
" I told you how 'twould be," says Pierre ;
" It's fit to make a bishop swear ! "
So growling forth, as if in spite,
Some words " unfit for ears polite,"
He started off, as in pursuit
Of his emancipated brute ;
While *Cerberus*, thinking it good fun,
Laugh'd at the mischief he had done.
Returning to his friend's abode,

A little way along the road,
Pierre didn't stop the dog to search,
Which thus had left him in the lurch,
Because, as you may take for granted,
The *dog* was not the thing he wanted ;
But this time, as was his intent,
He bagg'd the *calf*, and off he went.
The gensd'arme seeing him once more
With the same sack he had before,
Of course concluded 'twas the dog,
And onwards suffer'd Pierre to jog,
Observing archly, as he pass'd,
He saw he'd caught the dog at last,
And hoped Monsieur was none the worse
After his unexpected " course."
Pierre answer'd nothing, but within
Himself thought, " Let them laugh that win ; "
For, after cheating this old stager,
He gain'd his calf, and won his wager.

A. R. W.

AN APOLOGY FOR NOSES.

WE read in Romance, Poem, Novel, and Play,
Be the subject mysterious, tragic, or gay,
In Forget-me-not, Keepsake, and all other Annuals,
Voyages, Essays, Tales, Handbooks, and Manuals,
  Of soul-piercing eye,
  Of brow fair and high,
Of locks that with ravens' jet plumage may vie,
  Of cheeks that disclose
  Warmer blush than the rose,—
But tell me what poet has sung of the Nose?

  'Tis a cutting disgrace
  To each well-moulded face,
Its best feature by scornful neglect to abase :
  Ye, who write verse or prose,
  Will make thousands of foes,
If ye follow the fashion in slighting the nose.

As in eyes folks are apt to prefer black or blue,
As in hair a rich auburn's a popular hue,
As a maidenly blush is more charming to view
Than the loveliest flow'r that in garden ere grew,

As the lips should appear for a warm kiss to sue,
As the breath should be sweeter than rose wash'd with dew,
So the nose, to be perfect, (for tho' 'tis true, no man
Can be perfect, his nose may,) should surely be Roman.
There are noses of all sorts,—pugs, aquilines, crooks,
Cocks, Grecians, Dutch tea-pots, snubs, hat-pegs, and
    hooks,—
Nay, the list, I dare say, would admit of extension,
As the *genus* depends on the form and dimension ;
      And seldom, if ever,
      (I perhaps may add never,)
Will you find two alike, tho' for years you endeavour ;
Tho' a man search, unfetter'd by hind'rance or trammel, he
Need not expect to see two in a family.

      By many 'tis said
      That a mind may be read
By a critical glimpse at the bumps on the head,
      While others maintain
      That as daylight 'tis plain,
There's a method more easy such knowledge to gain ;
They profess all your habits and feelings to trace,
If you'll only allow them to look in your face.
Again, who does not from experience know,
Men are seldom admired if their foreheads are low ?
A fine open brow is imagined to be
A mirror wherein the whole heart we can see.
How often do poets say, we may descry
A proud haughty soul in a dark flashing eye ?
While a glance soft and tender (as who cannot prove ?)
Expresses confiding affection and love.

Ye bards, hide your heads—now a champion is come
To redress the wrong'd noses of Greece and of Rome,
And, defying the boasted success of Phrenology,
Will establish a science, and call it Nose-ology !

Now each learn'd M.D.
Will doubtless agree,
On the virtues of analysation, with me ;
Nor will any oppose
(When the facts I disclose)
My project of thus analysing the nose ;
Tho,'—if I would convince either silly or sensible,—
A few facts (or fictions) are quite indispensable.

Imprimis—a nose, be its form what it may,
Should be decently large, (or, as some people say,
A nose you could find in a bottle of hay,)
Not like those you may see in the street any day,
But something more out of the usual way,
Like (if well I remember) the nose of Lord Grey,
Or his, whose proud home you may pause to survey,
If towards Hyde-Park-Corner you happen to stray ;
(And here, I may venture a tribute to pay
Of respect to the nose, which in many a fray
Secured the brave leader's victorious sway,
In spite of Soult, Marmont, Massena, and Ney ;)
'Tis a fact, tho' a hero in mind and in body,
If a man has a small nose he looks a Tom Noddy.

I've hinted before,
(And none but a bore

Says a thing more than once, so enough on that score,)
    What shape I like best ;
    But I never professed
To lay down the law as regards others, lest
My readers might fancy my motives were sinister,
And trust me no more than they would a Prime Minister.

    Now I think every man
    Should give " sops in the pan "
To the fair-sex, when he conscientiously can ;
    So in this present case,
    With the very best grace
I own that, to set off a feminine face
Peeping 'neath a smart cap, with an edging of lace,
A Grecian nose is by no means out of place ;
But stop there, my dears, Lucy, Ellen, and Jacqueline,
It's no use your teasing, I can't bear an aquiline.

Paul Bedford, Paul Bedford, 'twould ill become me
To omit a poor tribute of homage to thee,
E'en now in my mind's eye I see thee once more,
Like a dignified lion beginning to roar ;
While the sound of thy voice thro' each startled ear
    goes,
And Echo, half frightened, repeats " Jolly Nose ! "
    Ah, Paul ! only think,
    Tho' men now-a-days shrink
From a song lest by chance it should tempt 'em to drink,
    It was not so with thee,
    As a proof of which, see
(Tho' so many are sold—out of print it may be—)

Thy portrait in every music *dépôt,*
Exclusively publish'd by D'Almaine and Co.
For thy chant is a triumph o'er dull melancholy,
And thy very phiz proves that the nose *must* be jolly.

Search History's page
From the earliest age,
Trace the portraits of warrior, poet, and sage ;
Or, to solve your doubts, seek
Any statue *antique,*
It matters not whether 'tis Roman or Greek,
For its nose to the truth of my doctrine will speak :
'Tis a prominent feature in worthies like Plato,
Or Socrates, Seneca, Cæsar, or Cato ;
But you'll find snubs predominate (Reader, I'm serious,)
In every bust that exists of Tiberius.
Besides, the mere name
Could formerly claim
For its lucky possessor no small share of fame,
As in his case, whose writings I once was quite pat in,
(And should be now, but I've forgotten my Latin,
Tho' I've left school some time, 'tis with shame that I
say so,)
I once was *so* fond of Ovidius Naso !
Look closely, and then contradict, if you can,
That the Nose is, and must be, a type of the Man.

CHARLES HERVEY.

THE THREE DAMSELS.

THREE damsels look'd down from the castle tower
　That frown'd o'er the winding vale,
Where, borne on his steed of matchless breed,
　Rode their sire in knightly mail.
" And welcome, Sir Father! and welcome," they cried,
" To thy daughters, who long for thy coming have sigh'd !
　　　　Oh, say, what gifts dost thou bring ?"

" On thee thy fond father hath thought to-day,
　My fair girl in yellow drest ;
For dear to thy heart is the toilet's art,
　And jewels and gems please thee best.
So take thou this chain of ruddy gold ;
I won it in fight from a gallant bold,
　　　　And that gallant bold I slew !"

The damsel hath flung that glittering chain
　Her swan-like neck around ;
And she sought out the spot where the gallant slain
　All drench'd in his gore she found.
" Oh, shame, that a knight like a knave should lie
The scorn and the scoff of each vulgar eye !
　　　　Hath my loved one no resting-place ?"

And his ghastly corpse in her arms she bore
  To the ground that the priests had blest ;
And she murmur'd a prayer as she laid him there
  In the tomb where her fathers rest.
And close round her neck the chain she drew
Till the last breath of life from her bosom flew,
      And she slumber'd by him she loved !

Two damsels look'd down from the castle tower
  That frown'd o'er the winding vale,
Where, borne on his steed of matchless breed,
  Rode their sire in knightly mail.
" And welcome, Sir Father ! and welcome," they cried,
" To thy daughters, who long for thy coming have sigh'd!
      Oh, say, what gifts dost thou bring ?"

" On thee thy fond father hath thought to-day,
  My fair girl that in green art drest ;
For dearly thou lovest to greenwood to stray,
  And the chase ever joys thee best.
Then take thou this javelin, my venturous child ;
I won it in fight from the hunter wild,
      And the hunter wild I slew !"

The javelin she took from her father's hand,
  Then roam'd to the greenwood away ;
But the horn that she wound gave a dirge-like sound,
  'Stead of hunter's roundelay :
And she saw 'neath a willow-tree's mournful shade
The youth of her heart in deep sleep laid,—
      The deep, deep sleep of death !

" Oh, true to the faith that I plighted, I come
   To our trysting-place, loved one, to thee !"
And quick in her heart hath she buried the dart,
   And sunk her beneath the tree.
And o'er the two fond ones sweet flow'rets spring,
And the birds of the forest at summer-tide sing
          The lovers' lullaby !

One damsel look'd down from the castle tower
   That frown'd o'er the winding vale,
Where, borne on his steed of matchless breed,
   Rode her sire in knightly mail.
" And welcome, Sir Father ! and welcome," she cried,
" To thy daughter, who long for thy coming hath sigh'd !
          Oh, say, what gift dost thou bring ?"

" Nay, think not thy sire hath forgotten thee,
   My fair girl that in white art drest ;
For dearer than gems are the soft flowers to thee,
   And the gardens e'er joy thee best.
From the gardener so skill'd, for my darling one,
This flow'ret, than silver far fairer, I won,
          And the gardener so skill'd I slew !"

" And hast thou then slain that gardener so skill'd,—
   That gardener so skill'd hast thou slain ?
My flowers did he rear with a father's care—
   Now they never will bloom again !
And he swore to his loved one, no fairer flower
E'er blush'd 'midst the beauties of Flora's bower
          Than the flow'ret he nurtured for me !"

Then next to her bosom so gentle she laid
   The flow'ret her father had given ;
And forth to the garden she dolefully stray'd,—
   That garden her home and her heaven !
There a small mound freshly raised she descried,
And the lilies, like mourners, were drooping beside ;
        And she sunk on that freshly-raised mound !

" Oh, could I but do as my sisters have done,—
   But die as my sisters have died !—
But my delicate flower to wound hath no power,
   And death at its hands is denied !"
Like the flower that she gazed on, so wan and pale,
Did she breathe out her life to the passing gale ;—
        Like her flower did she fade and die !

THE LOVE-MERCHANT.

A FABLE.

— ♦ —

It was not until after I had written the following fable that the similarity of its point to that of the beautiful song, "Who'll buy my love-knots?" occurred to me. I am aware that my case may be thought to resemble his, who, when accused of having borrowed his thoughts from the immortal Bard of Avon, replied, "It is no fault of mine that Shakspeare and myself should have had the same ideas." Nevertheless, I venture to assert that my humble muse is not more indebted to that of the "Modern Anacreon" for the conception of this fable, than is the midnight lamp for its glimmering rays to the glorious orb of day. It was entirely suggested by a "fresco" painting, still existing on the walls of a house in Pompeii; and if my readers could have watched, as I did, the process of removing the envious "lapilli" which had concealed it for so many ages, they would, I think, allow for the impression it was likely to produce, and acquit me of plagiarism. The painting represents the figure of an old man, with a long white beard and flowing garments. Before him stands a large cage, or basket, containing several imprisoned "amorini," one of whom he has raised from it, and is holding forth by the wings, to attract the attention of a group of females. On the foreground lie a pair of compasses, and a mathematical figure described on a tablet.

O'ER Cupid and his quiver'd band
    Chronos, who seem'd in beard a sage,
Had gain'd a most complete command,—
    Thanks to philosophy—or age ;
For 'twas a subject of debate
To which he owed his tranquil state.

The old assign'd the former cause,
  The young insisted on the latter,
And quite denied "that Wisdom's laws
  Had help'd the dotard in the matter."
But though one passion was assuaged
In Chronos' breast, another raged,
And gain'd unlimited control
  (Spite of the virtue rules confer)
Over the calculating soul
  Of that self-styled philosopher.
This stumbling-block was love of gold,
(A vice well suited to the old,)
Which led him to conclude "'twas vain
To triumph where he could not gain ; "
And, after some slight hesitation
As to such mode of speculation,
Induced him to sell off the prizes—
Loves of all characters and sizes,
Which he by some strange arts had won
From Venus and her fav'rite son.

  Nor did the miser Chronos stop,
As moderns would, to paint his shop ;
No brazen plate announced his trade,
But, o'er the baskets he display'd,
On a rude board, which served as well,
He simply chalk'd up " Loves to sell ! "

  Now Loves, though always in demand,
Had ne'er been kept as "stock in hand,"
Or shown for public sale before :

(I write of very ancient days—)
So, when our sage produced his store,
 The chronicle I quote from says,
That "there ensued a perfect race
Amongst the ladies of the place ;
That old and young, the gay, the staid,
Each wife, each mother, and each maid,
With one accord were seen to start,
And crowd and jostle round the mart,
If not to buy, at least to stare
Upon this novel sort of ware."

 I hear some blooming reader say,
"What had the old to do there, pray ?"
But I declare, by those bright eyes,
Although the fact may raise surprise,
E'en grandmammas were seen among
That motley and excited throng !
At their tenth "lustrum" men may cease *

---

 * Horace seems to have thought fifty a very proper age for retiring
from the field of amorous warfare.

     "Desine, dulcium
   Mater sæva Cupidinum,
   Circa lustra decem flectere mollibus
   Jam durum imperiis."

In a previous ode he had already declared his intention of reposing on
his laurels,

   " Vixi puellis nuper idoneus,
    Et militavi non sine gloriâ ;
    Nunc arma, defunctumque bello
    Barbiton hic *paries* habebit,
    Lævum marinæ qui Veneris latu
    Custodit."

To listen to fair Venus' call,
May offer up their prayers for peace,
   Suspend their trophies on her " wall,"
And with some quiet, dull employment,
Replace love's turbulent enjoyment.
   But,—when they once have raised on high
The scarlet flag of gallantry,—
Women will still prolong the war,
In spite of wrinkle and of scar !

Nay, frown not, fair one, for 'tis true—
Though, mark, I do not write of you.
Goddess of Courtesy forfend
That aught by me should e'er be penn'd
'Gainst one whose charms of form and face
Yield only to her mental grace !
I write (perhaps my muse is rash)
Of those to whom, like Lady ——,
A certain character is given,
   But who contrive to be " received,"
Because the mates they fit for heaven
   Are either patient or—deceived :
And I assert as my conviction,
Without much fear of contradiction,
That *such* will oft defer the age
For quitting Love's seductive " stage,"
Till Death, whose " management is certain,"
Cuts short the " farce," and " drops the curtain."

But let us turn from this digression
To Chronos in his new profession.

That cunning rogue, who knew how best
He should consult his interest,
Determined that his sale should be
A "Ladies' sale" exclusively ;
And, thinking that to flattery's art
Their strings alike of purse and heart
Would soonest yield, display'd his skill
To gain his customers' good will—
He held his Cupids high in air,
To move the pity of "the fair,"
And raised his profits "cent per cent,"
By many a well-turn'd compliment.

"First, I declare," the sage began,
"That I'll not serve one single man
Until each lady in the crowd,
　Who may to purchase be inclined,
Has been, with due respect, allow'd
　To choose a Cupid to her mind.
Then hasten, lovely dames, nor fear
To meet with disappointment here ;
For my capacious cages hold
Loves for the young and for the old,
Loves for the beauteous and the plain !
Though, pardon me, I see 'twere vain
'Mongst those assembled here to seek
A plain or e'en a wrinkled cheek.
Yet, though you're young and handsome all,
Love comes not always at your call ;
Or if it does, you do not find
Your *lovers* always to your mind.

Then haste with confidence to me,
And take what suits you best—for see !
These pretty captives do but wait
Your choice to free them from the state
Of thraldom into which they 're thrown
By me for your dear sakes alone."

As thus he spoke a cage he shook,
When, such was the imploring look
Of each poor pris'ner, as in turn
   He flutter'd to the close-barr'd side,
That every heart began to yearn ;
   And, whilst the poorer deeply sigh'd
To think that poverty's control
Must check the promptings of the soul,—
The richer dames, who could afford
To feel, approach'd with one accord,
And each, with mingled blush and smile,
Requested that from durance vile
The little Love she most approved
Should to her keeping be removed.

'Twas for the sage no easy matter,
Amidst so great a din and clatter,
To hear and satisfy the claim
Preferr'd by each aspiring dame ;
Yet so much patience he display'd
In carrying on his novel trade,
That, ere the shades of evening fell,
He'd not a Cupid left to sell.
And not alone did *men* complain

Of having tarried there in vain ;
But (since his wares had all been sold
At heavy prices to the old,
Or matrons " of a certain age,"
The next his notice to engage)
Full many a disappointed maid,
Who her last drachma would have paid
For e'en a feather from the wing
Of such a pretty flutt'ring thing,
Went home in anger and despair
To dream of joys she could not share.

The miser chuckled when alone
To see such piles of wealth his own—
At thoughts of having taken in
   The richest ladies of the place
His wrinkles gather'd to a grin,
   And tears of joy bedew'd his face.
But still one thought would dash his pleasure—
The dread of losing such a treasure ;
And whilst an extra cruse of oil
Was burnt in counting out his spoil,
His door that night was doubly barr'd,
The dearly-cherish'd wealth to guard.
Nor was the sage's caution vain ;
   For with the morning came a crowd
That sought admittance to obtain,
   With angry voices shrill and loud,
Together crying out—" You old
Curmudgeon, give us back our gold ;
For all our Loves have flown away ! "—

" I never told you they would stay,"
Said Chronos, peeping safely o'er
A broken panel in his door :—
" The Loves that ladies deign to buy
Have wings expressly made to fly !
I cannot now refund their price ;
But for your money take advice,
And, to insure affection true,
Seek not for love—let love seek you ! "

W. B. Le Gros.

THE DEATH OF PIERS DE GAVESTON.*

—◆—

" Now, by my soul, he dies ! Sir Knights, I've sworn ere
    I depart,
That Arden's black hound shall have blood, his teeth
    shall grind his heart !
The scornful stripling who has dared to beard me to my
    face,—
By Heaven, it makes me almost mad to brook such foul
    disgrace ! "

Fiercely, and with impassion'd voice, the Earl of
    Warwick spoke,
And the deep tones through the lofty hall a murmuring
    echo woke ;
The three knights sat in thoughtful mood, and by their
    half-drawn breath,
It seem'd as if their minds were one, and their resolve
    was death !

---

* Piers de Gaveston, although guilty of many follies, was the victim
of gross treachery. Confiding in a treaty, by which his life was to
have been spared, he became the dupe of Lords Warwick, Arundel,
Hereford, &c., whose knightly honour had been pledged for its fulfil-
ment. Guy de Beauchamp, Earl of Warwick, in conjunction with the
others, conveyed him to his own castle, and thence to Blacklow Hill, a
mile distant, where he was beheaded.

Then rose Earl Arundel, "Methinks Gaveston's fate is
    seal'd,
But there are things of grave import, I ween, should be
    reveal'd;
My Lord of Beauchamp! lead us forth, that we ourselves
    may see
How well the dainty Gascon and thy prison-hold agree."

On the mattress of a gloomy cell, in Warwick's ancient
    keep,
Lay a gallant form, and comely clad, whose eyes were
    closed in sleep ;
The locks fell loosely o'er a brow that seem'd surpassing
    fair,
And features that had lovely been, but for their haughty
    air.

A smile was on his pallid cheek, a sneer his proud lip
    wore,—
Was he thinking of some courtly fête he mingled in once
    more ?
Dark thoughts have veil'd that smile in shade, his hands
    are clench'd—he raves !
"*Ye* part me from my royal liege,—down, down, false
    abject slaves ! "

He waken'd with a start—his naked arm had touch'd
    the steel
That bound him to the stony floor, on which was placed
    his meal,

Rich leaven, with the choicest fruits and wines ; but all
    in vain,
For they were spread beyond his reach, to mock his
    burning brain !

The door creak'd harshly on its hinge, and then 'twas
    open'd wide,
And Gaveston beheld the knights advance, with stately
    pride ;
Their visors scarce conceal'd the ire that from their dark
    eyes burn'd,
But, unabash'd, each fiery glance the prisoner calm
    return'd.

"Methought ye would not wait for me to linger o'er yon
    food,
The vulture spurns the carrion cold, and slacks its thirst
    with blood !
Come on, bold traitors to your king ! wreak all your rage
    on me,
And murd'ring him who scorns ye all, complete your
    treachery !"

Then loudly laugh'd Earl Hereford—" Ay, call upon
    your king,
And see if Edward to thine aid his myrmidons will
    bring.
The childish monarch is, like thee, a suppliant for life,
And soon the grave will hold ye both, and with it
    England's strife !"

The words came to the captive's soul wing'd as a
      pois'nous dart,
The head bow'd low to hide a tear, a chill came o'er his
      heart !
The shuddering frame too plainly told the fears for which
      'twas moved ;
They were not for himself, but for the master he had
      loved !

"What, whining now !" Lord Beauchamp cried. "Right
      glad I am 'tis thus ;
The cub, in thinking of its sire, forgets to bark at us.
What say ye, lords, to this rare sport ? The singing-bird
      is mute,
No more to strain o'er wassail cups, or sing to lady's
      lute ! "

As a flash of lightning shoots athwart the gloomy folds
      of night,
Or a tiger glaring on his prey, the youth survey'd the
      knight :—
" It boots thy bravery to taunt a captive in thy cell ;
But were I with thee in the field, it might not suit so
      well ! "

" By my father's sword," the Earl replied, " one brief hour
      shall not pass
Before ye view the field ye crave, and mingle with its
      grass !

And even in death these towers of mine shall gaze upon
    thee still.
Mount! mount! my men, and lead him forth: he dies
    on Blacklow Hill!"

The torches shed a fitful gleam, as fast they spread along,
And the night-winds, ruffled by the tramp, pour'd forth
    a dirge-like song.
No time for prayer—the neck was bent—the blade hung
    glittering o'er—
"My king!" he murmur'd as it fell,—and Gaveston was
    no more!

Oh! lonely is that place of blood; a huge cross marks
    the site
Where fell dishonour stain'd the shields long gain'd in
    valiant fight.
Ye who may gaze with awe-struck soul on that unhallow'd
    spot,
Mar not the sleep of death!—let all his frailties be forgot!

WILLIAM JONES.

THE RED-BREAST OF AQUITANIA.

AN HUMBLE BALLAD.

—◆—

"Are not two sparrows sold for a farthing? yet not one of them shall fall to the ground without your Father."—St. Matthew, x. 29.

"Gallos ab Aquitanis Garumna flumen."—Julius Cæsar.

"Sermons in stones, and good in everything."—Shakspere.

" Genius, left to shiver
 On the bank, 'tis said,
 Died of that cold river."—Tom Moore.

I.

River trip from Thoulouse to Bourdeaux. Thermometer at ·0. Snow 1½ foot deep. Use of wooden shoes.

Oh, 'twas bitter cold
As our steam-boat roll'd
Down the pathway old
 Of the deep Garonne,—
And the peasant lank,
While his *sabot* sank
In the snow-clad bank,
 Saw it roll on, on.

II.

Yᵉ Gascon farmer hieth to his cottage, and drinketh a flaggonne.

And he hied him home
To his *toit de chaume;*
And for those who roam
 On the broad bleak flood

L 2

Cared he? Not a thought;
For his beldame brought
His wine-flask fraught
    With the grape's red blood.

III.

He warmeth
his cold
shins at a
wooden fire.
Good b'ye to
him.

And the wood-block blaze
Fed his vacant gaze
As we trod the maze
    Of the river down.
Soon we left behind
On the frozen wind
All farther mind
    Of that vacant clown.

IV.

Y⁰ Father
meeteth a
stray ac-
quaintance
in a small
bird.

But there came anon,
As we journey'd on
Down the deep GARONNE,
    An acquaintancy,
Which we deem'd, I count,
Of more high amount,
For it oped the fount
    Of sweet sympathy.

V.

Not y⁰
famous alba-
tross of that
aiucient ma-
riner olde
Coleridge,
but a poore
robin.

'Twas a stranger drest
In a downy vest,
'Twas a wee RED-BREAST,
    (Not an "*Albatross*,")

But a wanderer meek,
Who fain would seek
O'er the bosom bleak
    Of that flood to cross.

VI.

Y⁰ sparrow crossing yᵉ river maketh hys half-way house of the fire-ship.

And we watch'd him oft
As he soar'd aloft
On his pinions soft,
    Poor wee weak thing,
And we soon could mark
That he sought our bark,
As a resting ark
    For his weary wing.

VII.

Delusive hope. Yᵉ fire-ship runneth 10 knots an hour: 'tis no go for yᵉ sparrow.

But the bark, fire-fed,
On her pathway sped,
And shot far a-head
    Of the tiny bird,
And quicker in the van
Her swift wheels ran,
As the quickening fan
    Of his winglets stirr'd.

VIII.

Yᵉ byrde is led a wilde goose chace adown yᵉ river,

Vain, vain pursuit!
Toil without fruit!
For his forkèd foot
    Shall not anchor there,

Tho' the boat meanwhile
Down the stream beguile
For a bootless mile
    The poor child of air !

IX.

Symptomes
of fatigue.
'Tis melan-
cholie to fall
between
2 stools.

And 'twas plain at last
He was flagging fast,
That his hour had past
    In that effort vain ;
Far from-either bank,
Sans a saving plank,
Slow, slow he sank,
    Nor uprose again.

X.

Mort of yᵉ
birde.

And the cheerless wave
Just one ripple gave
As it oped him a grave
    In its bosom cold,
And he sank alone,
With a feeble moan,
In that deep GARONNE,
    And then all was told.

XI.

Yᵉ old man
at yᵉ helm
weepeth for
a sonne lost
in yᵉ bay of
Biscaye.

But our pilot grey
Wiped a tear away ;
In the broad BISCAYE
    He had lost his boy !

And that sight brought back
On its furrow'd track
The remember'd wreck
   Of long perish'd joy !

XII.

Condoleance
of yᵉ ladyes;
eke of 1
*chasseur
d'infanterie
légère.*

And the tear half hid
In soft BEAUTY's lid
Stole forth unbid
   For that red-breast bird ;—
And the feeling crept,—
For a WARRIOR wept ;
And the silence kept
   Found no fitting word.

XIII.

Olde Father
Proutte
sadly
moralizeth
anent yᵉ
birde.

But *I* mused alone,
For I thought of one
Whom I well had known
   In my earlier days,
Of a gentle mind,
Of a soul refined,
Of deserts design'd
   For the Palm of Praise.

XIV.

Yᵉ Streame
of Lyfe. A
younge man
of fayre
promise.

And well would it seem
That o'er Life's dark stream,
Easy task for Him
   In his flight of Fame,

Was the SKYWARD PATH,
O'er the billow's wrath,
That for GENIUS hath
   Ever been the same.

xv.

And I saw him soar
From the morning shore,
While his fresh wings bore
   Him athwart the tide,
Soon with powers unspent
As he forward went,
His wings he had bent
   On the sought-for side.

xvi.

But while thus he flew,
Lo ! a vision new
Caught his wayward view
   With a semblance fair,
And that new-found wooer
Could, alas ! allure
From his pathway sure
   The bright child of air.

xvii.

For he turn'd aside,
And adown the tide
For a brief hour plied
   His yet unspent force,

And to gain that goal
Gave the powers of soul,
Which, unwasted, whole,
    Had achieved his course.

XVIII.

This is y*
morall of
Father
Prout's
humble
ballade,

A bright SPIRIT, young,
Unwept, unsung,
Sank thus among
    The drifts of the stream;
Not a record left,—
Of renown bereft,
By thy cruel theft,
    O DELUSIVE DREAM!

L'ENVOY TO W. H. AINSWORTH, ESQ.

WHILOME, AUTHOR OF THE ADMIRABLE "CRICHTON," SUBSEQUENT
CHRONICLER OF "JACK SHEPPARD."

which he
wrotte by
waxlight in
the *hostel de
Gascoigne* at
Bourdeaux,
6 Jan. 1841.

Thus sadly I thought
As that bird unsought
The remembrance brought
    Of thy bright day;
And I penn'd full soon
This DIRGE, while the moon
On the broad GARONNE
    Shed her wintry ray.

                      FATHER PROUT.

THE COUNTRY SQUIRE.

AN ANCIENT LEGEND, SHOWING HOW THE FAIR HELD EVERY OCTOBER AT
NOTTINGHAM WAS FIRST CALLED NOTTINGHAM GOOSE FAIR.

In a small pretty village in Nottinghamshire
There formerly lived a respectable squire,
Who possess'd an estate from incumbrances clear,
And an income enjoy'd of a thousand a year.

The country he loved : he was fond of the chace,
And now and then enter'd a horse at a race ;
He excell'd all his friends in amusements athletic ;
And his manner of living was far from ascetic.

A wife he had taken "for better, for worse,"
Whose temper had proved an intolerant curse ;
And 'twas clear to perceive this unfortunate wife
Was the torment, vexation, and plague of his life.

Her face it was fair ;—but a beautiful skin
May sometimes conceal a bad temper within ;
And those who are anxious to fix their affections,
Should always look further than lovely complexions.

Nine years pass'd away, and, to add to his grief,
No infantile prattle e'er brought him relief ;
When at length, to his great and unspeakable joy,
He the father became of a fine little boy.

The father grew proud of his juvenile heir,
A sweet little cherub with dark eyes and hair ;
And yet, strange to say, his paternal anxiety
Soon debarr'd him the bliss of his darling's society.

For he thought (and with truth), to his termagant wife
Might be justly ascribed all the woes of his life.
" Had I ne'er seen a woman," he often would sigh,
" What squire in the county so happy as I ! "

In a forest retired, some miles far away,
(Whether Sherwood or not the traditions don't say,)
Our hero possess'd an Arcadian retreat,
A snug little hunting-box, rural and neat.

Strange fancies men have—it was here he design'd
To watch o'er the dawn of his son's youthful mind ;
Where, only approach'd by the masculine gender,
No room should be left him for feelings more tender.

To further his plans, he procured coadjutors
In two very excellent pains-taking tutors ;
Who agreed, for the sake of two hundred a year,
His son to instruct, and immure themselves here.

The boy was intelligent, active, and bright,
And took in his studies uncommon delight,
And his tutors declared him " a pleasure to teach,"
So docile, so good, so obedient to each.

No juvenile follies distracted his mind,
No visions of bright eyes, or damsels unkind,
And those fair demi-sisterly beings so gay,
Yclept pretty cousins, ne'er popp'd in his way.

Time sped quickly on, years succeeded to years,
Yet brought no abatement of fatherly fears,
Till at length this remarkably singular son
Could number of years that had pass'd twenty-one.

The autumn was come ; 'twas the end of October,
When summer's gay tints change to liv'ries more sober ;
And, the 3rd of this month, it is known far and near,
There's a large fair at Nottingham held every year.

Now the father had settled his promising son
Should his studies conclude when he reach'd twenty-one ;
And a view of the world was the only thing needed
To prove how his singular schemes had succeeded.

He fix'd on this fair as the place of *début ;*—
Strange resolve !—when to keep the *fair* out of his view
Had been his most anxious endeavours through life,
And a bone of contention 'twixt him and his wife

This point by his firmness he'd constantly carried,
(The only one gain'd ever since he was married,)
And he went with a heart beating high with emotion,
To launch his young son on life's turbulent ocean.

As they enter'd the fair a young maiden tripp'd by,
With a cheek like the rose, and a bright laughing eye :
"Oh ! father, what's that ?" cried the youth with delight,
As this vision of loveliness burst on his sight.

" Oh, that," cried the cautious and politic squire,
Who did not the youth's ardent glances admire,
" Is only a thing call'd a Goose, my dear son,—
We shall see many more ere our visit is done."

Blooming damsels now pass'd with their butter and cheese,
Whose beauty might even an anchorite please :
" Merely geese !" said the squire ; "don't mind them, my
        dear,
There are many things better worth looking at here."

As onwards they pass'd, every step brought to view
Some spectacle equally curious and new ;
And the joy of the youth hardly knew any bounds
At the rope-dancers, tumblers, and merry go-rounds.

Now it's known to all young damsels and swains
That an excellent custom at these times obtains,
When each to his friends is expected to make
Some little donation to keep for his sake.

And thus, when the tour of the fair was completed,
The father resolved that the boy should be treated ;
So, pausing an instant, he said, " My dear son,
A new era to-day in your life has begun :

" Though the plans I've adopted to some may seem strange,
You have never induced me to wish for a change ;
And each day that passes delights me to find
Fresh proofs of a sensible well-order'd mind.

" And now, in remembrance of Nottingham Fair,
As a proof of your father's affection and care,
Of all this bright scene, and the gaieties in it,
Choose whatever you like, it is yours from this minute."
" Choose whatever I like ! " cried the youthful recluse,
" Oh, thank you, dear father,—then give me a Goose ! ! "

Grig.

THIS WORLD OF OURS.

———

This world of ours, if free from sin,
　Oh ! would it not be fair ?
Sunshine above, and flowers beneath,
　And beauty everywhere !
The air, the earth, the waters teem
　With living things at play ;
Glad Nature from an hundred throats
　Pours her rejoicing lay.

Each balmy breeze that wanders by
　Whispers some angel tone ;
And the clear fountains have a voice
　Of music all their own.
Even the leaves of forest trees,
　Moved by the zephyr's wing,
Make a low murmur of content
　To little birds that sing.

The busy bees o'er garden-flowers
　A holy song attune,
Joining, with never-tiring mirth,
　The minstrelsy of June :

And the great waves upon the deep,
  Leaping, like giants free,
Add, in their hollow monotone,
  The chorus of the sea.

There's beauty in the summer sky,
  When from his ocean bed,
Like a strong man refresh'd by sleep,
  The Sun uplifts his head ;—
And when behind the western rocks
  At eventide he goes,
How beauteous are the crimson clouds
  That curtain his repose !

Are not the grassy valleys fair,
  Deck'd in their spring array ?
And the high hills with forest clad,
  How beautiful are they !
Look on the sea, that girdle vast,
  Wherewith the earth is bound ! .
Even in Fancy's wildest dreams
  Can aught more grand be found ?

Oh ! 'twere indeed a radiant world,
  A paradise complete,—
So redolent of lovely things,
  So fill'd with voices sweet,—
If Sin had not in evil hour
  Enter'd this pleasant clime,
Yielding them over unto Death,—
  Sad consequence of crime !

Hence is it that the choicest flow'rs
    Fall by a swift decay,
And hopes to which we fondly cling
    Pass suddenly away ;
Yet, 'mid all trials of our life,
    This blessed thought is given,
Earth is not our abiding place,—
    Man's native clime is Heaven !

W. G. J. BARKER.

A TALE OF TRANSMIGRATION.

ADDRESSED BY A MOTH TO A VERY BEAUTIFUL YOUNG LADY.

MORTAL, of material finer
  Than thy sisterhood of clay !
Hearken to me, purest china !
  While I " hum " a mournful lay.

List ! it is a dismal duty,
  And take warning from my fate ;
I was once a famous beauty,
  Courted by the rich and great.

Yes—but start not—these antennæ
  Once were fingers of a hand,
Sought in wedlock, too, by many
  Lords and nobles of the land.

Though now hateful to beholders,
  And a scouted creature grown,
I had once a neck and shoulders
  Quite as charming as your own.

Though so lovely, still my carnal
   Heart was fill'd with folly full :
Hasten to the loathsome charnel-
   House, and gaze upon my skull.

There observe a gentle rising,
   Like an island of the sea,
Its dimensions are surprising,
   'Tis the bump of vanity.

Love of dress and approbation
   Was a fatal snare to me ;
It has hurl'd me from my station,
   And has left me—what you see.

Many lovers was my passion :
   I beheld a youthful one,
Handsome,—and the height of fashion,
   And I mark'd him for my own.

Sadly now my soul confesses
   That I play'd a cruel part :
Yes ; I favour'd his addresses,
   And he loved with all his heart.

Would I could those days recover !
   Days for ever pass'd and gone,
When he was a humble lover,
   And I treated him with scorn !

I, without a spark of feeling,
　Mark'd the anguish of his soul,
By well-bred surprise revealing
　Heart as icy as the pole.

Death, however, cut me off—in
　Anger at my sinning ; and,
Though my bones are in the coffin,
　Still, in spirit, here I stand !

Once I sat in silk and ermine ;
　Naked now I creep the floor ;
Eating with my sister vermin
　What I only wore before !

Mothers, who have babes to dandle,
　Let not flirting be their aims ;
I am doom'd to court a candle,
　Penalty for courting " Flames ! "

Watch me as I wildly hover,
　And my dissolution mark ;
I, who never pitied lover,
　Meet no pity from " a spark ! "

F. LOCKER.

THE NOCTURNAL SUMMONS;

OR, THE GOSSIP GHOST.

A FACT.

———◆———

" Tuâ quod nihil refert ne cures."

How vast the number of mankind who fail
 T'obey the wholesome rule which I've selected,
 And, as a sign or frontispiece, erected,
To indicate the tenor of my tale.

Whate'er your sex ; whate'er your state of life ;
Bachelor, husband, widow, maid, or wife :
Whate'er your rank—peer, knight, esquire, or yeoman ;
Duchess, your ladyship, or plain good woman :
Whether you move 'midst equipages garish,
  Flattery and smiles,
Or barrows, slang, and grins : whether the name,
Ta'en from the Calendar to grace your parish,
  Be James or Giles ;
In one particular 'tis still the same :
 Namely, that, when ye congregate,
  Whate'er the nature of your cheer ;
 Choice viands, served on costly plate,
  Tea and turn-out, or gin and beer ;

No sooner have ye got together,
Saluted and abused the weather,
Than some curst babbler of the throng
Lets fly that venom'd shaft, her tongue,
And food for conversation lends
By spleen-fraught strictures on her friends.

Yes, in the first, each slice of scandal bitter
Is welcom'd by an universal titter.
While, in the second, they take aim,
With the same bolt, at minor game :
As, " Did you see our neighbour, Mrs. Dray,
On board the Margate steam-yacht t'other day ?
How she was dress'd ! her head deck'd out with curls
As long and jetty as her gawky girl's ;
When everybody knows her locks
Are red, by nature, as a fox ;
And, now the progress of old Time has spread
Some parsnips 'mongst the carrots of her head,
'Tis speckled like an old cock-pheasant's feather,
Or salt and cayenne-pepper mix'd together : "

If in the third, a sordid set
To pass a jolly night are met ;
To bolt their hot cow-heel and tripe,
And smoke, *en tour*, the smutty pipe ;
Some beldams, still for censure ripe,
Enjoy no greater solace from their labours
Than dealing condemnation on their neighbours ;
And every moment of cessation
From ribald singing and potation,

Is fill'd with boisterous oaths and jeering,
Upon their cronies out of hearing :
As, who fought booty in the milling ring ;
And who was hang'd when who deserved to swing ;
With many a volley of pestiferous stuff
  And spite,
Which ink poetic is not black enough
  To write.
Yet, to my cockney readers, be it known,
That not in the metropolis alone
Exists the inquisitorial emulation
For scrutinising other folks' affairs ;
No—every town and village in the nation
Boasts its arch gossip, whose domestic cares
Are half forgotten in the task
Of daily running forth to ask,
Of every human snake within her reach,
The morning's news, and to extort from each
Some rumour'd hint, or vague suspicion,
Already in its third edition,
Whose honey'd poison may regale
   The gaping ears
   Of such compeers
As may be strangers to the tale.
All this I own is mere assertion,
And dogmatism is my aversion ;
Therefore, (as holders-forth extemporaneous
Say, when, from wandering to discourse extraneous,
They feel themselves perplext,
And cannot justly on their subject pop,

But hem and ha, and make an awkward stop,)
" Returning to my text !"

The theatre whereon the farce was play'd,
 Which now demands the efforts of my muse,
Was a small village, in a fertile glade,
 Near the romantic stream of northern Ouse.
  At a crude guess,
There might be fifty houses in the cluster,
  Few more or less ;
Whose population, at its greatest muster,
Did but half fill the ivy-mantled church,
Shaded by stately trees of yew and birch,
Whither they every Sunday went ;
Haply some pious few to vent
The fervent prayer ; a greater number
To pass an hour in tranquil slumber ;
Many to meet their sweethearts there,
And greet them with a loving stare,
Like hungry cats surveying lumps of butter,
  To wink and smile
  Across the aisle,
And *look* the passion, which they dared not utter :
While others sat the service out
As culprits bear a flogging-bout,
So anxious were they for its end,
That they might meet, shake hands, and spend
  An hour in chatter.
  Amongst the latter,
Was Miss Griselda Wilhelmina Gaunt ;
A waning fair, who could, with justice, vaunt

Of gentle breeding : all her youth had been
Wasted within a city's bustling scene.
But, as butchers, sometimes, with their delicate meat,
　　　Resolved on a price far beyond its just merit,
Maintain their demand until, no longer sweet,
　　　They're compell'd to seek out some sly spot to inter
　　　　it,
　　　So, she'd set such high price,
In the hey-day of life, on her precious virginity,
That no honorificabilitudinity
　　　Or wealth could suffice
To content her, though many a suitor had tried
All the engines of courtship to make her his bride.
Till, finding her charms were no longer available,
Her cherish'd commodity grown quite unsaleable,
She sought, in our hamlet, a rural retreat,
And, in a small cottage, sequester'd and neat,
Adjoining the wall of the little churchyard,
O'er all the concerns of her neighbours kept guard :
For, in the village, not a pig could squeak,
　　　　Or cock could crow
　　　　But she would know
The cause, e'en though she sought it for a week :
No rustic urchin could play truant,
But in an hour or two she knew on't :
No fuddled churl could beat his wife,
But she would meddle in the strife :
No poor old mumbling dame could lose
　　　　An aching tooth,
But she would ferret out the news ;
And, once apprised, the scent she'd follow,

To know the truth,
And ask around,
Until she found
Who took it out, and if 'twas sound or hollow :
No fight, or game of quarter-staff
Was hid from her ; no foal, or calf,
Or brood of puppies could be born,
But she would know it ere next morn ;
When she would, ceaselessly, inquire
   Till she could reach
A perfect knowledge of the sire
   And dam of each.
No villager, female or male,
Could drink an extra pint of ale,
Or pass an hour in rustic frolic :
No washer-wench could have the colic :
No lad could break a school-mate's head :
No woman could be brought to bed :
No load to market could be carried :
No clown be sent to goal, or married :
No fishing-punt could be capsised,
Treating its inmates with a ducking ;
No peasant's brat could be baptised,
Cut its first tooth, or leave off sucking ;
     Fall sick, or die ;
     But she would pry,
Until her craving sense auricular
Had been full-fed with each particular.

This penchant, and her tongue censorious,
Had made our heroine so notorious

Amongst the country rabble,
That, to prevent of breath the useless waste,
And make her epithet imply her taste,
  They call'd her Grizzy Gabble,
Which neat appellative, so aptly suited
    For brevity
    And levity,
Had long time for her name been substituted.
E'en now I ventured to express,
That every hamlet doth possess
Some glib-mouth'd wench who rules the roast
    In mag ;
,I also may make bold to state,
That every village, small or great,
'Mongst its inhabitants, can boast
    Its wag !
Some witty bumpkin who delights in joke ;
  For feats of fun and mischief ever ripe ;
Who, o'er his evening goblet, loves to smoke,
  Alternately, his neighbour and his pipe :
And so could this—perhaps as queer a wight
As ever wrought by day, or drank by night.

He long had known that, when, perchance,
    Miss Grizzy
    Was busy,
And could not 'mongst her neighbours prance
To chat, she most intently listen'd,
  Hour after hour, to the church-steeple ;
And, every time she heard a bell,
Whether for chime, or peal, or knell,

For some one married, dead, or christen'd;
   That she might learn the news ere other people,
      She made no pause,
However cold the day, for cloak or hat;
But, in an instant, as nimble as a cat,
      To know the cause:
So that the sexton ne'er could ope
The belfry door, and pull a rope,
But, in an instant, Grizzy's clatter
Saluted him with "What's the matter?"

One autumn night, damp, chill, and dark,
Our mellow, laughter-loving spark
Betook him to the sexton's cot,
Just when the simple man had got
His solid supper spread upon the table,
And, looking as demure as he was able,
Turn'd up his eyes, and shook his head,
   Saying, "Lord bless us, Master Sexton!
   Heaven only knows who'll be the next un!
Would you believe it? Grizzy Gabble's dead!
And I was sent to you to tell
That you must go and toll the bell,
Late as it is, without delay!"
This said, th' informant walk'd away.

The knave of spades, astounded, left his fork
Stuck in a mound of fat, cold pickled pork;
      Threw down his knife,
      Gazed at his wife,
Utter'd a pious exclamation,

And hasten'd to his avocation ;
Namely, to run ('twas but across the road)
    To church, to toll
    The fleeting soul
Of the dead gossip to its long abode.

Grizzy, although the sexton thought her dead
  As Hecuba or Priam,
Was just that moment getting into bed,
  In as good health as I am :
Her night-gown on—one foot just placed betwixt
  The sheets, when straight, the bell's first sound
  Striking her ear, she, doubtingly, look'd round,
And, for a moment, stood like one transfixt.
She listen'd, and another dong
Convinced her she had not been wrong ;
When, such her speed and eagerness,
She huddled on scarce half her dress,
Lest, if delay'd, some neighbour should obtain
    The news before her ;
But, slipshod, seized upon the counterpane,
    And threw it o'er her,
Then sallied forth, resolved to ask
The reason of the sexton's task.

Meantime, old "Dust to dust" pursued
    His dreary work,
In pensive, melancholy mood ;
    Between each jerk,
In these sage terms soliloquising :
"Well, Grizzy's sudden death's surprising !

She wur a queer un! 'cod, if she wur living,
     'Tis just the time
     That she would climb
The belfry stairs! Her loss won't cause much grieving!
I'm devilish glad her earthly prattling's o'er,
And I shall ne'er be pester'd by her more!"

While he the last, half utter'd word
     Was speaking,
He dropt the rope, and thought he heard
     A creaking;
When, turning promptly round,
He at his elbow found
His constant catechist, enrobed in white:
His blood ran cold, his hair stood bolt upright:
He bounded from the spot, and roar'd aloud,
     "Oh, heavens! I'm lost!
     'Tis Grizzy's ghost,
Risen from the dead, and walking in her shroud!"
No answer to her loud demands he utter'd,
But ran and tumbled down the steeple stairs,
While, ever and anon, he faltering mutter'd,
A mingled exorcism—half oaths, half prayers.

Grizzy, astonish'd at his flight,
Unconscious of his cause of fright,
Hotly pursued, her question bawling;
He, sometimes running, sometimes sprawling,
Had just arrived without the church,
When she appear'd beneath the porch:
Again her piercing voice, assailing

His tingling ears
Enhanced his fears :
Onward he ran the tomb-stones scaling,
Deaf to Miss Gabble's loud appeals,
Who closely follow'd at his heels.

An open grave lay in his way,
Dug by himself that very day,
But, in his fear, no longer recollected ;
Thither, by chance, his footsteps were directed,
Just when the dreaded Grizzy's outstretch'd hand
Had seized his coat,
And her wide throat
Sent forth its shrillest tones to make him stand.

'Twas now too late her harpy hold to quit,
For down they fell,
Headlong, pell mell,
He hallooing,
She following,
O'er the loose earth, into the yawning pit.
Nor did their hap end thus : The spiteful Fates
So managed that their prone descending pates
Met, with such stunning contact, at the bottom,
That, if a score of grenadiers had shot 'em,
They scarcely could more motionless have laid them,
Than the rude shock (*pro tempore*) had made them.

Meantime, a straggling villager, by chance
Passing, half drunk,
The churchyard's bound,

Of Grizzy and the sexton caught a glance,
     Just as they sunk
     Into the ground.
Away he scamper'd, like a bedlamite,
Making a most outrageous knocking
     At many a door,
On which, his friends around him flocking,
     He roundly swore
He'd seen two ghosts, one black and t'other white.

During this space, the wag who had convey'd
  Of Grizzy's death the counterfeit narration,
Behind the churchyard wall had snugly laid,
  To watch his wily project's consummation;
Now, creeping from his lurking-place,
He smooth'd his laughter-wrinkled face,
     And, rushing in among
     The terror-stricken throng,
Vow'd that the clown who gave th' alarm was wrong;
  · Declared that he had also been
    Ocular witness of the scene,
    And that, in lieu of apparitions,
    Sent to confirm their superstitions,
    The forms which met their neighbour's view,
    (He'd stake his life upon't) were two
    Infernal *habeas corpus* knaves
    Come down from town to rob the graves,
"So if," said he, "you have the least regard
    For all your dear relations' bones,
    Prepare yourselves with sticks and stones,
And follow instantly to our church-yard!"

Away the crew,
Like lightning, flew,
Seizing such rustic arms as chance provided;
Sickles and flails,
And broken pales;
Then softly t'wards the cemetery glided.
Their chuckling leader pointed out
The well-mark'd grave, and made a stand;
Then whistled, and his little band
Press'd on, and compass'd it about,
Just as the vital spark, so long supprest,
Became rekindled in the gossip's breast,
And, starting from her hideous dream,
She utter'd a terrific scream,
Which half aroused the sexton's slumb'ring senses,
Who, still supposing that he lay
Beneath some spell, began to pray
Forgiveness for his manifold offences,
In such repentant, piteous terms,
That all the crowd, sans mercy or reflection,
Proclaim'd them ministers of resurrection,
Come to defraud the village-worms,
And swore, by all their fathers' graves around,
That, back to back, the culprits should be bound,
And lodged within the village cage
Without delay.—Just in this stage
The matter pended, when the peasants' wives,
Alarm'd by Grizzy's shriek,
And anxious for their darling hubbies' lives,
Resolved the truth to seek;
So, snatching each a lantern or a torch,

They moved, a flaring phalanx, t'wards the church ;
Mix'd with the gaping group, and threw a light
Upon this strange adventure of the night.

Reader, imagine, if you can,
　　(For, if I should attempt to paint
The scene, the likeness would be faint,)
　　What wonder through the circle ran,
When, to their sober senses, 'twas made clear
　That, 'stead of thieves, the pair they strove to seize
Were their old sexton, still half dead with fear,
　And Grizzy Gabble in her night-chemise !

After some score of minutes spent
　　　In explanation
　　　And gratulation,
All parties to their pillows went ;
But, from that moment Grizzy Gabble's face
Has ne'er been seen within the county's space !

THE MONKS OF OLD.

—◆—

LAUD ye the monks !
    They were not men of a creed austere,
    Who frown'd on mirth, and forbade good cheer ;
    But joyous oft were the brotherhood,
    In the depths of their sylvan solitude.
    The ruin'd abbey hath many a tale
    Of their gay conceits and deep wassail ;
    The huge hearth, left to the wreck of time,
    Hath echoed of erst the minstrel's chime ;
    The caves, despoil'd of their goodly store,
    Have groan'd 'neath their weight in days of yore !

Laud ye the monks !
    The wand'rer was their welcome guest,
    The weary found in their grey walls rest ;
    The poor man came, and they scorn'd him not,
    For rank and wealth were alike forgot ;
    The peasant sat at the plenteous board
    With the pilgrim knight and the feudal lord ;
    The feast was spread, and the foaming bowl
    Gave freshen'd life to the thirsty soul ;
    Round it pass'd, from the prince to the hind,
    The fathers adding their greeting kind !

Laud ye the monks !
 Many a blazon'd scroll doth prove
 The pains they took in their work of love ;
 Many a missal our thoughts engage
 With scenes and deeds of a bygone age ;
 Many a hallowing minster still
 Attests the marvels of olden skill !
 The broken shaft, or the altar razed,
 The mould'ring fane, where our sires have praised,
 Are beautiful, even amidst decay,
 Blessing the men who have pass'd away !

Laud ye the monks !
 For they were friends of the poor and weak.
 The proud man came to their footstool meek,
 And many an acre broad and good
 Was the forfeit paid for his curbless mood :—
 The penance hard, and the peasant's ban,
 Would make him think of his fellow-man ;
 The mass and dirge for his parting soul
 Would wring for the needy a welcome dolc.
 The cowl bow'd not to the noble's crest,
 But kings would yield to the priest's behest !

Laud ye the monks !
 Tranquil and sweet was monastic life,
 Free from the leaven of worldly strife ;
 The desolate found a shelter there,
 A home secure from the shafts of care !
 Many a heart with sorrow riven
 Would learn to dream of a shadeless heaven !

And plenty smiled where the convent rose,
The herald of love and deep repose ;
The only spot where the arts gave forth
The hope of a glorious age to earth !

WILLIAM JONES.

THE SABINE FARMER'S SERENADE.

BEING A NEWLY RECOVERED FRAGMENT OF A LATIN OPERA.

———◆———

I.

Erat turbida nox
   Horâ secundâ mané
Quando proruit vox
   Carmen in hoc inané ;
Viri misera mens
   Meditabatur hymen,
Hinc puellæ flens
   Stabat obsidens limen ;
   Semel tantum dic
  Eris nostra LALAGÉ ;
   Ne recuses sic
  Dulcis Julia CALLAGÉ.

II.

Planctibus aurem fer,
   Venere tu formosior ;
Dic, hos muros per,
   Tuo favore potior !
Voce beatum fac ;
   En, dum dormis, vigilo,
Nocte obambulans hâc
   Domum planctu stridulo.

I.

'Twas on a windy night,
　At two o'clock in the morning,
An Irish lad so tight,
　All wind and weather scorning,
At Judy Callaghan's door,
　Sitting upon the palings,
His love-tale he did pour,
　And this was part of his wailings :—
　Only say
You'll be Mrs. Brallaghan ;
　Don't say nay,
　　Charming Judy Callaghan.

II.

Oh ! list to what I say,
　Charms you've got like Venus ;
Own your love you may,
　There's but the wall between us.
You lie fast asleep
　Snug in bed and snoring ;
Round the house I creep,
　Your hard heart imploring.

Semel tantum dic
Eris nostra LALAGÉ ;
Ne recuses sic,
Dulcis Julia CALLAGÉ.

III.

Est mihi prægnans sus,
   Et porcellis stabulum ;
Villula, grex, et rus [1]
   Ad vaccarum pabulum ;
Feriis cerneres me
   Splendido vestimento,
Tunc, heus ! quàm benè te
   Veherem in jumento ! [2]
Semel tantum dic
Eris nostra LALAGÉ ;
Ne recuses sic,
Dulcis Julia CALLAGÉ.

IV.

Vis poma terræ ? sum
   Uno dives jugere ;
Vis lac et mella,[3] cùm
   Bacchi succo,[4] sugere ?
Vis aquæ-vitæ vim ? [5]
   Plumoso somnum sacculo ? [6]
Vis ut paratus sim
   Vel annulo vel baculo ? [7]
Semel tantum dic
Eris nostra LALAGÉ ;
Ne recuses sic,
Dulcis Julia CALLAGÉ.

Only say
You'll have Mr. Brallaghan ;
　Don't say nay,
Charming Judy Callaghan.

III.

I've got a pig and a sow,
　I've got a sty to sleep 'em ;
A calf and a brindled cow,
　And a cabin too, to keep 'em ;
Sunday hat and coat,
　An old grey mare to ride on.
Saddle and bridle to boot,
　Which you may ride astride on.
　Only say
You'll be Mrs. Brallaghan ;
　Don't say nay,
Charming Judy Callaghan.

IV.

I've got an acre of ground,
　I've got it set with praties ;
I've got of 'baccy a pound,
　I've got some tea for the ladies ;
I've got the ring to wed,
　Some whisky to make us gaily ;
I've got a feather-bed
　And a handsome new shilelagh.
　Only say
You'll have Mr. Brallaghan ;
　Don't say nay,
Charming Judy Callaghan.

V.

Litteris operam das ;
   Lucido fulges oculo ;
Dotes insuper quas
   Nummi sunt in loculo.
Novi quod apta sis [8]
   Ad procreandam sobolem !
Possides (nesciat quis ?)
   Linguam satis mobilem.[9]
   Semel tantum dic
Eris nostra LALAGÉ ;
   Ne recuses sic,
Dulcis Julia CALLAGÈ.

VI.

Conjux utinam tu
   Fieres, lepidum cor, mî !
Halitum perdimus, heu,
   Te sopor urget.   Dormi !
Ingruit imber trux—
   Jam sub tecto pellitur
Is quem crastina lux [10]
   Referet hùc fidelitèr.
Semel tandem dic
Eris nostra LALAGÉ ;
   Ne recuses sic,
Dulcis Julia CALLAGÉ.

FATHER PROUT.

v.

You've got a charming eye,
   You've got some spelling and reading ;
You've got, and so have I,
   A taste for genteel breeding ;
You're rich, and fair, and young,
   As everybody's knowing ;
You've got a decent tongue
   Whene'er 'tis set a-going.
   Only say
You'll be Mrs. Brallaghan ;
   Don't say nay,
Charming Judy Callaghan.

vi.

For a wife till death
   I am willing to take ye ;
But, och ! I waste my breath,
   The devil himself can't wake ye.
'Tis just beginning to rain,
   So I'll get under cover ;
To-morrow I'll come again,
   And be your constant lover.
   Only say
You'll be Mrs. Brallaghan ;
   Don't say nay,
*Charming Judy Callaghan.**

* The above English lines are a portion of a ballad by the late Tom Hudson, grocer, publican, and vocalist.—Ed.

NOTULÆ.

NOTUL. 1.

1° in voce *rus.* Nonne potiùs legendum *jus,* scilicet, *ad vaccarum pabulum?* De hoc *jure* apud Sabinos agricolas consule *Scriptores de re rusticâ* passim. Ita *Bentleius.*

Jus imo antiquissimum, at displicet vox æquivoca ; jus etenim *a mess of pottage* aliquando audit, ex. gr.

Omne suum fratri Jacob *jus* ven
    didit Esau,
  Et Jacob fratri *jus* dedit omne
    suum.

Itaque, pace Bentleii, stet lectio prior.—*Prout.*

NOTUL. 2.

Veherem in jumento. Curriculo-ne ? an ponè sedentem in equi dorso ? dorsaliter planè. Quid enim dicit Horatius de uxore sic vectâ ? Nonne "*Post equitem sedet atra cura*" ?— *Porson.*

NOTUL. 3.

Lac et mella. Metaphoricè pro *tea :* muliebris est compotatio Græcis non ignota, teste Anacreonte,—

ΘΕΗΝ, θεαν θεαινην,
Θελω λεγειν εταιραι, κ. τ. λ.
      Brougham.

NOTUL. 4.

Bacchi succo. Duplex apud poetas antiquiores habebatur hujusce nominis numen. Vineam regebat prius ; posterius cuidam herbæ exoticæ præerat quæ *tobacco* audit. Succus utrique optimus. —*Coleridae.*

NOTUL. 5.

Aquæ-vitæ vim, Anglo-Hybernicè, "*a power of whisky,*" ισχυς, scilicet, vox pergræca.—*Parr.*

NOTUL. 6.

Plumoso sacco. Plumarum congeries certè ad somnos invitandos satis apta ; at mihi per multos annos laneus iste saccus, Ang. *woolsack,* fuit apprimè ad dormiendum idoneus. Lites etiam *de land* ut *aiunt caprinâ,* soporiferas per annos xxx. exercui. Quot et quam præclara somnia !—*Eldon.*

NOTUL. 7.

Investitura "*per annulum et baculum*" satis nota. Vide P. Marca de Concord. Sacerdotii et Imperii : et Hildebrandi Pont. Max. bullarium.—*Prout.*

Baculo certè dignissim. pontif. —*Maginn.*

NOTUL. 8.

Apta sis. Quomodo noverit ? Vide Proverb. Solomonis cap. xxx. v. 19. Nisi forsan tales fuerint puellæ Sabinorum quales impudens iste balatro Connelius mentitur esse nostrates.—*Blomfield.*

NOTUL. 9.

Linguam mobilem. Prius enumerat futuræ conjugis bona *immobilia,* postea transit ad *mobilia,* Anglicè, *chattel property.* Præclarus ordo sententiarum !—*Car. Wetherall.*

NOTUL. 10.

Allusio ad distichon Maronianum, "Nocte pluit totâ, *redeunt spectacula manè.*"—*Prout.*

      κ. τ. λ.

THE SIGNS OF THE ZODIAC.

A GASTRONOMICAL CHANT.

———•———

Sunt Aries, Taurus, Cancer, Leo, Scorpio, Virgo,
Libraque et Arcitenens, Gemini, Caper, Amphora, Pisces.

I.

Of a tavern the Sun every month takes "the run,"
    And a dozen each year wait his wishes;
One month with old Prout he takes share of a trout,
    And puts up at the sign of THE FISHES. ♓
'Tis an old-fashion'd inn, but more quiet within
    Than THE BULL ♉ or THE LION ♌—both boisterous;
And few would fain dwell at THE SCORPION ♏-hotel,
    Or THE CRAB ♋ .. But this last is an oyster-house.

II.

At the sign of THE SCALES ♎ fuller measure prevails;
    At THE RAM ♈ the repast may be richer;
Old Goëthe oft wrote at the sign of THE GOAT, ♑
    Tho' at times he'd drop in at THE PITCHER; ♒
And those who have stay'd at the sign of THE MAID, ♍
    In desirable quarters have tarried;
While some for their sins must put up with THE TWINS, ♊
    Having had the mishap to get married.

III.

But THE FISHES ♓ combine in one mystical sign
   A moral right apt for the banquet ;
And a practical hint, which I ne'er saw in print,
   Yet a Rochefoucault maxim I rank it :
If a secret I'd hide, or a project confide,
   To a comrade's good faith and devotion,
Oh! the friend whom I'd wish, though he *drank* like a *fish,*
   Should be *mute* as the tribes of the ocean.

THE BATTLE OF HASTINGS.

ACROSS the ocean's troubled breast
    The base-born Norman came,
To win for his helm a kingly crest,
    For his sons a kingly name ;
    And in his warlike band,
    Came flashing fair and free,
The brightest swords of his father's land,
    With the pomp of its chivalry.

What doth the foe on England's field ?
    Why seeks he England's throne ?
Has she no chiefs her arms to wield,
    No warrior of her own ?
    But lo ! in regal pride
    Stern Harold comes again,
With the waving folds of his banner dyed
    In the blood of the hostile Dane.

The song—the prayer—the feast were o'er,
    The stars in Heaven were pale,
And many a brow was bared once more
    To meet the morning gale.

At length the sun's bright ray
   Tinged the wide east with gold.
And the misty veil of the morning grey
   Away from his forehead roll'd.

And all along each crowded track
   His burning glance was thrown,
Till the polish'd armour sent him back
   A lustre like his own.
   Still flash'd his silver sheen
   Along the serried lines,
Where the deadly wood of spears was seen
   To rise like forest-PINES.

In either host was silence deep,
   Save the falchion's casual ring,
When a sound arose like the first dread sweep
   Of the distant tempest's wing;
   Then burst the clamour out,
   Still madd'ning more and more,
Till the air grew troubled with the shout,
   As it is at the thunder's roar.

And the war was roused by that fearful cry,
   And the hosts rushed wildly on,
Like clouds that sweep o'er the gloomy sky
   When summer days are gone.
   Swift as the lightning's flame
   The furious horseman pass'd,
And the rattling showers of arrows came
   Like hailstones on the blast.

The island phalanx firmly trod
    On paths all red with gore ;
For the blood of their bravest stain'd the sod
    They proudly spurn'd before.
    But close and closer still
    They plied them blow for blow,
Till the deadly stroke of the Saxon bill
    Cut loose the Norman bow.

And the stubborn foemen turn'd to flee,
    With the Saxons on their rear,
Like hounds when they lightly cross the lea
    To spring on the fallow-deer.
    Each war-axe gleaming bright
    Made havoc in its sway ;
But, in the mingled chase and flight
    They lost their firm array.

From a mounted band of the Norman's best
    A vengeful cry arose,
Their lances long were in the rest,
    And they dash'd upon their foes
    On, on, in wild career ;
    Alas for England, then,
When the furious thrust of the horsemen's spear
    Bore back the Kentish men.

They bore them back, that desp'rate band,
    Despite of helm or shield ;
And the corslet bright and the gory brand
    Lay strew'd on the battle-field.

Fierce flash'd the Norman's steel,
    Though soil'd by many a stain,
And the iron-tread of his courser's heel
    Crush'd down the prostrate slain.

But still for life the Saxons ply,
    In hope, or in despair ;
And their frantic leader's rallying-cry
    Rings in the noontide air.
    He toils ; but toils in vain !
    The fatal arrow flies,
The iron point has pierced his brain,
    The island-monarch dies.

The fight is o'er, and wide are spread
    The sounds of the dismal tale ;
And many a heart has quail'd with dread,
    And many a cheek is pale.
    The victor's fears are past,
    The golden spoil is won,
And England's tears are flowing fast,
    In grief for England's son.

                ALEXANDER McDOUGALL.

THE CHRISTENING OF HER ROYAL HIGHNESS THE PRINCESS ALICE MAUDE.

———

Refrain.

MOLLY, my dear, did you ever hear
　　The likes of me from Cork to Dover?
The girls all love me far and near,
　　They're mad in love with " Pat the Rover."

Molly Machree, you didn't see
　　THE PRINCESS AILLEEN'S royal christening;
You'll hear it every word from me,
　　If you'll be only after listening.
To see the mighty grand affair
　　The *Quality* got invitations;
And wasn't I myself just there,
　　With half-a-dozen blood relations?
　　　　　　　　Molly, my dear, &c.

What lots of Ladies curtsied in,
　　And Peers all powdhered free an aisy!
Miss Biddy Maginn, and Bryan O'Lynn,
　　Katty Neil, and bould Corporal Casey.

Lord Clarendine, and Lord Glandine,
  Each buckled to a Maid of Honour,
The Queen of Spain, and Lord Castlemaine ;
  The Queen of France, and King O'Connor,
                Molly, my dear, &c.

There was no lack, you may be sure,
  Of writers, and of rhetoricians,
Of Whigs and Tories, rich and poor,
  Priests, patriots, and politicians.
The next came in was Father Prout,
  With a fine ould dame from the Tunbridge waters,
And Dan O'Connell, bould and stout,
  Led in Rebecca and her Daughters.
                Molly, my dear, &c.

Some came in pairs, some came in chairs,
  From foreign parts, and parts adjacent !
"Ochone ! I'm alone !" says the Widow Malone,
  " Is there nobody here to do the daycent ?"
There was Peggy O'Hara, from Cunnemara,
  And who her beau was I couldn't tell, sir ;
But the Duke of Buccleuch danced with Molly Carew,
  And Paddy from Cork with Fanny Ellsler !
                Molly, my dear, &c.

We every one sat down to tay :
  The toast and muffins flew like winking ;
Before or since that blessed day
  I never saw such eating and drinking.

We had pigeon-pies, and puddings likewise
We walk'd into the pastries after ;
We'd D'Arcy's whiskey, and Guinness's stout,
    Impayrial pop, and soda-water !
              Molly, my dear, &c.

And when there was no more to sup,
    The Prince cried, " Piper, rouse your chanter !"
The band of blind fiddlers then struck up,
    And scraped, "God save the Queen" *instanter*.
Her Majesty she danced, d'ye see,
    An Irish hornpipe with Sir Bobby ;
We piled the chairs upon the stairs,
    And pitch'd the tables on the lobby.
              Molly, my dear, &c.

The clargy then at last came in—
    Says he, "Ladies and gentlemen, will ye's all be
      sayted ?"
" Faith," says I, "I wish you'd soon begin ;
    I long to see the job complayted."
And so on it was.   The young Princess
    Was stood for by my gossip's daughter ;
And didn't Father Mathew bless,
    And sprinkle her with holy water ?
              Molly, my dear, &c.

HEALTHY LODGINGS;

OR, "TAKEN IN AND DONE FOR."

———•———

"Full many a dire exposure spring, we
See, from one mere *lapsus linguæ*."—ANON.

WHERE London's dome exalts its towering head
O'er the urn'd ashes of th' illustrious dead :
While many a jostled bumpkin, passing under,
Lifts his strain'd eyes, and opes his mouth with wonder ;
Where, all around, in rich display, we find
Provisions for the stomach, limbs, and mind :
Where—but, kind reader, I surmise,
From these faint hints you'll recognise,
  (Or else 'tis very hard
  Upon your bard)
  Saint Paul's churchyard.
Well—near this memorable minster
There dwelt a certain aged spinster,
  Who had a phthisic,
So firmly rooted in her constitution,
  That all the physic
Which fifty doctors had prescribed,
And she, by gallons, had imbibed,
Wrought, in its force, no jot of diminution ;
  But, for the golden lining of her purse,

That, I confess,
Grew daily less,
In ratio as her malady grew worse.

This (as their *bleeding* patient still was rich,)
Ne'er gave the doctors' consciences a twitch ;
But was, of course,
The fertile source
Of anxious cares
To her next heirs ;
A couple of necessitous and sly
First cousins,
Who, seeing thus the guineas daily fly
By dozens,
Resolved, if possible, to check
Their long-expected fortune's wreck.
They sought the suffering invalid,
And on their knees began to plead,
That of her life she'd take more heed.
" Yield," argued they, " to our advice,
And 'twill relieve you in a trice.
Discard your doctors ; nauseous drugs forbear ;
Quit London's smoke, and try a CHANGE OF AIR !
Depute to us the pleasing duty
To find a genial spot to suit ye ;
And you shall find our loving plan
More efficacious
Than all the med'cine-monger clan,
With hands rapacious."

The feeble patient gave consent,

And to their task the cousins went.
For many a day, beyond the city's bound,
The busy pair pursued a weary round,
And many a rural village had they paced,
Ere they could find an air to please their taste.

At length, to finish their perambulations,
An accident fulfill'd their expectations;
For, passing through a snug churchyard,
  A welcome symptom met their view,
Which with their wish precisely squared,
  For *nearly half the graves were new.*
Resolving here to make a stand,
They turn'd their eyes on either hand,
When, *à propos*, before their faces,
Scarce distant half a hundred paces,
A neat, lone, wood-built house appear'd, whose door
With full-blown eglantine was mantled o'er;
     And, to complete their luck,
     A glaring placard stuck
Upon a *board*, intelligence afforded
That, in this house *of boards*, you might be boarded.
      Thither they steer'd,
       And ask'd to see
       The landlady,
      Who straight appear'd.

The cousins, in a sigh-fraught simper,
(Something between a smile and whimper)
Their pious errand faltering told:
" We have a *valued* sick relation,

Who, being now infirm and old,
Has singled out this situation;
Hoping that your *salubrious* air,
For some few years her life may spare.
But, hark ye! we have cause to fear
That *deaths* of late are frequent here.
This we entreat you not to mention,
For 'twould defeat our kind intention.
To-morrow morning she shall come;
      But mum!
      Don't drop a word
      That you have heard
Of death, for years, within a mile!"
" No," said the housewife, with a smile;
" You need not fear—my tongue ne'er slips:
No word of *death* shall 'scape my lips."
Next morn the fragile lodger came:
With eager haste th' officious dame,
      At her approach,
      Flew to the coach,
Dropt her best curtsey—lent her shoulder,
To be the lady's crutch, and told her
Thus, " My first floor has been prepared:
The fires are good, the beds well air'd;
I'm quite convinced that, on inspection,
The rooms will merit your election
And, if th' improvement of your case
Can be obtain'd by change of place,
No spot's so well adapted to insure
      Your perfect cure;
      Our air's so pure,"

Continued the loquacious wife,
"'Twould almost raise the dead to life."
Finding old Goody thus verbose,
The tottering lady craved repose,
Thanking the gossip for her cares ;
But, when prepared to mount the stairs,
She found no friendly balustrade,
To yield her hand the wonted aid ;
For, though its clumsy rails were oaken,
            'Twas broken !

"Good hostess," (croak'd the hectic fair,)
"Your stairs of all support are bare ;
And ne'er can be by me ascended,
Unless the balustrade be mended."

This speech the dame's good-humour marr'd,
And threw her somewhat off her guard :—
"The Devil take the stairs," quoth she,
"They're an incessant plague to me.
Madam, 'tis true as I stand here,
Only within the last half year,
SIX TIMES the joiner I have paid
For mending that same balustrade ;
And yet, with all th' expense and care,
I cannot keep it in repair ;
For, every time 'tis done, just when
    'Tis fix'd as firm as hands can make it,
THE CURSED UNDERTAKER'S MEN,
    IN BRINGING DOWN THE COFFINS, break it !"

                        HILARY HYPBANE.

THE HAUNTED CHAMBER;

OR, THE PEDLAR'S PANIC.

A TALE OF BLOOD.

—◆—

Les ombres quelquefois font paroître *des substances.*

THINK not, kind reader, here to find
  A tissue of poetic fancies ;
If such will satisfy your mind,
  You'll find enough in stale romances :
Where, 'twixt the time-gnawn, mouldering walls
Of man-deserted gothic halls ;
    Witches and devils
    Join in revels,
And ghosts and fairies hold their midnight balls.
  Where bleeding nuns, with gory vests,
  And daggers sticking in their breasts,
Through drear churchyards their algid airing take,
    In doleful dumps :
  Where errant elves, and spell-driv'n sprites
  Flit through the air like northern lights,
And armour'd *armless* heroes groan and shake
    Their bloody stumps.

Where shade of murder'd miser, knight, or prince,
    Deserts his tomb,
To visit cut-throats' beds ; and, when they wince
    And almost stare their eyeballs out,
      Gives them a gentle hint about
        Their future doom.
Or calls, *en passant*, at his old château,
To see if spouse's tears have ceased to flow :
Or, silently and slily as a dun,
    Through well-known passages and chambers stealing,
Peeps o'er the shoulder of his spendthrift son,
    As drunk to bed the scape-grace rogue is reeling.
Where letters, traced with sulphury flame,
    Glare on the floor, or tapestry, or ceiling ;
Showing some vile assassin's name,
    Or other dreadful mystery revealing ;
      Which, in true novel-weaving guise,
      Is hidden from the reader's eyes ;
Nor by the cautious author e'er unravell'd,
Till through three long, dark volumes he has travell'd.
    Where flickering flambeaux flash and flare,
      (By powers supernal borne and lighted)
    In gambols through the murky air,
      To guide the errant chief, benighted,
    Into some lonely haunted tower,
    To break some fell enchanter's power.
Where mingled noises, harsh and risible,
Seem to proceed from things invisible :
    Where sorcerers' cauldrons bubbling boil,
      And goblins flock from cave and flood :
    Where rusty hinges creak for oil,

And poniards, dripping victims' blood,
 Dance, jig, and hay,
 In grim array,
And scare the plodding peasant on his way.
Where the adventurous knight approaches
 Some castle's dragon-guarded door :
Draws his all-conquering sword, and broaches
 The monster's heart ; and with the gore,
Which flows in torrents from the hideous wound,
Inscribes his mistress' name upon the ground ;
 Then ventures in, and finds the hall
 Full of fierce griffins—slays them all ;
Rushes resistless on from room to room,
 While dwarfs and griffins fall beneath his sword,
As spiders fall beneath the housemaid's broom ;
 Meets with the mighty mansion's giant lord,
 Whose steeple stature and ferocity
 Repress not his impetuosity,
Pierces his heart, spite of his brazen mail,
As south-sea mariners harpoon a whale ;
 Explores each subterranean maze,
  By moans directed,
 Till a fair damsel meets his gaze,
  Pale and dejected ;
Kneels, prays, and wins; then back to daylight gropes;
And with the grateful franchised maid elopes.

 I say, if *fables* such as these
 Suffice your appetite to please,
 Stop here ; or, haply, I may miss
 The target of your taste ; for this,

For which your patience now I crave, is
A literary *rara avis ;*
    A something new :
A story of an apparition,
      Yet strictly true,
As grave, historical tradition :
A ghostly tale, yet fact, I dare engage,
As ghostly text e'er breathed by ghostly sage.
As some usurper of a gay domain
  Thrusts from his native seat some milder lord ;
Employs rude arms his conquest to maintain,
  And bids the hall's late hospitable board
No more be spread to greet the welcome guest ;
Its couch no more afford the traveller rest :
Strips from his vassals, while they quake with dread,
  The livery worn through many a happy day,
And on each sighing churl bestows, instead,
  The sombre symbol of his iron sway ;
Killing, with merciless severity,
Such as would shrink from his austerity :

So tyrant Winter, with his chilly blast,
  Had rudely driv'n rich Autumn from her throne ;
His sable, storm-fraught clouds around had cast,
  And made the empire of the plain his own :
    Had seen before his withering breeze
        Each flower expire ;
    Had shaken from the sturdier trees
        Their green attire ;
    And now began to clothe their boughs
    In the white mantle of his snows.

When, o'er a bleak and barren moor,
A travelling pedlar, near threescore,
      At close of day,
      Toil'd on his way :
      A weighty pack
      Strapp'd on his back,
Seem'd to require his utmost strength ;
A crabstick of enormous length
He held, whereon his weary limbs he propt,
As ever and anon for breath he stopt.

Keen blew the loudly-whistling northern wind,
      Driving apace,
      Plump in his face,
Huge flakes of snow, which almost made him blind.

    His hands, benumb'd, he blew and flapp'd ;
    His tatter'd cloak around him wrapp'd ;
And, like a tether'd donkey, oft-times turn'd
  His rump, to bide the pelting of the storm ;
Sigh'd o'er the cheerless trade by which he earn'd
  His daily bread ; and, writhing like a worm,
      As on the crackling frozen snow
      He fell, and rose again to go,
And fell again, and, patient as a lamb,
Drew forth his little flask to take a dram.

A tawny, tailless terrier, cowering, crept
On his lee-side : the pedlar almost wept
    The little trembling brute to see,
    Whimp'ring and fawning on his knee ;

And, patting the fond creature, thus he spake :—
  "Poor faithful Crop !
'Twould glad my heart if thou couldst also take
  A little drop
 Of this exhilarating stuff !"
 The grateful animal cried "Whuff !"
And shook his hide and bark'd,—as if to say,
"Courage, my generous patron ! let's away !"
At least 'twas thus the partial pedlar judged ;
 So rose, and, for the timely hint, caress'd
His four-legg'd monitor, whom, as they trudged,
 In social mood, he in these terms address'd :—
  "Well, if I'm spared to reach some hut,
  And get an ounce of food to put
  Within my famish'd lips, I swear it,
  My good old dog shall fairly share it ;
  And, if I find a smiling fire,
  (Which both of us, Heaven knows, require,)
  I vow that thou, poor quaking elf,
  Shall sit as near it as myself."
  Crop frisk'd about, and wagg'd his tail ;
  But, fearing this alone might fail
  To show his gratitude's extent,
  Close to the pedlar's side he went,
  And lick'd his hand, and gave a squall
  About the key A *natural*,
   (Tail wagging faster)
  Which persons learned canine chat in,
  Affirm is excellent *dog latin*
   For "Thank ye, master."

Darker and darker grew the sky :
No hospitable roof was nigh :
    No moon that night
    Display'd her light :
No evening star with friendly radiance twinkled ;
  The blackthorn bushes show'd their snow-clad tops,
  Like May-day sweeps bewig'd with new thrum mops,
Or negro-lackeys' heads with flour besprinkled.
    Mile after mile the drooping pair
      In silence paced
      The trackless waste,
    And almost yielded to despair :
    When, seized with pleasure and surprise,
    The hope-cheer'd pedlar strain'd his eyes,
    And, still half doubting, dimly spied
      A glimmering light :
      With all his might
    He rallied his frail limbs, and onward hied.
At length a lonely mansion met his view,
    Through the few half-opaque remains
    Of whose bepatch'd and shatter'd panes
The taper gleam'd which his attention drew.
    The fabric was an antique tower,
  · Which, when the exercise of power
    Was unrestrain'd by wholesome laws,
    And lords cut throats for hairs and straws,
    Had weather'd many a fierce attack,
      Without a crack,
And many a bold intrusive force driv'n back :
      But an old knight,
      Sir Tempus hight,

Had since besieged it with his battering balls,
And made some woful breaches in its walls.

 The glare of the surrounding snow
 Sufficed our traveller to show
 The tumbling tenement's extent,
 And guide him to the door : he went,
 And with his trusty crab-stick knock'd,
 And strove to open it,—'twas lock'd !
 He would have whistled, but the frost
   Had made so stiff
   His lips, that if
 The failure had existence cost,
 He ne'er had overcome the puzzle
 Of screwing up his mournful muzzle.
 At length, within, the landlord cried,
 "Who's there?"   The pedlar straight replied,
   " A frozen friend !
   For Heaven's sake, lend
 Attention to my piteous plight,
 And give me lodging for the night."

 The landlord ope'd the door, 'tis true,
 But just sufficiently to view
   The would-be guest
   Who broke his rest.
 This, when the anxious pedlar saw,
 He thought he'd best adopt club-law ;
 So raised his tough crab-staff, and put it
  Between the threshold and the door,
  A further parley to secure,
 In case the churl should strive to shut it.

"Hark ye, mine host," the pedlar said,
  "Give me but shelter, fire, and food,
And, by the mass, you shall be amply paid!"
  "Good!" quoth the landlord, "very good!
      But, on my soul,
      There's not a hole,
As large as would receive a mouse
In this old weather-beaten house,
But what contains some snoring wight,
Driven in by this tempestuous night.
I mean in all the *habitable part ;*
  For ('tween ourselves) there is a spacious room,
  Which many a year hath seen nor guest nor broom,
But heaven forbid that I should have the heart
To such a dimsal place to invite ye ;
For, by the saints, I tell no lie t'ye,
'Tis by a *hideous spectre* haunted,
Which many a valiant heart hath daunted.
However, if you think you dare
Take, for the night, your lodging *there,*
I'll make you up a blazing fire ;
  As good a bed and supper, too,
As any traveller need desire."
  An owl i' th' ivy cried—"Whoo, whoo!"
The pedlar started at the voice :
The landlord said, "Come, make your choice !
Hunger and thirst, wind, snow, and frost ;
Or bed, fire, liquor, food, and GHOST !"

Cold as he was, when the last word prophetic
      Struck on his ear,

It acted like a dose diaphoretic.
  Sweating with fear,
He started like a Bedlamite,
And almost bade the host good night ;
  But, as the snow-fraught blast blew fiercer still,
Anxious the proffer'd cheer to share,
He faintly mumbled half a prayer,
  And ponder'd which might be the minor ill.

" If I proceed," thought he, " I'm lost,
  On such an awful night ;
And, if I stay and meet the ghost,
  I shall expire with fright !
Which shall I do ?—go on or stop ?"
The answer was supplied by Crop,
Who, setting up a piteous yell,
  Reproach'd him with his late pledged oath,
Beseeching him his fears to quell,
  And keep his word, however loth.

The pedlar own'd the dog's appeal,
Craving the promised fire and meal,
    Was strictly just.
    A sudden gust,
Replete with hail, that moment caught him,
And nearer to decision brought him ;
  That is, the smiling cherub, Hope,
Came peeping through the cloud of doubts and fears,
Just as the hailstones rattled in his ears,
  And for his prudence gave more scope.
" Wherefore," quoth he, " should *I* so dread

This apparition of the dead ?
I have *no motive* for alarm :
I ne'er did human being harm :
My conscience bears no murder's stains :
   I ne'er have been in vice a meddler ;
Then why should spectres take the pains
   To scare a poor benighted pedlar ?
Nay, should they in the room appear, I
Am so cold, and wet, and weary,
That, if I once to bed could creep,
And get myself fast lock'd in sleep,
      Deuce take me
If I believe that all the ghosts
That any moderate churchyard boasts
     Could wake me !"

This said, our hero boldly ventured,
  And, calling Crop to follow, enter'd.
The shivering landlord led the way,
  Through many a passage dark, and lone, and long,
Where foot had never trod for many a day,
  Stumbling the fallen fractured stones among,
Which strew'd their dreary path, they reach'd
A rude stone stair, where many an owlet screech'd,
And many a toad, and many a mouse and rat,
Stared, wond'ring what the deuce the men were at,
And seem'd displeased that their asylum
Remain'd not undisturb'd, as whilom.

  Onward the tristful trio went,
  And enter'd on the stair's ascent,

O'er whose disjointed steps they needs must clamber
Ere they could reach the pedlar's destined chamber.
At length, the rugged steep ascended,
The host pronounced their task was ended,
And, striding o'er the creaking floor,
Show'd the appointed room, whose door
To many a million hungry worms had lent
Their fill,
Till nearly all its *substance* it had spent ;
But still
It held its form and power of motion,
And almost seem'd to inspire the notion
That 'twas the spectre of a door,
Which had been once, but was no more.

The *story* where this chamber lay
Was lofty ; though I cannot say
It either taste or elegance could boast ;
'Twas big, black, broken, barbarous, and bare,
Peculiarities by no means rare
In *stories* which contain *a Ghost.*
They enter'd, and the host essay'd to raise
An ample fire : forthwith the genial blaze,
Spreading its influence round the room,
Began to dissipate the gloom.
Crop wagg'd his tail, crept to the hearth,
Seem'd quite contented with his berth,
Turn'd himself round, and cosily reclined,
Nor thought of ghost or snow, or frost or wind.
Meanwhile the landlord was not still ;
But, by a generous impulse speeded,

Began his promise to fulfil,
　And with such vigilance proceeded,
That e'er a full half hour his guest
　Before the fire his seat had taken,
And gain'd a little warmth and rest ;
　An ample dish of eggs and bacon
(The best his dwelling could afford)
Was, smoking, placed upon the board.
This, with some potent home-brew'd beer
　　　And household bread,
　　　The landlord said,
Must constitute his evening cheer.
His watering chops the pedlar smack'd,
And straight the savoury meal attack'd ;
　　　Nor did he stint
The motion of his nimble jaws,
Until he felt Crop's two fore-paws,
　　　By way of hint,
Placed eagerly upon his knee,
Seeming to say, "Remember me !"
When, knowing well what was the matter,
He instantly gave Crop the platter.

While thus the dog and master fed,
The busy landlord made the bed,
Which now he told him was prepared,
With store of rugs and sheets well air'd,
Whenever he might deem't expedient
To go to rest.　"Your most obedient,"
Pursued the host, " I'll to my nest,
And wish you, sir, a good night's rest !"

"Thank ye," the cheerful pedlar said ;
" Believe me, friend, I'm not afraid."
In fact the happy man had quaff'd
    Such draughts of courage from the oft-fill'd horn,
That now, pot valorous, he laugh'd
    The simple landlord's childish fears to scorn.
However, when the host had fairly left him,
        The cheerless scene
        Brought on the spleen,
And almost of his fortitude bereft him.
    So, to protect his mind from dread,
    He stripp'd and hasten'd into bed ;
    And, that he might forget the place,
    Pull'd up the bed-clothes o'er his face.

    That fleeting shades of murder'd wights
    Should rise and prowl this world o'nights,
    Their various injuries to avouch,
    And scare the assassin on his couch,
    Making him blab by terror's dint,
    May have some show of justice in't ;
        But, by my bardship,
        'Tis a great hardship
    That a poor simple snoring elf,
    Who would not hurt Old Nick himself,
    Should be disturb'd.   The crazy floor
    Shook like an aspen leaf : the door
    Upon its rusty hinges creak'd :
    The pedlar raised his head, and shriek'd :
    The roaring thunder peal'd around,
    And seem'd to move the very ground :

The waken'd dog set up a hideous yell,
And cower'd beneath the bed ; when, strange to tell,
   The fire, which scarce had shown its light,
   Was kindled up with flames most bright,
   As if to add more terror to the sight ;
The horrid sight ; for, with a hollow groan,
Which almost turn'd the pedlar's heart to stone,
A grizzly *Ghost*, with solemn stately pace,
And glaring eyeballs, stalk'd along the place.
   Its vest was streak'd and clotted o'er
   With purple stains of human gore :
   A ghastly wound yawn'd on its brow,
   Whence sanguine streams appear'd to flow ;
And thrice, with heavy step, it pass'd the bed ;
And thrice it groan'd, and shook its bloody head.
   The pallid pedlar nearly swoon'd with fright ;
He thought the very devil possess'd him :
   His blood ran cold : his hair stood bolt upright :
   At length the gory apparition
   (Seeming to pity his condition)
The awful silence broke, and thus address'd him :—
   " Six twelvemonths since I chanced to be
   Benighted, driven in here, like thee.
   Far from my home (that home, alas !
   Whose threshold I no more might pass),
   Laden with treasure, all my own ;
   Too dearly won ; for, not alone
   By honest industry 'twas gain'd,
   But by deceit and fraud obtain'd.
   I craved for wealth.   Let every knave
   Receive a lesson from my grave ;

And turning from his dangerous folly, see
That honesty's the safest policy.
Just when I 'gan myself to hug,
Quite sure I held my treasure snug,
Mark how it ended!   On that very bed
I laid my weary limbs and anxious head ;
When, at the hour of midnight, e'en when most
I thought myself secure ; my treacherous host
Came to my chamber, clad in spectre's guise,
Flashing a flaming torch before my eyes ;
And, as I lay transfixt with fear and wonder,
Remorseless, plunder'd me of all my plunder ;
Then, that my murder ne'er might come to light,
Dash'd out my brains, and thrust me out of sight.
Behold this gash! yet let it not alarm thee !
I come for thine advantage, not to harm thee !
The barbarous villain ne'er enjoy'd the spoil,
For, every night, his quietude to foil,
I came to haunt him ; till, o'ercome with dread,
He left his house, and from the country fled.
His blood-stain'd booty still lies buried near :
'Twill make you rich.   Arise! dismiss your fear,
And follow me ! I'll show you where 'tis hidden ! "
The listening pedlar rose as soon as bidden,
Such magic power did hope of wealth impart,
To brace his limbs, spite of his fluttering heart.

"Hold !" said the *Ghost*, "ere we one step proceed,
Swear to perform for me one pious deed ;
'Tis all that I demand.   Beneath the stones
Which form yon hearth, repose my mouldering bones.

Remove them thence, and see them safe convey'd
To holy ground, and there in burial laid:
So shall my wandering spirit be at rest,
And you with ease and opulence be blest!"
The pedlar pledged his oath, and onward hied,
At humble distance following his grim guide.
With perfect ease they pass'd the broken stair,
And speedily arrived i' th' open air.

The northern blast, which erst had blown so keenly,
Was now quite hush'd; the moon had risen serenely,
And on the snow-spread earth diffused her light
So brightly, yet so palely, that the night
Seem'd like the ghost of day. Silent they pass'd
O'er many a spacious field, until, at last,
The *Ghost* stopp'd short, and, pointing to the earth,
Said, "Here lies buried all that I was worth
Of worldly wealth: I give it all to you—
Mark well the spot—be to your promise true—
So shall your fears of future want be banish'd!
Farewell! remember me!"—this said, it vanish'd.

The pedlar's hair stood bristling still on end,
And, when deserted by his ghostly friend,
Shuddering with mingled fright, and cold, and joy,
   He look'd around
For something which, *as mark*, he might employ;
   But all the ground
Was clothed with snow, and neither bush nor tree,
Nor stick nor stone, was near the spot, that he
Could use to be his beacon for the morrow.
I'll not attempt to paint the poor man's sorrow,

When he perceived no chance, but there to stay,
And wait th' arrival of the following day.

No month of darkness to the mariner,
   Whose ship lies frost-lock'd in a northern sea :
No voyage to a sea-sick passenger,
   Sighing from waves and puking to be free :
No livelong route, which pious pilgrims take,
   Famish'd and sick, o'er Afric's burning sands :
No father's lifetime, to the spendthrift rake,
   Eager to squander his paternal lands :
No lingering week, with Christmas at its end,
   To longing urchin, daily flogg'd at school :
No period which th' offender's doom'd to spend,
   With sheet enrobed, on the repentant stool :
No sleepless night to the expectant wench,
   Whom next day's noon is to behold a bride :
No space by culprit pass'd before the bench,
   While judge and jury on his fate decide :
No day to galley-slave, when labouring hard,
   Unfeeling knaves with stripes his toil requite :
No last rehearsal to a starving bard,
   Whose firstling play's to be produced at night,
E'er seem'd more tedious, long, and wearisome,
   Than to the pedlar's mind the sluggish hours :
He thought the wish'd-for dawn would never come :
   Nay, almost thought Sol had withdrawn his powers,
      And that he did not think it worth
      His while to shine upon the earth,
      Whilst the bright moon, that beauteous doxy,
      Served him so well by way of proxy.
      At length a sudden gleam of thought

His strain'd imagination caught :
'Twas this—to breathe some little vein,
  Or slightly wound a thumb or finger,
And thence a crimson stream obtain,
To sprinkle o'er the virgin snow,
The spot whereon he stood to show,
  So that he need no longer linger ;
But neither pin nor needle, thorn nor knife,
Had he, or could he gain, to save his life.
Long time he ponder'd how to act,
His mind with various projects rack'd :
          At length, again,
          A novel train,
Of fancy flash'd across his brain,
And eased his breast of many a throe :
This was to give his nose a blow,
And, with the blood it would give vent to,
To form the long-desired memento.
He clench'd his fist, strung every nerve
  To bear the self-inflicted shock ;
Nor did he from his purpose swerve,
  But gave himself *a thund'ring knock !*
His eyes flash'd fire—moon, trees, and snow
Like lightning vanish'd with the blow ;
And now such objects met his view,
That, yawning, he had much ado
          To understand 'em :
His nose was swoln as big as two !
With blood his pillow was wet through !
In short, all night he'd soundly slept,
And all had been *a dream*—except
          HIS MEMORANDUM ! ! !

SONGS AMONG THE FLOWERS.

I.—SPRING AND ITS MEMORIES.

No longer the dark earth looks sad ;
　　The land is glad,
And hope renew'd hath touch'd each living thing.
　The world arises as from death ;
　　Beneath the breath
Of balmy, laughter-loving Spring.

In death fast lay the silver lake :
　　'Tis now awake ;
And, from its bright and crystal plain,
　The mirror'd beauty from on high,—
　　The azure sky—
In all its pride flings back again.

The snowdrop's scentless life is o'er ;
　　She is no more
Who once, in sweetly drooping grace,
　Bloom'd through a brief, chill, wintry day,
　　Then pass'd away ;—
Her scented sisters fill her place.

The yellow cowslip now is there;
  And, on the air,
Th' anemone and primrose wreathe
 A world of odours rare and sweet;
 And 'neath our feet,
The violets their perfumes breathe.

The joy of Spring!—It comes, that joy,
  Without alloy;
And Winter's stern dominion o'er,
 The heart declares Spring's sunny brow
 And radiant glow,
Never look'd half so bright before.

And when her time of bloom is flown,
  Her flowers gone,
And Winter spreads his sable wing,
 The heart's fond memories will stray
 Back to the day
When first we pluck'd the flowers of Spring.

So in life's Winter, if there come
  That age of gloom,
The stricken man recalls the bliss—
 The Spring-time of his heart,—the maids—
 The vows—the glades—
And Love's first flower that blooms,—the kiss.

II.—MAD RHYMES FOR MAY.

WHO would not be gay ?
'Tis May !   'Tis May !
'Tis Nature's fav'rite holiday !
There's melody gushing from every spray ;
And now from old Winter we turn away.
   For, over the plain,
   Comes tripping again,
The Spring's sweet daughter, blushing May !

Who would not be gay ?
Let life as it may,
Be tinged with shadows, gloomy and grey,—
They all disappear in the sun's bright ray ;
And the waters sparkle, the zephyrs play,
   As they haste to greet
   The sandall'd feet,
Of laughing, life-giving, lovely May !

Who would not be gay,
To see young May,
As she passes along her magic way,
Kissing the buds that through Winter lay
In Death's cold arms, as cold as clay ;
And, from her bright hair,
Shaking chaplets fair,
To deck those we love, as we love young May ?

Who would not be gay,
When the early May,
Awakes the Lark, and he wings away
To carol his cheerful roundelay,
At the fount of light, and the gates of day ?
　　Whenever did song,
　　Float so gaily along ;
As the song of the Lark, in early May ?

Who would not be gay ?
Young maidens, say,
Is this not the month when lovers stray,
In pairs, at eve ? and when,—but nay,
Far be it from me to tear away
　　The mystic veil,
　　Or tell the tale
Of the stolen joys that are favour'd by May.

Who would not be gay ?—
But, maidens, pray,
Like a sage as I am, allow me to say,
In vulgar terms, you had better make hay
While the sun doth shine, while yet 'tis day ;—
　　Lest Lover, like Lark,—
　　Excuse the remark,—
Turn silent and sulky, after May.

III.—THE LOVER AND THE FLOWERS.

How longs the heart to speak
Of her it loves !   In solitary hours
To discourse hold, and into musings break,
      Amid the flowers ?

  Thus, to the violet
I bend ; and, as its perfum'd breath I sip,
I gently murmur, sweet thou art, but yet,
      I know a lip

  Oh, richer far in sweets
Than violet e'er breathed upon the air ;
And yonder blushing rose, my view that meets,
      Is not so fair.

  The lily of the vale
Looks meekly upward, deck'd with modesty ;
Sweet, too, her beauty, soft her hue, though pale,—
      'Tis just like thee !

  The water-lily, too,
As trembling on the liquid stream it lies,
Shows its mild colours of transparent blue,
      Just like thine eyes.

Unlike the tulips bright,
Which in proud beauty, without sweetness, grow :
Both are united in those eyes of light,
 And on thy brow.

But, as the fair thatch-palm,
Which not alone shows beauty to the eye,
But tells how deep the soil, and rich the balm,
 That 'neath it lie ;*

So, in thy gentle face,
When looking on its radiant smiles, we find
Proofs of a deeper and a richer grace,
 That decks thy mind.

---

* "In some places are vast groves of the Latamia, or thatch-palm, the sight of which always gives pleasure to the beholder, not more from the singular conformation and beauty of the tree, than from the circumstance that it indicates with unerring certainty a rich and deep soil underneath."—*Edward's Historical Survey of St. Domingo.*

J. D.

THE EPICURE;

OR, WOODCOCKS NO GAME!

A TALE FOUNDED ON FACT.

—◆—

> " Colui che compra gatta in sacco,
> Merita traversia, per Bacco ! "

METHINKS I 've heard some stories blown about
   Touching the great Sir Isaac Newton,
That he on some occasions hath gone out,
   Having one slipper and one boot on ;
And that he caused an aperture
To be cut through his study door,
So that his favourite cat could get in ;
   And, when 'twas finish'd, told the man,
   To make another, half the span,
That puss might also bring her kitten.
Nay, I myself once knew a wight,
Who made as gross an error quite,
Though he'd as good a share of wit and sense
As has your bard, or (pray don't take offence)
   Even the learn'd reader may be.
Bound on a long sea-trip, he took the boat,
And went on shore to buy his wife a goat,
   To give her milk to feed her baby.

He soon return'd ; but when the prize
Met the delighted lady's eyes,
    It proved a male !
    But to my tale,
Which, like the anecdotes above,
Will have a tendency to prove,
That men whose genius and sagacity
  Almost inspire their friends with wonder,
Sometimes, despite of their capacity,
  Are caught in some egregious blunder.

There dwelt within a country town,
  A man well known amongst the peasants,
For wondrous skill in knocking down
    Partridges, woodcocks, snipes, and pheasants.

His accuracy was so great,
His friends would scarcely hesitate
To stake the bulk of an estate,
    Or take an oath,
That, when preparing to let fly,
He cock'd his piece, and *shut one eye*,
The fated game as certainly
    Forthwith *shut both*.

But this prodigious deadly aim
Was not the compass of his fame ;
He was renown'd, in many a court of law,
For length of head and nimbleness of jaw ;
    For depth of reading,
    And skill in pleading.

And framing many a fine-drawn quibble,
　　The cash of litigants to nibble ;
Who oftimes found that, though their *suits* were gain'd,
　　　　Their *suits* were lost ;
That is, their purses were in contest drain'd ;
　　And, though their *causes* might go well,
　　Their *clothes* they were obliged to sell
　　　　To pay the cost.

I've known full many a skilful shot,
　　Who almost made the chase his sole employment ;
Yet cared not for the game a jot,
　　Being contented with the mere enjoyment
Of walking twenty miles a-day,
　　And lugging home a bag of prey ;
Then sending round, in presents to his friends,
　　　　The hard-earn'd spoil ;
Thinking the pleasure amply made amends
　　　　For all his toil :

The more especially if those who got it
Praised the precision of the hand which shot it.
But this was not the temper of our hero :
He for the *pastime* scarcely cared a zero ;
　　For, whatsoever his pursuit,
　　He loved to taste its *solid fruit.*

Whether in practice or in sport ;
Whether in thicket or in court ;
Whether conveying lands and moneys,
　　Or shooting pigeons, hares, and coneys ;

Whether he wielded tongue or gun,
Trigger or brief, 'twas all as one.

It was not for the empty satisfaction,
   That friends of his dexterity might brag ;
No : he endured the labour of each *action*,
   To try what *game* or *cash* his hand could *bag*.

Of all the furr'd or feather'd throng,
   And, faith, he loved them all full well !
(Few epicures will deem him wrong,)
   He thought the WOODCOCK bore the belle.
Through copse and bog he'd grope and wade,
   His little favourite's haunts to trace ;
And think his trouble well repaid
   When he obtain'd a single brace.
Then, with some cozy neighb'ring squire,
   It often was his evening boast
To roast them at his parlour fire,
   And spread the trail on butter'd toast :
The which, he said, required such watchful care,
   That he the office always undertook,
Ne'er trusting so momentous an affair
   To the dull talent of his clumsy cook.

At length, one year it so befel,
He traversed every swamp and dell,
But not a woodcock could be found
Within the space of ten miles round.

It seem'd as if they had deserted,
   With one consent, their former favourite spot,

And 'mongst themselves a scheme concerted
   To leave off flocking thither to be shot.
Whether this really was the reason
I know not ; but for one whole season,
Of every other bird he had his fill,
But ne'er could set his eyes on one *long bill ;*
Which (as he held them in such estimation)
Was to *his* mind a source of great vexation.

Though all his wrangling clients, I'll be sworn,
Such disappointment cheerfully had borne,
      Nor e'er had taken huff ;
For, whatsoe'er his fortune in the field,
His *law-game-bag* was always sure to yield
      For them *long bills* enough.

It chanced, one morning, as he sat,
Correcting this, and conning that ;
Now culling from some learn'd philologist
   Choice terms to deck his next oration ;
Now skimming o'er some ornithologist,
   On *woodcocks*, and their strange migration ;
A letter summon'd him to roam
Some five-and-twenty miles from home ;
To wait upon a wealthy friend,
   Whose thread of life was nearly spent ;
And make arrangements for his end
   By drawing up his testament.

Mounting his fleetest horse, away he rode,
And hasten'd to the invalid's abode ;

Quickly perform'd his business of attorney,
And wish'd his dying friend a pleasant journey;
   Then, to return, restrode his steed,
   And urged him to his former speed;
   Being engaged at home to meet,
Within three hours, a man for whom he pleaded
   Of efforts in his cause to treat,
And tell with what success his suit proceeded.

But, ere a dozen miles he could complete,
(Passing a certain city's busy street,)
Finding the winter blast too biting,
   He stopt before a well-known inn,
And ate and drank (without alighting)
   A biscuit and a glass of gin.
Which done, his palfrey's side he spurr'd,
But at the very juncture heard,
Behind the house, a pedlar cry,
"Come, buy my woodcocks! cocks! who'll buy?"

"Bless me!" the man of law exclaim'd,
"I've ofttimes heard this spot was famed
For woodcocks; but could ne'er have thought
That they of hawkers could be bought!
Hostler, methinks (although my ears I doubt)
I heard a man cry *woodcocks* hereabout!"

"Ees," said the lad, "I knows the man as cries 'em;
He brings 'em faster nor the people buys 'em;
And yet, for one as brings 'em to your door,
Sixpence a-piece is cheap enough I'm sure."

" Sixpence a-piece ! " replied the cavalier,
" Egad ! to-night I'll have delicious cheer !
Here, take this money—I've no time to waste—
I shall but be in time with utmost haste—
Buy me six brace—get them pack'd up with care,
And send them by the coach this evening—there—
That's my address—now, for your life, don't fail ;
Here's half-a-crown to get yourself some ale."

The clown, delighted, promised to obey ;
And Latitat, delighted, rode away.

Arrived at home, and business past,
He took a chop to check his fast ;
Still leaving ample appetite
To grace his dainty meal at night ;
Then sent a pressing invitation
To an old crony 'cross the street,
Adding, by way of stimulation,
That he'd procured a certain treat,
Which for their supper should be drest,
Crown'd by a bottle of *the best*.
And, to fulfil his generous design,
He from his cellar brought a full supply,
Cull'd from the strongest ale, and oldest wine ;
For both the codgers loved to wet an eye.

The willing guest made not a moment's pause,
But brought his answer in his watering jaws ;
His hand the happy host with fervour prest,
And thus his welcome visitor addrest :

"My good old friend, 'tis thirteen months, at least,
Since you and I enjoy'd our favourite feast ;
But, as I've had the fortune now to light on't,
Faith, I'm resolved we'll have a jovial night on't.
　　Betty, by my express desire,
　　Has made us up a roaring fire,
　　And brought my parlour-spit and dish,
　　That we may cook to our own wish.
　　　　Here's ale in prime
　　　　To 'guile the time,
　　Tables, dice, box, and bread for toast ;
　　　　So, here we'll sit,
　　　　And play our hit,
　　And tipple while we rule the roast."

They sat, and play'd with various luck,
Till twice the tedious clock had struck ;
And now they watch'd the dial's hand,
And almost thought 'twas at a stand ;
So tardily it seem'd t' approach
The hour appointed for the coach.

At length the hour and coach together came,
When, anxious as a young, expecting dame,
The lawyer sent a servant for the game.

Ere long the breathless messenger return'd,
　Bearing beneath his arm the neat rush-basket ;
His master seized the prize, as much concern'd
　As if 't had been of precious stones a casket ;
Praised to the skies the hostler's punctuality,
And hasten'd to explore his bargain's quality.

The vivid fire burnt clear and red ;
Betty brought up the toasted bread ;
The package on the table laid,
Master and friend, and man and maid,
Forming an eager group around,
Ope'd it; and, what d'ye think they found?
You'll recollect, to aid your divination,
  He purchased them by ear, and not by eye :
Nor gave his agent any explanation,
  Save the mere mention of the vendor's cry.

Six brace of *cocks*, 'tis true, there were,
But such as ne'er had flown in air.
Woodcocks they were, in honest truth,
But somewhat hard for human tooth.

In short, the lawyer blush'd, and all the rest
  (Stifling their feelings, though to laughter moved)
    Look'd blank as cossets :
For, 'stead of dainties of the promised zest,
  To their astonishment the WOOD-COCKS proved
    SPIGOTS AND FAUCETS !

HILARY HYPBANE.

DAINTY FARE;

OR, THE DOUBLE DISASTER.

—◆—

" Multa cadunt inter calicem supremaque labra."

Soho, my Pegasus ! gently, my boy !
   The bard, in serious mood, designs to talk :
Cease for a while your pinions to employ
   In fitful, freakish flights absurd,
And bear me in a calm, majestic walk !

     Now ! off we go,
        At measured pace,
    Stately and slow,
        To show the place
At which the mirthful scene occurr'd.
'Midst the recesses of a Cambrian vale,
Long famed for mutton, pedigrees, and ale,
Where many an *Ap*, of princely lineage born,
His wealthy *nameless* neighbours laughs to scorn ;
Instead of palace, some lone hut inhabits,
And daily dines *in state* on headless rabbits.
Where Nature, like a gay coquette, displays
Her choicest charms to court the stranger's gaze,

Whose eyes enraptur'd o'er the landscape glide,
And find some beauteous trait on every side :
On that a blushing orchard—and on this
Some grassy slope or break-neck precipice.
There ocean's wide expanse, bespeck'd with shipping ;
Here playful goats o'er craggy passes skipping.
Copses where feather'd songsters warbling flutter,
And towns whose names 'twould break one's jaws to utter.
Oxen and cows in verdant meadows lowing ;
Or some bold river, in blue mazes flowing,
With glassy surface, round the mountain's bases,
Where pretty milk-maids view their pretty faces ;
Where pretty skiffs expand their pretty sails,
And " pretty fishes wag their pretty tails,"
While angling peasants watch, with fell intent,
To snatch them from their native element.

Hills piled on hills in crescent form recede,
Where bleating flocks in dewy pastures feed,
And Alpine mountains bound the eye's extension,
Bedeck'd with hues *too numerous to mention.*

'Midst the recesses of this Cambrian vale
Had dwelt from birth the hero of my tale.

Observe ! this scene is not a mere creation,
Coin'd in the die of my imagination,
Like empty puffs of London auctioneers,
(To trap the cash of thoughtless wealthy peers,)
Who with such skill descriptive subjects handle,
When they've *estates to let by inch of candle ;*

" Romantic sites ! tall woods ! meand'ring streams !
Extensive plains !" and twenty idle dreams :
Fictions invented to enhance the rent,
And only found *in the advertisement.*
My picture's drawn from nature, gentle friends,
Which for its faults perchance may make amends.

Methinks full plain my mental optic sees
The russet steeple peeping o'er the trees ;
And now, approaching nearer to the spot,
I see the snug farm-house,—the smart white cot,
Whose sign proclaims, to all who read or spell,
That 'tis inn, tavern, alehouse, and hotel,—
The ruddy clowns returning from their tillage,
And all the objects of the rural village.

Thanks, my good steed ! you've shown obedience readily,
And o'er the *heavy road* hath march'd so steadily,
That, by Apollo and his female cronies,
  I ne'er was better *borne* since I was born.
(Excuse me, gents, but to *poetic ponies,*
  An ounce of praise is worth a ton of corn.)
I'll give you now a looser rein,
  Nor longer regulate your journey's measure,
But let you play your pranks again,
    And flit at pleasure !

Just in the centre of a straggling street,
  (The only one our hamlet's name possest,)
As if resolved each wandering eye to meet,
  One small neat house advanced beyond the rest :

Its window was—i'faith I can't tell what,
  For buildings rules afford no term to call
    Its figure whereby—
'Twas not a bow or bay, nor was it flat,
  But modestly projected from the wall,
    Enough to swear by.

Three globes of colour'd liquor graced its panes,
  Whose brilliant hues of crimson, blue, and green
  Look'd wondrous pretty ; e'en in daylight seen
By truant children from the fields and lanes.
But in the night three meteors they seem'd ;
  For then, (with farthing candles stuck behind 'em,)
Full in each passing ploughboy's eyes they gleam'd,
    Threat'ning to blind 'em.

Over the door was placed a board, to teach
The sick and maim'd that there lived DOCTOR LEECH.

Within his shop, a sightly show to make,
  Shone drawers and jars, each with its classic label ;
But, as the drawers were *shut*, and jars *opaque*,
  No passenger nor customer was able
Whether they full or empty were to tell,
Though Doctor Leech the *latter* knew full well.

These, with some bullocks' bladders,
    And half a dozen adders
        Preserved in spirits,
        Beyond their merits,
With empty phials, a prodigious host,
Were all our pharmacopolist could boast.

In med'cine's science and chirurgic art
 His studied mind and practised hand were skill'd ;
Nay, I have heard it said (reader, don't start !)
 He cured a greater number than he killed !
  For not alone the human race
  His patient-list conspired to grace ;
  He doctor'd horses, sheep, and cows,
  Cropp'd terriers' ears, and physic'd sows ;
  Besides attending at the labours
  Of all his breeding female neighbours ;
  And curing gripes amongst the male,
  When they perchance had drunk sour ale ;
  Or making lotions for their sprains,
  And bruises, and rheumatic pains.

"Why," you'll exclaim, "with such extensive practice,
He surely must have thriven !" But no ; the fact is,
 The country was so *cursed healthy*,
 He could not for his soul grow wealthy.
Nay, *au contraire*, though from his youth he'd follow'd
 The Æsculapian trade in all its branches,
  So far from riches,
His fees scarce furnish'd the coarse meals he swallow'd,
 Or suffer'd him to clothe his bony haunches
  In decent breeches.
And, though he kept his credit pretty level,
 Striving to make the best of his affairs,
The which invariably he made a rule, yet
 He was in truth, almost as poor a devil,
As thread-bare, woe-begone, and full of cares,
 As Shakspeare drew in " Romeo and Juliet."

Year after year he starved and wrought,
Nor ever would admit a thought
Of quitting that dear spot of earth
Which gave his meagre carcase birth.

Somewhat resembling a domestic cat,
  Left in a house where first he saw the light,
Who, having murder'd every mouse and rat,
  Still hugs his native place in famine's spite,
And stalks from room to room with hunger gaunt,
Rather than wander from his favourite haunt.
By Jove, the meanest slave or poorest bard
Could scarcely hold his life on terms so hard !
Sometimes he lived on porridge made of leeks
          For weeks :
          Or toasted cheese,
          Or boil'd grey peas.
Nay, in extremity, he sometimes fed
For many a cheerless day on barley bread.

Yet, when dame Fortune, (the capricious beldam)
Deign'd him a savoury meal, which was but seldom,
Our son of Galen thought it no iniquity
  To gormandise like Heliogabalus,
Or any other glutton of antiquity,
          Real or fabulous.
And now the goddess, in propitious mood,
Vouchsafed to glad his sight with luscious food ;
But who bestow'd the choice donation
Requires some farther explanation.

I should have told you that the doctor's soul
  Bore to his fortune great disparity :
And, though his scanty purse forbade a dole,
  He oft perform'd some act of charity.

One deed above the rest conspicuous shone ;
He took beneath his care a widow's son,
    To teach him *gratis* how to read
    And write, and tug out teeth, and bleed ;
    Blister, and purge, and hack, and heal,
    And in galenicals to deal ;
With all the arts and mysteries he knew,
Which, as I said before, were not a few.
    But not to give his pupil board ;
    For this his house could not afford ;
    Nor did the grateful youth desire it,
    Nor did his mother's means require it ;
    For, though not affluent, she had enow,
    Lived prettily, and kept a breeding sow ;
    On one of whose portentous farrow
    Hinges in part our story's marrow.

    The anxious widow's heart had spent
Many a tedious hour, and day, and week,
    Anticipating the event,
When she should hear the new-born porklings squeak,
That she with *solid thanks* her friend might greet,
And give his stomach a delicious treat.

At length the day of parturition came,
To crown the hopes of the expectant dame :

When straight, with exultation big,
　　She mark'd the largest, healthiest pig,
With which her sow's fecundity had stock'd her ;
　　And made it her diurnal care
　　To see it suck an ample share
　　Of milk, to make it plump and fair—
A worthy present for the worthy doctor.
Full well her charge repaid her assiduity ;
　For, ere he thirty days of life could boast,
His fat had grown almost to superfluity,
　And every mouth pronounced him " fit to roast."

　　But here I beg you to excuse
　　One small omission of the muse.
　　Do not compel me to dilate
　　Minutely on the sufferer's fate ;
Describe the *piercing* steel and *piercing* cries,
　Rending the atmosphere with din infernal ;
The sanguine gurgling wound ! the staring eyes !
　And the responsive grunts of agony maternal !
　　For, to be plain, I'm not in cue
　　Such tragic subjects to pursue.
Let it suffice to say, the butcher's knife
Deprived the *tender innocent* of life.
And now suppose him in a basket pent,
And by our youngster to his patron sent,
About that juncture of a Sabbath day
When the church-bells were chiming, "Come and pray !"

　　Kind reader, did you ever see
　　Th' inside of a menagerie

About the usual feeding-time,
   When all the beasts, with hunger prime,
Roll their fierce eyes upon the man who caters,
  As if the paroxysm of famine's rage
  Would make them burst the limits of their cage,
And swallow half a score of the spectators ?
    If not, I pray you to walk up,
    And see the rampant rascals sup ;
    For, lest you do, I must take leave
    To say you never can conceive
How Doctor Leech's glaring optics gloated
On the tid morsel to his maw devoted.

It seem'd for once benignant Heaven's behest
To give the dainty a superior zest,
And make his craving paunch supremely blest.

    Methinks I need not tell the reader,
    That Madam Fortune, when we need her,
Oft sends her eldest daughter in her stead,
  And pays *her* visits when we least expect her.
Thus, though she ne'er had been our hero's friend,
Yet now, to make a semblance of amend,
She shower'd a *double dose* upon his head,
  And crown'd his rich *ambrosial* feast with *nectar*.

Among his patients, one Lucretia Lloyd,
An antique maiden, long had Leech employ'd ;
  But rather as her friend, or old acquaintance,
     Than her physician ;
For all the patching of her crazy health

Had never added sixpence to his wealth.
   Yet he ne'er breathed a disapproving sentence
      Of his condition ;
And, though he could not *bleed* the female miser,
He still remain'd her body's supervisor,
Made all her fancied ills his constant care,
And kept her nervous system in repair :
While she, at every autumn when she brew'd,
   Pickled, preserved, prepared her wines, *et cetera,*
      Sent him (by way of annual *douceur,*
In token of her ardent gratitude,)
   Back'd by a most conciliating letter, a
      Full pint of that delectable *liqueur*
Elixir vitæ, alias cherry-brandy ;
Which every country housewife who is handy
   Makes once a-year to grace the Christmas frolic,
Or, by its sweet exhilarating power,
To cheer her spirits in a languid hour,
      Or cure the colic.

That two such presents should be centred
In one short day, could ne'er have enter'd
   The wrinkled tenant of the doctor's wig ;
     Yet so the busy fates contrived,
     The cordial beverage arrived
E'en at the self-same moment with the pig.

Forthwith an ample fire was raised,
   Spread to the utmost of the grate's expansion,
More fierce than e'er before had blazed
   Within the gloomy walls of Leech's mansion.

The meat, suspended from a rusty hook,
  Revolved before its glowing front ;
While orphan Davy was appointed cook,
  (A trade·to which he'd ne'er been wont,)
And in an easy chair was posted,
To watch the dinner whilst it roasted,
To baste it well, and keep it turning,
And guard its tender skin from burning.

For Doctor Leech esteem'd it most convenient
To go to church—not to the call obedient—
  Or that he strove t'avert celestial ire
        By worship's law ;
But lest his hunger, if he stay'd at home,
(Like the Imperial epicure of Rome,)
  Should make him snatch the viand from the fire
        And eat it raw.
Yet, ere he went, one difficulty rose :
  To place his brandy in a secret station,
To leave it safe from every prying nose,
  And shield the precious draught from depredation ;
For neither cupboard, drawer, nor chest,
In all his house a lock possess'd,
And well he knew 'twould not be prudent
To trust its keeping to his student ;
For e'en the promise of a basting
He fear'd would not prevent his tasting.

At length he hit upon an odd invention,
To rid his mind from further apprehension,
And obviate all cause for his detention.

He recollected having chanced to see,
When autumn's gifts hung ripe on every tree,
That cautious gard'ners, to preserve their hoard,
Wrote in large characters upon a board,
(To terrify the predatory chaps,)
"Within these grounds beware of guns and traps ! '
    And though nor trap nor gun were found
    Within the teeming garden's bound,
    Yet, by their stratagem acute,
    They managed to protect their fruit.

    "Egad," thought he, "if such deceit
    A set of practised knaves can cheat,
      Spite of their pilfering avidity,
    With confidence I may employ
    Such means to guile an artless boy,
      And check his lickerish cupidity."

So lest the treasure he should lose,
(Resolving to adopt the *ruse*,)
He from a dusty shelf took down
An ample square of *whited-brown* ;
And, folding it at one end taper,
He wrote " RANK POISON " on the paper,
In letters almost large enough
To grace a glaring London puff ;
Then, taking Miss Lucretia's bottle,
Affix'd the placard to its throttle,
Placed it within the cupboard-door,
And gave these orders o'er and o'er :
"Davy, beware ! this potent mixture

Must on this spot remain a fixture !
You must not dare yourself to broach it,
Nor suffer mortal to approach it ;
For 'tis so virulent, that half a gill
Were quite sufficient instantly to kill
The strongest man that ever wore a head
'Twixt Snowdon's ice-clad top and Severn's mud-clad bed!"

This task achieved, with caution due,
He soon arrived within his pew ;
But had the seat been stuck with pins,
Or swarms of hornets stung his shins,
Or had his ears been full of fleas,
He scarcely had been less at ease.
Alternately he sat and rose,
Wriggled and writhed, and blew his nose,
And rubb'd his beard, and scratch'd his jazy,
As if he'd been bewitch'd, or crazy.

He seem'd to care no more for Paul's Epistles
Than for his roasting grunter's useless bristles ;
Nor for the Sermon, Litany, or Creed,
   A fig ;
So much his yearning bowels long'd to feed
   On pig.
And though he felt his restlessness was wrong,
 Yet all his consciousness could nought diminish it ;
He thought the service irksome, flat, and long,
 And wish'd with all his soul, the priest would finish it.

Here, then, we'll leave him for a little space,

(As happy as an owlet in a rookery,)
While on the wings of fancy we change place,
    To take a peep at Davy and his cookery.
'Tis passing strange! but so it oft'imes chances,
That when some wretched being fondly fancies
    Of Pleasure's cup he's just about to sip;
The Destinies (a set of squabbling elves)
Proceed to loggerheads amongst themselves,
    And snatch the goblet from his pouting lip.
E'en so it fared with ill-starr'd Doctor Leech;
For (ere the pious parson ceased to preach)
Old Somnus in their service they enlisted,
Whose leaden powers no mortal e'er resisted.

One tedious hour the lad obedient sat,
Twirling his charge, and bathing it with fat;
When from the soporific god,
Morpheus, descending, waved his rod,
And made him blink, and yawn, and nod.

But all the dire effects of sleep's indulgence
Burst on his frighted soul with dread effulgence;
And, swearing not to yield without a battle, he
Rummaged the shop for snuff, or sal-volatile;
But not a single particle could find
To drive the hideous spectre from his mind.

He, therefore, ceasing from his fruitless search,
    Reel'd to his station, and resumed his ladle;
But, long before his master came from church,
    Sunk like a sated infant in its cradle.

For now, resolved no more to be opposed,
   The drowsy god, to smother his alarms,
By force his heavy quivering eyelids closed,
   And lock'd him firmly in his ebon arms.

Then, more to tantalise his fallen victim,
He with a gay delusive vision trick'd him ;
Caused him to dream his toils were o'er at last,
And he was seated at the rich repast :
The generous doctor bade him eat his fill,
And eulogised his culinary skill ;
While, slice on slice, with apple-sauce and gravy,
Were heap'd upon the plate of *Dainty Davy.*

I know not if my reader be well versed,
   In that *delightful* author, Mrs. Glasse :
Nay, banter not, my friend, for I'll be curst
   But she in sterling merit doth surpass
Many a grave, profound metaphysician,
Who (should his eyes encounter this position)
   Will shudder the comparison to brook ;
Although, perchance, his most elaborate folio
Is scarcely worth " directions for an olio,"
   Penned by the fingers of the good old cook.

Whether her book be to your mind familiar,
Or not, I dare presume you not so silly are,
But you are perfectly aware
That roasting meat demands some care ;
For, if the person charged to keep
It turn'd and basted, falls asleep,

'Tis seized upon with fury dire
By that unbidden guest, the fire,
And metamorphosed in a trice
Into a *burning sacrifice.*

Thus it befel !—the dangling pig stood still !
No guardian hand was near to ward the ill !
Awhile it crackled, squirted, smoked, and hiss'd,
Seeming to ask the wonted friendly twist,
Till, borne along the streams, ignition came,
And wrapt the unctuous mass in one devouring flame.

Upward the flaring havoc spread,
And sever'd the suspending thread,
    When down it plum'd
      Into the dripping.
    Whose pan, thus thump'd,
      Untimely slipping,
Fell with its ponderous load beneath the grate,
  With grease bedrenching it ;
Nor did the copious flood improve its state ;
  For, 'stead of quenching it,
It served to aggravate the keen disaster,
And make it burn the fiercer and the faster.

I have remark'd in my short life's dull measure
  The Sisterhood who o'er our actions reign,
Though oft they keep us *fast asleep* to pleasure,
  Take care to make us *wide awake* to pain !
Thus 'twas with Davy, for, the mischief o'er,
He op'd his eyes as widely as before.

Oh ! what a spectacle now met his view,
    Contrasted with his late delightful fiction !
He hoped that, like the last, it was not true,
    But found it past the power of contradiction.
Convulsed with fear, the fatal chair he quitted,
    And where he stood could scarcely form a notion ;
Yet urchins, when some fault they have committed,
    Never forget their power of locomotion.
Bounce to the door he darted, to elope ;
    But, ere his trembling hand could raise the latch,
One instant served to bar his utmost hope ;
    For, through an open pane he chanced to catch
A transient glimpse of Leech's earnest face,
Advancing to the house with rapid pace.

Thus foil'd, he to the cupboard lightly stepp'd,
And, to elude the storm, within it crept ;
But, what his frantic rashness perpetrated,
Oh ! arduous task ! remains to be related.

Oh ! that my pen were fashion'd from a feather
    Pluck'd from the wing
  Of Pegasus, 'stead of a goose's !
  Or that Apollo and the Muses
Would jostle their prolific heads together
    To help me sing
The ranting, roaring rage the doctor flew in,
When, entering he beheld the reeking ruin !
Not e'en the great Napoleon, when he saw
His eagles fall beneath the lion's paw ;
And his *invincibles*, or fall, or run,

Before the conquering arm of Wellington.
Not e'en the Guardian of the Tower,
(In that momentous, trying hour,
When Spa-field's rabble braved the state,
And vow'd they'd force the fortress gate,)
Could with more rancour bluster, rave, and fume,
Than Leech : from room to street, from street to room
Distractedly he paced, and scarce believed
The scene was real which his eyes perceived ;
And that his sapid, sucking son of Sus,
Had proved a perfect *ignis fatuus.*

At length (as rapier-blades are wrought ;
   First heated to a crimson glow,
Then, to their *perfect temper* brought,
   By wafting swiftly to-and-fro,)
When many a hearty curse, and hasty stride,
Had caused his *red hot* choler to subside,
He found that grief and anger were stolidity,
And made some efforts to regain placidity.
Quoth he, "Though of my meal bereft,
Thank Heaven ! a sovereign balm is left ;
   And while th' occasion serves,
Lest further ill should come to pass,
I'll draw the cork, and take a glass
   To tranquillise my nerves."

He op'd the cupboard with a testy jerk :
But, had he been an Algerine or Turk,
Maugre his angry mood, he had relented,
To see the piteous figure there presented.

Forth from his durance vile the culprit crawl'd,
And, while before his patron's feet he sprawl'd,
With streaming uplift eyes and falt'ring speech,
He thus began for mercy to beseech :
" Oh ! let my penitence for pardon plead !
I'll tell the genuine truth ! I will, indeed !
But must be brief, while Heaven affords me breath !
One minute more will seal my eyes in death !
I slept—the pig was burn'd—I would have fled—
But, peeping through the window, saw your head ;—
And when your frowning brow I set my eyes on,
   Remorse, despair, and terror, fired my brain ;
   I hasten'd back, a lurking-place to gain,
Pray'd for my soul, and DRANK OFF ALL THE POISON ! ! !"

HILARY HYPBANE.

THE FISH-STREET CATASTROPHE;

OR, THE TENDER NEPHEW.

—◆—

"Ma chair m'est plus proche que ma chemise."

WHERE the broad bosom of majestic Thames
    Presents his stream, which near a mile embraces,
To Kent's athletic sons and courteous dames,
    To brew their ale, and wash their ruddy faces.

Where oft the Briton sees, with heart elate,
    The ship of war with banners all unfurl'd,
Launch'd from her parent stocks in pompous state,
    Old England's pride—the terror of the world.

Where from each house-top the projecting spout -
    Its little tributary torrent sputters;
And many a common sewer its charge pours out,   -
    Each the grand confluence of a thousand gutters.

Where, each returning tide, we also view
    The merchant's rich-fraught ships from foreign seas;
Or outward-bound their traffic to renew,
    In hope and search of competence and ease.

Where reeking steamboats up and down are hieing,
    From all the cares of sail and rigging free ;
Their boiling kettles double boons supplying
    The vessel's impetus—the ladies' tea.

While colliers, lighters, barges, boats, and hoys,
    In groups promiscuous down the current scud ;
Drown'd puppies, cabbage-stalks, and dirty boys,
    Mingling in all the majesty of mud.

When thus old Father Thames's refluent wave,
    Seaward some miles from London Bridge hath glided,
(Bearing from every spot his waters lave,
    The various treasures to his care confided.)

His surface oft, with conscious exultation,
    Reflects that memorable stately dome,
Raised by a generous and grateful nation,
    To bless her veteran warriors with a home.

I say, he *oft reflects*, lest critics chide,
    And think me ignorant of this objection ;
That Thames's breast, like every breast beside,
    When *ruffled*, is *unfitted for reflection.*

Here the infirm and weather-beaten tar,
    From hottest action never known to skulk,
When no more equal to the toils of war,
    Finds a safe mooring for his batter'd hulk.

With splinter'd limbs, and store of nautic knowledge,
　　Fights o'er again the battles he has seen ;
Mumbles his two-days quid, stumps round the college,
　　Swigs his small beer, and sings GOD SAVE THE QUEEN !

But hold ! my rambling Muse, you're grown too prolix,
　　At such digressions you're by far too ready ;
Endeavour to restrain your devious frolics ;
　　Bridle your tongue, and let your tale be steady.

Here let us leave the river to his bed,
　　And pensioners to stump about the college ;
For of " My Uncle " we have nothing said ;
　　Not even brought him to the reader's knowledge.

Thus, then, the story runs :—Within a mile
Of the aforesaid venerable pile,
But East, West, North, or South, I cannot tell—
　　Nay, whether 'twas an hundred years ago,
　　Or whether more or less, I do not know,
A reputable tradesman chanced to dwell :

Fortune had bless'd him with good store of gold,
Which from his neighbours he would ne'er withhold ;
His house seem'd Hospitality's abode :
　　Whene'er a needy person sought his door,
　　Though he had never seen his face before,
On him a largess quickly was bestow'd.

Nay, lest the poor should wander in distress,
Or from *another's* bounty seek redress ;

To guide the welcome traveller to his walls,
   High on his house's front you might behold,
   Glittering like gingerbread enwrapt in gold,
The triple trophy of the brazen balls.

As shipwreck'd papist sailors fly to thank
Their patron-saint, who sent the timely plank
To snatch their drowning bodies from the brine;
   And think the favour amply is repaid,
   When they by rote a dozen prayers have said,
And left an *offering* before his shrine;

So, all this liberal-minded man required,
For granting thus whatever was desired,
To wretches who for his assistance sued,
   Was, that each person, on his boon receiving
   Should recognise the benefit by leaving
Some small memento of his gratitude.

But, we are told, that when a shrine's well stock'd,
By ardent zealots who have thither flock'd,
The cunning priests who o'er the place preside,
   Acting as proxies in his saintship's cause,
   Take all the gifts into their reverend paws,
And most *religiously* the spoil divide.

So, when a twelvemonth's crowd of hungry elves
Had laid their offerings on My Uncle's shelves,
So that his magazine could scarcely hold 'em:
   That he might have a vacant house again,
   Still, to pursue his philanthropic vein,
He carried them to London, where he sold 'em.

Now it will somewhat singular appear,
That though this generous wight from year to **year**
Dealt forth a dole to every hapless stranger;
   Still there were some whose hearts were so **malign**
   As to assert that e'en his very sign,
As well as benefit, imported danger.

For though a man restoring a donation,
Obliterating thus his obligation,
Might claim his token, if he so esteem'd it;
   Yet, that the posture of the balls denoted,
   When once a pledge to Nunky was devoted,
'Twas *two to one* the owner ne'er redeem'd it.

In short, they said he was a very Jew:
But whether the sarcastic taunt was true,
Or the mere fiction of some envious elf,
   I know not; but it might with truth be said,
   That (having forty years pursued the trade)
He was a perfect Jew in point of pelf.

No kindred circle graced My Uncle's house,—
No brother, sister, or attentive spouse,—
No playful group of ruddy girls and boys
   Promised to cheer the evening of his life;
   He never had encounter'd wedlock's strife,
Nor ever had experienced wedlock's joys.

And, although half the people in the county
(Perhaps from having ofttimes shared his bounty)
Agreed to call him "Uncle," just as I do,

Yet 'twill be plainly seen 'twas but a whim :
They'd no more consanguinity with him
Than I have with the Pope, or he with Dido.

But, two there were who call'd him so in truth :
These were bereft of parents in their youth ;
Our hero's only sister was their mother,
    Who, having nought to leave them when she died,
    Thinking their wants would all be well supplied,
Kindly bequeath'd them to her wealthy brother.

But Nunky relish'd not her poor bequest ;
And though obedient to her last behest,
To leave them all his riches he was willing :
    Yet, lest their heritage should be impair'd,
    During his life, he solemnly declared,
Without a pledge they should not have a shilling.

Sometimes we see spring from one-parent root
Branches producing different kinds of fruit ;
And thus it happen'd with My Uncle's heirs ;
    For neither fire and water, day and night,
    Summer and winter, nor e'en black and white,
Had properties more opposite than theirs.

The first-born merits to be first described :
He from his loving father had imbibed
Good morals and a useful occupation ;
    And when an orphan, he with tranquil heart,
    And empty purse, pursued the useful art
Of hammering people's *soles* for their salvation.

Not their *immortal souls*,—though I believe
Hundreds of ranting fanatics conceive
That *souls* prepared for heav'n and *soles* for jumping—
 Those by soft velvet cushions struck by bones,
 These by broad hammers upon massive stones—
Are benefited and preserved by *thumping*.

Only this *striking* difference seems pat,
The blows have scarcely force to kill a cat,
Which would the *first* from fate *infernal* guard ;
 Yet (though the self-same hand oft thumps for both)
 In beating for the *last*, I'll take my oath,
The stone and blows are both *infernal* hard.

I say, the elder nephew, from a child,
Had been devout, industrious, and mild,
Stedfast alike to chapel and to trade ;
 Thus all his actions in succession ran ;
 Week after week the thrifty, pious man
Pray'd, stitch'd, and hammer'd—hammer'd, stitch'd, and
  pray'd.

For constantly each Sunday he was seen,
With countenance demure and placid mien,
Attending sermons, evening prayers, and matins ;
 And every working-day, from morn to night,
 Striving 'gainst poverty with all his might,
He stuck to boots and shoes, and clogs and pattens.

Not so the younger : he with vice innate,
Had from his boyhood been a profligate—
A fellow who would rather steal than labour—

A swindler, glutton, gamester, sot, and wencher,
Who knew no joys but woman, bowl, and trencher,
Or cards and dice, to rob th' unwary neighbour.

The elder painfully his courses view'd,
And with a brother-like solicitude,
From some untimely exit strove to save him :
　　Giving him oft *good counsel* and *good shoes*,
　　But he the *latter* only deign'd to *use*,
Trampling alike on all his brother gave him.

Rare were his visits to his native place—
He ne'er beheld his chiding brother's face,
Save when compell'd by dire starvation's calls ;
　　His *talents* brook'd not so confined a scene,
　　Long in the great metropolis he'd been,
Prowling for prey 'twixt Wapping and Saint Paul's.

His careful Uncle, too, by age though bent,
Delay'd to make his will and testament,
Uncertain how his fortune to divide ;
　　And to allow him time for reformation,
　　Still persevered in his determination
To make it his last action ere he died.

Now father Sol, who steadily drives on,
(E'er since he lost his proxy Phäeton,
Whom once he trusted to his great reproach ;
　　For though his team were prime well-*seasqn'd* tits,
　　Used to the road, with Vulcan's patent bits,
The blundering blockhead overturn'd the coach ;)

With wheels of flame, and *four-in-hand* divine,
(Taking a dram at every well-known *sign*,
Which like our whips below he never misses,)
 Had once more gallop'd o'er his annual track,
 Through all the *turnpikes* of the zodiac,
From Aries starting-house *bang up* to Pisces.

Since last the vehicle from Uncle's door,
Bore off the pledges of twelve months before,
To grace the halls of London's auction mart ;
 While many a neighbour (but, alas ! too late)
 Sat weeping o'er the useless duplicate,
For goods committed to the fatal cart.

And now repentant tears again they shed,
For shirt, or watch, or gown, or smock, or bed,
Whose produce they've consumed in gin and beer ;
 For Nunky, true to the appointed date,
 To town escorts his miscellaneous freight,
The tributes of another fruitful year.

But Fate, who oft our brightest hopes doth foil,
(While thus he reap'd the harvest of his toil,
Thoughtless alike of sickness or of death,)
 Had issued the omnipotent decree,
 That he should meet a dire catastrophe,
To stop at once his traffic and his breath.

Here, Muse, be circumspect ;—the Hero falls !
The rich, the ancient knight of Lombard's balls !
Like Uncle Toby, " shew the very spot ;"

Lest future commentators miss the mark,
And lead their readers wandering in the dark,
To find where Uncle his *quietus* got.

Just where the glorious sons of reformation
Have raised a fabric, to inform the nation
That Papists in the second Charles's reign,
When they no longer could indulge their maggots,
With bonfires made of Protestants and faggots,
Vented their *pious flame* in Pudding Lane.

Behold the anxious man ; his stedfast eye
Fix'd on the full-charged wain, which, jogging nigh,
Toils up the steep ascent, by slow approaches ;
Till at the pillar's base 'tis forced to stand,
The busy street choak'd up on every hand,
With chaises, waggons, chariots, drays, and coaches.

Now, though a Bard, whose lays we all admire,
Has flatly call'd the Monument a liar,
Swearing its founders each deserved a rope,
(A thing of course—for, whatsoe'er their tricks,
'Tis natural that Roman Catholics
Should find a stanch defender in their *Pope;*)

Uncle, who held the legend of the column
True as a chapter of the Sacred Volume,
(Justly abhorrent of the atrocious deed,)
With veneration his long visage raised,
Upon its lofty fire-capp'd summit gazed,
And most *devoutly* damn'd the Romish creed.

Reader, if e'er you climb'd old Fish Street Hill,
Each inch of which the concourse used to fill,
I dare be sworn you fully are aware,
   That, 'stead of gaping upwards as you went,
   Your eyes below required to be intent,
Nay, you might e'en have used a second pair.

But at this juncture every passenger
His limbs as well as eyes began to stir,
As if he fear'd that even these might fail
   To save his carcase from hard kicks and knocks :
   For scampering down the hill appear'd an ox,
A host of slaughterers shouting at his tail.

Through many a street, almost to frenzy driven,
He hitherto by speed alone had striven :
But beasts, when press'd, will turn though butchers chase
     them ;
   So, finding now a stop to his career,
   And scores of hostile cudgels brandish'd near,
Foaming with rage, he wheel'd about to face them.

Firm as the monarch of the woods, at bay,
His flashing eyes and roaring seem'd to say,
" *Furor fit læsa sæpius patientia,*
   Come on, ye braggart hinds ; your valour shew,
   Whate'er the numbers of your clamorous crew,
By great Osiris I 'll no longer blench ye."

They fled in turn ; for though the butcher feels
No dread of danger at a bullock's heels,
But all his bellowing and kicking scorns ;

Yet if the brute resolves to bear the brunt,
And shows the terrors of his lordly front,
Not one in ten admires to face his horns.

Uncle (his thought recall'd from *things above*)
Not an iota from his cart would move ;
For " watch and pray " was his unvaried maxim.
   The ox surveys indignantly around,
    And, finding one who still maintains his ground,
Darts to the spot, and furiously attacks him.

The fugitives return'd the sport to see,
Judging that Nunky's utmost risk would be
Slight bruises or prostration in the mud ;
   But, 'stead of mirth, it proved a tragic fray,
    Writhing in death the mangled victim lay,
Trampled and gored, and weltering in his blood.

Scarce had the hapless mortal breathed his last,
When straight a youth, distracted and aghast,
Rush'd through the pitying crowd : "It is !" he cried,
   " It is my honour'd uncle ! cruel fate,
    He is no more ! I have arrived too late
To gain his parting blessing ere he died !"

So natural, so frantic was his grief,
Every spectator held a firm belief
That he sincerely mourn'd his murder'd kinsman ;
   But, reader, (*entre nous,*) to tell the truth,
    In spite of all his well-dissembled ruth,
The harden'd rascal did not care two pins, man.

" Call me a coach !" the vile impostor bawl'd ;
" Call me a coach !"   Forthwith a coach was call'd,
Which, when the *quick and dead* were placed within it,
  Drove from the fatal spot with rapid pace,
  Leaving full many a sympathising face,
Hied o'er the bridge, and vanish'd in a minute.

Meanwhile at home the senior nephew wrought,
Grave as a tomb, nor e'er of mischief thought,
Humming a hymn, his daily task to cheer ;
  But, borne on rumour's wings, the tidings spread,
  And ere 'twas night, the words, " Your uncle's dead,"
From twenty mouths were echo'd in his ear.

Not Brutus, when he breathed his stern decree,
Display'd more stoic equanimity,
Or firmness, to behold his offspring die,
  Than he, when first the melancholy tale
  His neighbours told ;—his spirits did not fail,
Nor did he shed one tear, nor heave one sigh.

'Twas thought by some religious resignation ;
But no ; his grief was curb'd by exultation,
That he should quit the labours of his stall.
  The accident made his advancement sure ;
  To him, by right of primogeniture.
His uncle's *end* secured his uncle's *all.*

When by condoling gossips left alone,
Srraight to the house, which now he call'd his own,
He sped to wait his brother's sad approach,

Hour after hour towards the street he gazed,
And each succeeding hour was more amazed ;—
There came nor brother, message, corpse, nor coach.

In sable weeds, belied by cheerful breast,
Of opulence and leisure now possest,
Leather and tools tools he hasten'd to resign.
    His coarser food, which toil had long made sweet,
     Was changed for daintiest poultry, fish, and meat ;
And sour small beer for generous ale and wine.

Of all My Uncle's *friends* there was *but one*
Who felt severe regret that he was *gone ;*
He drew a face as long as any quaker,
    To *lose* a friend he'd known for many a year,
     Nor will you doubt his sorrow was sincere ;
I'll tell you why—*he was an undertaker.*

Three weeks had Crispin pass'd in fruitless search,
Ranging the capital from church to church,
Curious where Uncle was interr'd to know ;
    At length one morning as he sipp'd his tea
     Snugly at home, he was surprised to see
His scapegrace brother in the garb of woe.

The reprobate felt all his courage drop ;
For though, when driven to seek his brother's shop,
Whate'er reproof he met he stoutly bore it ;
    Yet such command can affluence assume,
     That now, in entering that same brother's room,
He fear'd his discipline, and shrunk before it.

He look'd just like a disobedient hound
That drops his tail and crouches on the ground,
In dread of kick, or stripe, or such disaster,
　　When *nature,* 'stead of *education,* following,
　　With currish appetite he has been swallowing
The game he should have brought unto his master.

At length this adage to his mind arose;
That "whether men contend by words or blows,
"He who first speaks or strikes, 'tis odds he wins."
　　Therefore, anticipating the assault,
　　He promised to refrain from future fault,
And to atone for all his former sins.

The welcome, but unhoped-for, protestation
Dispell'd at once his brother's indignation,
Who said (and kindly hugg'd him to his breast,)
　　That if he proved his penitence sincere,
　　He would esteem his friendship doubly dear,
And all the past should in oblivion rest.

Nor did his love stop here; the generous heir
Promised his convert should his fortune share;
Then with a soothing air, and voice pathetic,
　　(While *tête-à-tête* o'er their repast they sat,
　　Mingling inquiry with *familiar chat,*)
Commenced this conversation catechetic.

SENIOR.

"I hope you'll make a hearty breakfast, brother;
Where have you been since last we saw each other?

(Take some more ham) and pr'ythee, let me ask
  Why was not Uncle's body home convey'd,
  That when his relics in the earth were laid,
I might have shared the melancholy task ? "

JUNIOR.

" Brother, your proffer'd reconciliation
Precludes concealment or prevarication :
Let not th' acknowledgment your love decrease ;
  'Twas to secure his jewels, watch, and cash,
  That I might revel, drink, and cut a dash,
While they supplied me with a single *piece*.

And that my sense of grief might seem acute,
I sold his watch to buy this mourning suit."

SENIOR.

" I thank your frankness ; but have still to crave
  That you his place of burial will make known ;
  And we will raise a monumental stone,
To tell his hapless end, and mark his grave."

JUNIOR.

" First let me trespass on your condescension,
By owning *one more cause* of his detention."

SENIOR.

" With all my heart ; I'll gladly hear you out.
  Only inform me where his bones repose ;
  And whatsoever follies you disclose,
They all shall be forgiven, you need not doubt."

JUNIOR.

"Hoping, although my uncle bleeding lay,
That life remain'd, I hurried him away,
With all the speed two well-flogg'd hacks could muster;
  Nor could I count ten minutes from his fall
  Ere he was laid within an hospital,
With twenty surgeons round him in a cluster."

SENIOR.

"'Twas kind!"

JUNIOR.

                "I thought, if death he could elude,
I should ensure his lasting gratitude,
And gain some *solid proofs* of his affection.
  But all their efforts fail'd—his soul had fled!
  So, finding him irrevocably dead "—

SENIOR.

"Alas! and then ? "—

JUNIOR.

"I SOLD HIM FOR DISSECTION."
                                HILARY HYPBANE.

THE NORTHERN TOWER.

A TALE, PARTLY OF FICTION AND PARTLY OF FACT.

—◆—

In the feudal days of RICHARD THE FIRST,
When children in armourers' forges were nurst,
　　　When sword and shield
Were the very first things they were tutor'd to wield,
　　　When the anvil and hammer,
　　　And all kinds of clamour,
　　　Served the dears for a rattle,
And the clashing of steel and of iron convey'd
Some idea of what a magnificent trade
They'd no doubt carry on, on some future fine day,
When they'd have it entirely all their own way
　　　In some desperate battle—
We sing of those times when your chieftain was prouder
　　　Of the feats that he did
　　　Beyond what he was bid,
　　　Of the splendid array
　　　That was brought into play,
　　　Of that dauntless degree
　　　Of inspired chivalrie,
And those deeds in the thick of the conflict's alarms,
Surpassing your modern encounter of arms,

Than others can be
Of all the fine fun
They have luckily done,
Since combustible SCHWARTZ introduced his gunpowder.

Well—a knight who had sprung up
From some martial stew,
(Such as one we have herein depicted to you,
Where sires bring their young up,)
Having gather'd some laurels
In those pretty quarrels
Which RICHARD with SALADIN carried on then,
Having fought his way through
A battalion or two
Of the Saracen's biggest and bravest of men,—
Why, SIR REGIMOND cross'd again over the seas
To enjoy his ease,
That climax of comfort so welcome to all,
Which "*otium cum dignitate*" they call.
Our hero held state
With the brave and the great,
In a famous strong castle his family built,
By the wages of honour (or may be of guilt,)
But of which—why, it is not worth while to relate—
Suffice it to say,
It was certainly one of the best of its day,
Had ramparts well guarded,
A drawbridge and moat,
A portcullis, and gates that were worthy of note,
Which a fine stalwart warder each evening well bar
did.

One night, dispensing wine and wassail,
(Good things which have titles now, foreign and grand,
But were then better known as " the fat of the land,")
To table brought by page and vassal,
     In which he in reality,
Like every fellow of true hospitality,
       Very much prided,
       And *at* which he presided !
While guest and host at board were seated,
And both with grape juice slightly heated,
       When mirth prevail'd,
And many a chief his tale got through
Of what he had done—or meant to do,
       Of terrible hobbles
       Got into by squabbles,
       Through following exemplars
       They were set by the Templars,—
       The disbursement of marks
       For what are now called " larks,"
       And other such squandering,
       Resulting from wandering—
At this critical moment their ears were assail'd
       With a terrible sound,
       Which made them all quake,
       And enough was to shake
The castle, and all it contain'd, to the ground.

       In utter disorder
       In rushes the warder,
And whisper'd some words in his chieftain's ear,
Which the latter one did not like to hear.

" The night is dark "—" *What*, knight ?" cried he.
" As dark," he replied, " as a night can be !
The sky is seam'd with pitch, and shorn
Of a single star, but never I ween
      Was there ever seen
Anything half as black, since the world was born,
As he who now blew the castle horn."
(Though nothing, they say, a hero's nerve dashes,
Yet the cheek of *our* hero turn'd pale as ashes.)
" His helm and mail which o'er him clink,
And the cloak he is wrapped in, are black as ink :
He bridles a horse of gigantic growth,
Which, black as *they* are, is as black as both :
He summons you to him, and seems to say,
The matter between you brooks no delay !"

Sir Regimond's spirit suddenly sunk
And a shudder or two he was seen to give—
In short, if the hero had happened to live
      In the present day,
      We should certainly say
He was what may be call'd in a bit of a funk ;
But as knighthood is bound to meet any defiance,
And face it, as well as he can, with reliance,
      He springs from his seat,
      Makes a hasty retreat,
(But first, as he is of politeness the essence,
He begs they'll excuse for a moment his presence,)
      Darts across the quadrangle
      Orders down the draw*bridge*,
      And then stands on the ridge
Of the moat, well prepared for a bit of a wrangle.

" *Well* met,—*well* met,"
Said he encased in the black helmet,
In voice with tone such as mortal ne'er gave,
But liker to that they say comes from the grave,—
" Your time is come,
Exceeding the limits I've given to some—
The fame you have purchased by compact with me
Report has well varnish'd :
Your sword and feather
Kept true, and untarnish'd ;
And now we, together,
Will add to the ranks of that good companie
Awaiting the doom of ETERNITY !"

He seized upon REGIMOND'S arm as he spoke ;
But the latter, not liking it, hastily broke
From his gripe, and, appalling
To mention, was very near falling !
" When first," quoth he, " that charm you gave,
Which had power my body and soul to enslave,
You promised some token forerunner should be
Of the time you required the penalty ;
And therefore to come, without notice, to ransom one,
Is acting a part which I don't think a handsome one."

The knight, already black as jet,
Contrived to look much blacker yet,
And though, for the day,
Thus foil'd of his prey,
He bore it as calmly as any knight may,

In order to prove, however absurd,
That the Devil himself is a man of his word !

“ I've some faint recollection,”
  Quoth the horseman in sable,
“ And I'll meet your objection
  As far as I'm able.
Look upon this !”—and e'en as he spoke
He drew from underneath his cloak
  An old-fashioned lamp
   Of the tint of the raven,
   Whereon were engraven
  Words of a cabalistic stamp ;
   It emitted a flame
   Of a brimstone glow ;
   And as REGIMOND gazed
   On the light as it blazed,
    From whence it came
   'Twas a riddle to know !

“ I will never,” the Black Knight said, “ return
While the fire of this lamp shall continue to burn :
   Guard it, by day,
   From the sun's bright ray ;
   Veil it, by night,
   From the moon's chaste light ;
   And place adamant bars
   Between it and the stars !
   For their purer gleam
   Will extinguish its beam !

Darkness must cover it ;
Breath not blow over it ;
Heat come not near it ;
For either will sear it !
Nor shake it, nor break it, and then it will burn on
As long as the great globe its axis shall turn on."

SIR REGIMOND listened, as well he might,
And the legion adds, in a deuce of a fright,
  Which was somewhat increased
    When the warning ceased,
And he, who its mystic matter spoke,
Had vanished as quick as in air the smoke !
SIR REGIMOND pauses, then seizes his prize,
And carefully back to the castle hies ;
      Reflects as he goes
       On the power it bestows,
And says, "Bright as *my* star it appeareth that none
    shines,
And so I'll not fail to make hay while the sun shines !"

The time rolls on ; but the time's not lost,
For SIR REGIMOND built up with caution and cost,
A keep, in his castle's *Northern Tower,*
To hold there in safety. this type of his power ;
Impervious, as to the tempest the rock,
Is its deep recess from the lightning's shock ;
     The wind and the rain
      May assail it—in vain.
The words of the Black Knight fulfilled are, and done,
And, like a taut vessel, his " keep " stands A 1.

Time continues his course ; for nor fortune nor clime,
Which can stop other movements can ever stop Time ;
And once more SIR REGIMOND fearlessly hies
To that land where his hope of preferment all lies,
   Where his fame used to shine—
   His beloved Palestine !

Well, once more our hero is destined to gain
Immortal renown upon *Ascalon's* plain.
   His deeds unsurpassed
   Set his comrades aghast :
He fights, and he beats down with sword and shield
The infidel rogues who had vowed not to yield.
   And, the conflict now o'er,
   He sails back once more,
With esquires and pages his retinue swelling,
   To the family dwelling !

Though glory be made of pleasantish stuff,
'Tis a thing of which people may soon have enough ;
   And, to tell you the truth,
   In SIR REGIMOND'S youth
   'Twas to him just the same,
Whether the weather was gentle or rough,
   For he lived upon fame,
And *never* had what people call *quantum suff*.
But, as we grow older our energies falter,
   And things deucedly alter ;
And *how* with our hero, and *to* what degree,
   You shall instantly see !

A fearful catastrophe, grieve we to tell,
SIR REGIMOND's castle one evening befel ;
To believe 'twas by chance we of course must incline,
For surely such things are not done by design ;
    THE CASTLE's ON FIRE ! ! !

Though the bravest its ravage appals,
Yet the serfs scale the walls ;
Ply water ; hew beams down ; ascend to the roof,
Which was not, we're sorry to say, fire-proof ;
Shout to those underneath to take care of their head,
For the heat was beginning to melt all the lead ;
Throw goods out of window—a very odd plan ;
Seize jewels, (and pocket whatever they can) ;
Give orders not to let the mob in,
They've such an ugly taste for robbing ;
In short, cut off communication,
In hopes to stop the conflagration !

Though SIR REGIMOVD having worked hard as the rest,
Sits down for a respite, fatigued, and oppressed,
Yet servants, dependants, and peasants, don't shirk
One instant for hurrying on with the work.
Now a calm succeeds, while the ruin smoulders ;
    Now red are the skies ;
    Then it breaks on the eyes
Once again of the frightened beholders !
At length, by the dint of incredible labour
Of household, of kinsfolk, of friend, and of neighbour,
They hasten to apprize the master
They'd reached the end of the disaster,

By buckets of water ; by an opportune shower
   The great scene of danger they'd managed to dout,
   And every bit of the fire was out,
Save a trifling blaze in the old *Northern Tower*.

Sir Regimond rose, and again fell back,
Then shrieked loud enough all his muscles to crack :
"The *Northern Tower !* the *Northern Tower !*
'Tis the secret deposit of all my power !
The mine of my wealth, the stronghold of my fame ;
The prop of my house, and support of my name.
       Save it ! save it !
Great as the danger, whoever will brave it,
      May claim at my hands
      One half of my lands !"

They rushed, one and all, to their lord's behest,
And squire, and vassal, and serf did his best,
      In vain—in vain !
The element mastery seems to gain ;
When Sir Regimond's spirit gets madder and madder,
And he screams for his axe, and a scaling-ladder !

On the topmost height is seen his form,
Like that of a demon directing the storm,
He lashes about his "morning star,"
      (That nice little flail
With which they used, then, all tough things to assail,)
      Then seizes a bar,
And hurling it out with a giant's force,
Why, in the wall goes, as a matter of course !

On the self-same spot where, in years gone by,
The talisman lay, it was seen now to lie ;
  Its sulphury light
  Was precisely as bright
As if at that moment lit up for the night.
  SIR REGIMOND grasped it,
  With ecstacy clasped it,
And uttered a loud, exulting shout ;
   But whether that motion
   In jeopardy brought it,
   Or a puff of wind caught it,
   Or the free, common air
   Was not welcome in there,
   We haven't a notion,
 But—THE LAMP WENT OUT !

The walls and the ceiling began to scorch,
As if newly lit up by APOLLYON's torch ;
  The floor gave in
  With a booming din ;
  The casements were shattered,
  Their fragments were scattered
Away on the winds, that howled afar
For the total eclipse of SIR REGIMOND's star !

  As the dun smoke cleared,
   By the blast hurried off,
  An outline appeared
To SIR REGIMOND's eye, which made all his frame tremble,
So much did its figure THE BLACK KNIGHT resemble !

It hovered and fluttered,
    And then, with a scoff,
Maliciously muttered,
    "My prey! my prey!
The warning you asked for has passed away!"
And castle, and chieftain, and spirit, they say,
Were lost to the light on the breaking of day!

The drift of this tale is, to bear well in view,
With anything wicked have nothing to do;
For, as certain as fate, whether squire or knight,
Like all that *is* wick-ed, *it must come to* LIGHT!

ALFRED BUNN.

A BROAD HINT;

OR, THE HORNS OF A DILEMMA.

—·—

" È massimo prudent' e saldo,
  Batter' il ferro mentr' è caldo ;
  Ma questo rend' un doppio prode,
  Ad una calda far' due chiodi."

A TRITE historian somewhere tells
That the two sees of Bath and Wells,
Some centuries ago, were fated
At the same time to be vacated ;
And Satan, ever on the watch
For such stray sheep as he can catch,
Succeeded many souls to fish up,
For want of their protecting bishop :
At length the sov'reign, taking pity
Upon the flock of either city,
Sent for a certain dean of note,
Whom he was anxious to promote,
And bade the worthy priest to choose
Which diocese should meet his views.

The happy dean, before he breathed his wishes,
  Paused for some half-score moments to reflect
  (A caution 't had been folly to neglect,)
Which gave the greatest store of " *loaves and fishes.*"

At length, his cogitation o'er,
He made obeisance to the floor ;
Assured the King that his beatitude
Was only equal'd by his gratitude,
And said, " My liege, I pray you give me Bath."
But (*entre nous*) the man of sable cloth
Pronounced with such a broad provincial twang
　　　The whole harangue,
That, 'stead of *Bath*, you might have ta'en your oath
　　　He had said *both.*
We ofttimes lose by being over modest !
　For, though his Majesty thus understood,
And deem'd his answer somewhat of the oddest,
·　Yet, being in a bishop-making mood,
　　　The generous and complacent prince
　　　　　Straight coincided,
　　　And join'd the sees, which never since
　　　　　Have been divided.

　　　'Twill be but justice to confess
　　　　　This little tale
　　　　　Is somewhat stale
　　　In sober prose ; but, ne'ertheless,
　　　　　As 'twill be new
　　　　　To not a few,
　　　I've clothed it in a doggrel dress,
　　　Making a sort of parallel
　　　To what my Muse is going to tell.

Reader, I take for granted that you've been
In London's bustling streets, and ofttimes seen,

Amongst the numerous huge machines vehicular,
 Some which excel
All others of the throng in this particular :
 That they so well
Evince how swimmingly their masters thrive,
 That, in surveying them, your mind's in doubt
 Which are the most gigantic, sleek, and stout,
The animals which draw, or those who drive.

Led by this hint, methinks you cannot fail
 Forthwith to ween
 That those I mean
Are cumb'rous cars, with porter fraught, and ale ;
 One of which useful equipages
 The hero who my Muse engages
 For many a year had driven : his name,
 Or patronymic, or sponsorial,
 Never within my knowledge came ;
 But his amazing powers corporeal,
 And lusty limbs, by prototypon aid,
 Nomen supplied, and cognomen his trade ;
So joining both, of might and malt the types,
His crony carmen dubb'd him " SAMPSON SWIPES."

 Amongst the goodly guzzling train
 Whose cellars eased his weighty wain,
 A tough old widow, without fail,
 Each month received her cask of ale,
Which honest Sampson, in his punctual round,
Had long supplied, nor e'er complaint had found.

At length, one day,
The brewer's dray
Arrived before
The well-known door,
When, 'stead of the accustom'd hailing,
"Good morrow, Sampson !   How d'ye do ?"
The housewife in a passion flew,
Thus, with shrill pipe, his ears assailing :
"Arn't you ashamed to sell such stuff
As last you brought me ?   'Twas enough
To turn the stomach of a pig !"
"Indeed !" cried Sampson; "dash my wig !
That's queer !
'Twas the same beer your neighbours had,
And no one else has found it bad,
I'll swear."
"How ?" cried the widow in a pet,
D'ye disbelieve ?   I have it yet !
'Tis such vile stuff that we must waste it :
I'll draw a quart, and you shall taste it."

"I thank you, ma'am," quoth he; "you're vastly kind
And generous when your liquor's sour, I find.
I've brought you humming ale, as sound and strong
As e'er was brew'd with malt and hop ;
But, while 'twas good, you never wagg'd your tongue
To offer me a single drop,
Although," pursued the man of malt,
"However bad
The ale you had,
You know full well 'twas not my fault ;

So let my master come and taste the beer ;
For devil take me if I volunteer
To lay my lips against your tankard's brink,
Unless 'tis fill'd with something fit to drink."

The widow instantly her clamour hush'd,
    And, though she lived some fifty years and odd,
    And laid three husbands' bones beneath the sod,
(Would you believe it ?) absolutely blush'd ;
        And, feeling that her ill-timed huff
        Had given just cause for his rebuff,
        A brace of bottles she brought out,
        Strong brandy one, and one brown stout ;
        A silver pint the latter graced ;
        A glass beside the first she placed,
        And bade the drayman, at a word,
        Inform her whether he preferr'd
    A foaming tankard or a potent dram.
" Come, that's too good an offer to refuse,"
Quoth Sampson, " but I don't know which to choose ;
    For, to confess the truth, *just now I am*
So pinch'd with colic, and so parch'd with thirst,
That, 'pon my soul, I don't know which is worst ! "

HILARY HYPBANK.

MEDITATIONS AT A KITCHEN WINDOW.

SPIRIT of Hunger, who dost love
With threadbare sons of song to rove
Through some blind alley's dark retreat,
The Muse's old-establish'd seat,
Clinging to them close the while
In a most uxurious style;
Or, to mock them when alone
They scrape a clean-pick'd mutton-bone
In some ethereal attic, where
The wind howls up the creaking stair—
Taunting Spirit of Starvation!
I feel thy fullest inspiration,
While, standing by this kitchen-window,
With phiz as grave as any Hindoo,
I mark yon partridge—dainty bit!—
Gently wheeling round the spit.

Savoury bird! thy very sight
Lends an edge to appetite,
And my stomach, while I gaze,
Rumbles volumes in thy praise!

Some in sonnet, ode, or tale,
Laud the maudlin nightingale;
Some exalt the cooing dove;
Some, the royal bird of Jove,
Fond of new-born lamb, the glutton!
And not indifferent to mutton;
Some, the mountain condor, who,
Crafty as a polish Jew,
Seldom from his lodgings hies out,
Save to peck a dead man's eyes out;
Some, the rook of solemn clack,
Dressed, like parsons, all in black;
Some, the woodcock; some, the widgeon;
Some, the well-conditioned pigeon,
Who, to gastronomic eye,
Looks so lovely in a pie;
But the partridge, plump and white,
Is my feather'd favourite;
Dress'd as epicure could wish,
   And crisp of breast and wing,
" Isn't he a dainty dish
   To set before a king?"*

But, hark! the clock from yon church-tower
Shrilly strikes the wish'd-for hour,
And the butler, grave and steady,
Proclaims the tidings,—"Dinner's ready!
Dinner's ready!" Proclamation,
Source of liveliest delectation;

   * *Vide* the old nursery song.

All who hear it mutely bless
The messenger of happiness!
Dobbs, a lawyer, grim and spare,
Leaps in transport from his chair;
Hobbs, a fat old city bore,
Weighing twenty stone or more,
Cuts a long dull story short
About the Aldermen's last Court;
Pretty Mrs. Colonel Cox,
A widow shrewd as any fox,
To her dandy neighbour's sighs,
And his whisper'd flatteries,
Turns awhile a careless ear,
Better pleased, I ween, to hear
The tuneful rush of whizzing cork,
And clatter of the knife and fork!

"Dinner's ready!"—Down they go,
Two by two, a gallant show,
Attracted by the rich perfume
That floats around the dining-room.
Now they're seated, and, methinks,
Commence 'mid cheering nods and winks,
And interchange of social greeting,
A course of serious, steady eating.

In imagination, I
Join the festive company,
And, on schemes of havoc bent,
Waste no time in compliment,
But placed, by her express command,

At my hostess's right hand,
Set to work with heart-felt glee
On callipash and callipee,
Victimise the venison pasty,
Punish the calve's-head so tasty,
Pitch into the pigeon-pie
With a shark's voracity,
Flirt with jelly, custard, ice,
Like the Arab Ghoul with rice,*
And quaff the sparkling cool champagne,
As thirsty meads drink in the rain,
Obedient to dame Nature's laws;
While my ever-restless jaws
Convey a very vivid notion
Of the poetry of motion!

Glorious enterprise!   But, hark
How the guests in whispers mark
Their sense of wonder and affright
At a poet's appetite!—
"There's a mouthful!—did you ever?"—
"He's bolted all the pasty!"—"Never!"—
"Goodness gracious, what a swallow!
Sure he beats an ostrich hollow!"
"Try him with a tough ship's cable!"—
"Oh, good Lord, he'll clear the table!"—
Such the pert, facetious sneers
Mutter'd in his neighbour's ears
By each guest, to mark his sense
Of my rare ventripotence!

* *Vide* the story of the Ghoul, in the Arabian Nights.

Well, I grudge them not their grin,
Those are tolerant who win ;
And I have bravely won, I swear,
A dinner fit for my Lord Mayor.

Mere empty boast !   An envious cloud
Wraps my vision in its shroud ;
Vanish'd is the banquet-hall,
Host and hostess, guests and all,
And I stand musing here, the winner
(In fancy only) of a dinner !—
Day-dreams of imagination,
Could ye but repress starvation,
How supreme in joy would be
The gifted poet's destiny !
But, alas ! with magic sway
Ye rule us, only to betray ;
And gladly I'd exchange, heaven knows,
All delusive Fancy's shows
(Though brilliant as a comet's tail)
For a rump-steak and pot of ale ! !

A HUNGRY POET.

A LEGEND OF REVOLUTION.

—◆—

> Upon my soul it's true,
> What'll you lay it's a lie?
> *Major Longbow.*

THERE's not a doubt
That Byron's Lord,—*id est*, the Poet,—
When his high genius was a little mellow,
Was what they call a very funny fellow;
At least his writings show it,
When you precisely know what they're about;
For instance, he says in *Don Juan*, "Revolution
"Alone can save the earth from hell's pollution."

But doctors differ, as we know full well;
For some maintain,
In precept very plain,
That revolution's nothing else *but* "hell!"
We'll put the case before you, gentle reader,
With all the cunning of a special pleader
In his full practice,
Stating exactly what the fact is,
Then say if it be what, in your solution,
'Tis most advisable that we and you shun!

We will not talk of kings,
For they *are* call'd Ambassadors of Gods ;
  Though they are brittle things,
Shiver'd·whene'er the infuriate rabble nods.
  We'll speak of household matters,
   Of all the ties
  Which gaunt rebellion shatters,
   Where'er her pinion flies,—
Kindred, house, home, wife, mother, daughter,
Swept down alike in one wild scene of slaughter
Where blood, uninterrupted, rolls like water !
   Youth, innocence, defiled,
   The parent and the child,
Mow'd down without respect, as if, in play,
Death and his scythe were making holiday !

The principle of all whom an *émeute* empowers
Is to make *theirs* to-day what once was *ours*,—
To level all distinctions, to bring down
The worth of all things, from a copper to a crown,—
To aim at every prize, and try to win 'em,
And as for those who *hold* " the stocks," to put them *in* 'em.
This is some part of revolution's pastime,—
At all events it *was*, the last time
  𝕿𝖍𝖊 𝕸𝖔𝖇
Thought it divine to kill, and right to rob !

Ergo—if in these days the world is quiet,
  When monarchs reign supreme,
  And when their subjects seem,
If not misled, to be averse to riot,—

When nature's bounties all the globe embalm,
Making those blush who would disturb her calm,
If, in this bless'd estate, 'tis " revolution
" Alone can save the earth from hell's pollution,"
We should be glad (not being too particular)
Just of one word, writ or auricular,
 To tell us WHAT can save it
 From those who would enslave it,
From scenes of murder, rapine, and of terror,
Such as we 've here described,—perhaps in error !

Without, then, even seeking to convince,
 Or asking you *which* doctor's right or wrong,
 What arguments to either side belong,
What scenes had pass'd *before*, or happen'd *since*,
 We'll lead you into one which, you will see,
 If it occurr'd, took place in '93,
When *France* play'd tricks which other states thought
 scurvy,
And tried to turn their kingdoms topsy-turvy,
And when Party display'd, what she 's certain to do,
" The madness of many for the gain of a few."

The spot was one, the PLACE DE *GRAVE** they call,
And justly so, for 'tis the tomb of *Gaul*,—
 And thereupon, as being quite select,
  A scaffold stood erect,
 And, rising high in air, the rack
  (The guillotine
  We mean)

  * Quere, *Grève ?*—Printer's Devil.

Was, like the boards which bore it, clothed with black,
　　　Soaked through with stains
　　Of human gore,—for, strange to say,
　　　E'en in that awful day,
When those condemned *to* death *we* hung in chains,
France hung *her* palaces *of* death in cloth, to prove
How much in all things *England* she's above ;
And if we thrash her every time we fight her,
In matters, or of *goût*, or blood, she's much politer.

　　'Twas a fearful night of which we speak ;
　Not a star shone out upon heaven's cheek,
　They were all, the weather-wise say, in doubt
　　　Whether on earth if they ventured to stare
　　　At the sanguined rivers billowing there,
　The spray of the waves would not put their light out

　The city was hushed, and its places of death
　Were, like a volcano out of breath,
Reposing from action, in order to borrow
A little more force for the fun of the morrow !
The wine, which had streamed as freely and red
As though 'twere gore, had now muddled each head ;
　　　A calm as profound
　　　Pervaded around,
As if, though hotter its vengeance might wax,
There was not another wretch left for the axe !
　　　The drowsy guard
　　　Were snoring hard ;
　　　The headsman slept ;
And if the grief of some one awake,

That terrible silence seemed to break,
It came from a broken heart, that wept
    In desperate agony
Over those who were dead, or about to die !

On the night in question a **German youth**,
Who lived on hypothesis rather than truth,
And who also lived in a street hard by,
And slept on a bed where 'twas hard to lie,
In a chamber (but that we shall tell you about
When we have resolved other matters of doubt,)
Who had visited Paris, to study the arts :
But when *quite* " at home," why, he dwelt on the **Hartz**,
A pleasant abode, both extensive and airy,
    Inhabited, if not by Christians or Jews,
By plenty of others, from devil to fairy,
    And possessing, in very fine weather, fine views !
There are one or two lakes for the web-footed elf,
    There are plenty of trees, and a capital glen
    For the famous Demon's banded men,
Where the traveller 's advised to take care of himself.
        If he 's partial to fish,
There are plenty herein, and e'en GROVE cannot match 'em,
If one could but invent any process to catch 'em ;
        And, better than all,
        That choice viand they call
        " The cameleon's dish."

Well,—wending home on this murky night,
    With thoughts so full of " the metaphysick,"
    'Twas enough to give all the city the phthisick,

The mournful tone
Of a voice unknown
On his sensitive hearing chanced to alight ;
Was it the wind
That sought in some hollow a shelter to find ?
Or was it a moan
From a re-opened grave, of the spirit there
Wanting to take a little fresh air ?
—The devil a bit !
'Twould the fancy strike
Of a sober person, as much more like
The groan of one fallen down in a fit.
He hurried as fast as he could to the spot,
(The identical scene
Of the guillotine,)
And all preternatural matters forgot ;
But the ground was so clammy, not having yet sipped
The moisture thereon, that he nearly tripped.
—'Tis an odd sensation
In any—no matter whatever *the*, nation,
When, thinking you're slipping about in mud,
To find it's a fellow-creature's blood ! ! !
But this is an episode, slightly comparative,
Which must not impede the course of our narrative.—

At the foot of the fatal stairs which conducted
To yonder Engine,
By ingenuity so well constructed,
That, without any twinging,
Writhing, or gasps, or kicks,
Which vulgar hanging inflicts,

It can slice off your head,
Before you've any idea you're dead—
We say—on those stairs, by a dash of the moon,
    Which had been fast asleep,
    Or been playing bo-peep
Through an ebon cloud, hung up for a curtain,
Our German youth felt pretty certain
A figure reclined, just got out of a swoon.
He was perfectly right ; and how high you may rate your
Ideas of science, yet one touch of nature
Will settle all questions regarding humanity,
Much sooner than doctrines that verge on insanity.
    Flesh and blood 's the criterion,
And always has been, since the days of *Hyperion !*

'Twas a female form, and never had eye
Been permitted to gaze on such symmetry :
    On her ashen cheek
    One livid streak
   Of animation seem'd to stray ;
    And her hair, as black
    As the raven's back,
  Strew'd o'er it in careless play ;
Her bosom as white, and of course as pure,
As the snow on the mountains of *Ukasure,*
    Was painfully heaving,
    As if some grieving
    Had robb'd that breast
    Of its hallow'd rest.
She was robed in velvet of jet, to betoken
The heart within it was utterly broken,—

And those exquisite arms,
Where nature had almost exhausted her charms,
Rich bracelets of gold presumed to deck,
And a *bandeau* of diamonds encircled her neck—
In short, she was beautiful,—and as he gazed
The student felt something much more than amazed,
And it would not a conjuror puzzle to tell
He was both beside *her*, and himself as well !

" Is there aught I can do ?" he frantic, cried,
As the sister of sorrow despairingly sigh'd.
  " Is there any relief
   To that canker grief,
  Consuming a thing so fair,
    Which an anxious heart
    May dare to impart ?
In short, if I'm not breaking
   The rules of society,
   Of decorum, or piety,
   Or suspending attrition,
   Or a liberty taking,
May I ask what a lady of your condition
  Can at such an hour be doing there ?"

  " I mourn for the dead,"
She replied, in a voice whose tones seem'd to enter
His panting heart, and stick fast in its centre—
  " In the ruthless fray
   Of the bygone day,
  On the spot where now ye stand,
   By murder's purple hand,

My brother lost his head !
There is not a tie, how little the worth,
Which binds me now to this guilty earth,—
    I have not a home, nor a friend
    A sheltering hand to extend—
A fond one I left for this scene of strife,
In the hope to save that brother's life ;—
And I ask but a boon you will not deny—
—To remain where I am, and here to die ! ' "

The student had no such idea, and so
He turn'd a deaf ear to this tale of woe.
" Not a friend, nor a home !—though you *have* lost your
    brother,
I'll be to you one, and will find you the other.
    Leave this terrible place,
    Envelop that form and face
In this cloak."—In fact, o'er his frame
A sudden odd sort of tenderness came.
The night and scene alike were dreary,
The lady was sad, and exceedingly weary,
And probably peckish, and so he resolved
The duty to fill which upon him devolved.
    He raised her up, and by her side,
In a tone between pity and selfishness, cried,
    " There are reasons you don't now see
    For intrusting yourself to me.
I've a room, and a trifle, I think, to eat,
And a fire I'll make for those delicate feet ;
And, should such inducements as these plead in vain,
There's one that will not—IT'S BEGINNING TO RAIN ! ' "

"Have you sister, or mother ?"
 The victim exclaim'd.
"Neither one nor the other,
 To own I'm asham'd !"
She rose up with dignity, look'd him quite through,
To see if by chance any feature she knew—
 With the pride of her sex,
 Quite enough to perplex
All logicians on earth, when the heart's in a mask.
 She then ventured to ask,
"Do you think, *entre nous*, it would *really* be prudent
For me to go home with a young German student ?"

 With a fancy highly wrought,
 He spurn'd at the very thought.
"Madam ! I hope *you* do not suspect
That honour on which man don't dare to reflect.—
 Von Humbuggrim's a name
 That is well known to fame,
 And, though people may bully it,
 I would not sully it !
My apartments are snug, notwithstanding they're small,
But that's not consider'd a drawback at all ;
Sufficiently warm for those who're rheumatic ;
 And for those who are not,
 It's a fine open spot,
And classical too, for they're up in an *attic !*
Then, if on a delicate point I might verge,
There's a lady to wait on you, call'd the *concierge ;*
Mine '*ancient*' "—(from which appellation, 'twould seem
She belong'd to the days of the *ancien regime*)—

"Well, I'll show you the door, and, that there may be no
    sin with it,
I'll give you the key, too, to lock yourself in with it!"

    There was really some reason
    Her feelings to seize on,
      In all that he said;
    It was plain, and well-bred—
    Then 'tis fit we should state
    It was getting quite late,
    And bear also in view
    She was nearly wet through—
So you can't be surprised she accepted the offer
The student *Herr* 愛. was so kind as to proffer!
They reach'd his home, and, though long the walk,
He beguiled the time with such charming talk,
    That, though she well knew
He ought on the instant to bid her adieu,
She said, while his cap in his hand he twirl'd,
She would not be left there alone for the world!

If he jump'd before by starts and fits,
He now very nearly jump'd out of his wits!

On that *very* "spare" bed, as her frame reposed,
And the lid on the eye underneath had closed,
    He heard an intermittent sighing,
      Then again so calmly she dozed,
    He really thought she was dying;
And if she were so, he couldn't outlive it.
Then, his attention completely to rivet,

The *bandeau* of diamonds continually glitter'd—
Then she gnash'd her teeth; and apparently titter'd !

In deep abstraction at last he sank,
    And, seeing the rich things she wore,
    Though he had not much doubt before,
He concluded she must be a lady of rank ;
For this *bandeau* for ever arrested his eyes,
Its brilliants appear'd of such very large size !

       'Twas getting near dawn,
         As he knew by the cock,
       That infallible "herald of morn,"
         When, his feelings to shock,
       She was seized with a spasm,
And ask'd him to get her a cataplasm !
       Though up five pairs,
In a twinkling he sprang down stairs ;
       He knocked *up* the *concierge*,
And, on her attention the matter to urge,
       He gave *her* a good d—,
       And her *door* a good slam ;
Then seeking a doctor, in great alarm,
He nearly knock'd *down* a brace of *gens-d'armes.*
"*Sacré nom de Dieu !* *qu'est ce que c'est que ça ?* "
Said one, and the other exclaim'd, "*Ha ! ha !*"

He utter'd a most inarticulate phrase,
Which kept these good people in greater amaze :
"A lady is dying—I don't know her name—
Run to *numéro trois,* there, and then *au cinquième—*

While I run for a doctor;"—and he took to his heels
With the speed of the *Birmingham* railway wheels;
While the men, as it was not a very great distance,
Were soon on the spot to offer assistance.

The HERR was not very long away,
But whether he managed to fly,
To get back in the wink of an eye,
The legend does not exactly say;
But certes it is, he burst into the room
Precisely in time to hear his doom!

She who had bound his soul
In feeling's fond control,—
She, who'd no stain upon her,
Although she *had* done him the honour
To come to his house,—she, his heart's pride,
(For he'd sat up all night by her side,)
She, who was all mystery,
For he didn't know her history,—
She—had been seized with hysterics and cramps, and raved
In a manner, 'twas clear her life couldn't be saved—
She gasp'd, drew her lip in, as though she would suck it,
And kick'd, till at last she kick'd—the bucket!
Thus, though they had scampered fast,
Ere they came she had breathed her last.

'Twere vain HUMBUGGEIM's grief to paint,—
Suffice it to say, he was ready to faint.
He quickly recover'd, and flew to the bed,
And then began swearing she couldn't be dead.

"Not dead!" said the man-at-arms,—and it seem'd
An incredulous smile on his visage beam'd,
He open'd his hand, put his thumb to his nose,
(A sign of cognition which all the world knows,)
"MEIN HERR, other people this stuff you may cram on,
But really with us you are 'coming the gammon.'
Not dead!" and he gave his fellow a nudge,
Who acted at once both as jury and judge;
  "Why, my comrade and I
  Were standing by,
Only yester noon, and chanced to have seen
Her head taken off by the guillotine!"

He reel'd—then his arms he began to extend,
  His eye had a demon's glare,
  And his head's "each particular hair,"
Like the curly tail of a pig, "stood on end"—
"Guillotined!" he yell'd; "why, some hours ago
She was pacing this chamber to and fro—
She'd been walking the streets—that very chair sat in—
And, before she retired, we'd an half hour's chatting.
Abuse as you please my rhapsodical nation,
But I never yet heard of such mystification."
[He forgot that KING CHARLES, though the notion some
  scoff,
  Both walk'd,
  And talk'd,
Half an hour AFTER *his* head was cut off!!!!]

  The reader perchance will believe,
  Or can readily conceive,

While change upon change thus continued to pass,
The tragedy promised to turn out a farce !

The " *gens-d'arme* " gave a significant leer
At MEIN HERR—and his comrade standing near,
Then he gave a shrug, and a moment after
He burst out into a fit of laughter.
" If you won't believe *me*, or rely upon *my* sight,
You cannot object to believe your *own* eyesight."
He went up to the couch, and with instant grasp
He seized the *bandeau* and its diamond clasp,
Ripp'd it off her neck with malicious frown,
And surely enough HER HEAD ROLL'D DOWN ! ! !

(The bed-curtains here of themselves withdrew,
And a fleshless figure appear'd in view,
The Cap of Liberty cover'd his head,
And, with bony finger fix'd on the dead,
The legend affirms, he was heard to say,
" Death and the Devil will have their own way !")

It were not a difficult thing to describe
The wink of the *gens-d'arme's* eye, and his gibe,
The student's horror, his vacant stare,
And an evident doubt of all passing there—
The trunkless head, that had roll'd on the ground,
And the *bandeau* which circled it tightly round—
The old *concierge*, who had dropp'd on her knees,—
And the worthy old *medecin* diddled of fees ;—
But, treating all that as a child does its coral,
We had better at once go direct to the M

Its purpose is twofold, as a legend's should be ;
And as to a tale, when *our* legend has told hers,
    You will fully agree
    It behoves us to see
That we *have* got a head, and it's fast on our shoulders !

To a person of sense this first point is clear,
And the next just as plain to the world will appear,
That when body and head cease to hold all communion,
It is what *may* be call'd—A REPEAL OF THE UNION !

ALFRED BUNN.

THE OMEN.

BEFORE the bombardment of Bergen-op-Zoom,
  (*Not* the fatal attack when Skerret and Gore,
  Macdonald, and Carleton, and numberless more
Were lost to their country, and plung'd us in gloom ;)
But the siege when, old Cumberland acting as hat-holder,
Maurice of Saxony warr'd with the Stadtholder ;—
Still, as the fire of his batteries got MORE range,
Redoubling the cry of—" No quarter to Orange !"—
So that, when the poor city surrendered,—'twas sack'd,
Which seems a great shame, and is call'd a great fact !—

Well,—before THAT bombardment of Bergen-op-Zoom,
  In one of the aisles of that stately cathedral,
To all English travellers, a wonderful tomb
  Was specially pointed to note by the bedral.—
And the moment the eye of the stranger espied it,
Though others more showy by half stood beside it
Every monument there, whether urn, bust, or slab, he
Held cheap, as the tombstones in Westminster Abbey,
Which headless and dusty, look shockingly shabby :—
      Or St. Paul's, where on payment
      Of twopence a head,

In a temple to pray meant
They peep-show the dead ;
Where beadle and verger
So cruel a scourge are,
And keen Dean and Chapter
To screw one so apt are,
That Sir Christopher Wren would their *robbing* disown,
Could he do in St. Faith's what he pleas'd with his own.
On marble Archdukes
In flowing perukes,
A Dutch burgomaster
In pure alabaster ;
Electors in steel, and
Archbishops of Zealand,
All mitred and crosiered,
(You'd fancy their prose ye heard.)
People listlessly gaz'd, like the cockneys who go
To stare at the wax-work of Madame Tussaud,
Stiff as pokers or pikestaffs, and ugly as sin,
Lord Palmerston,—Nap,—and Commissioner Lin !—
But awful to view was the wonderful tomb,
Beside the high altar of Bergen-op-Zoom ;
Its emblems mysteriously hinting a doom
That might take out the shine in cadaverous gloom
Of the tales of Monk Lewis, Ann Radcliff, and Co.,
Once the popular authors of *gens comme il faut.*—

To remind us that fragile as glass human fate is,
A lesson old Time still imparts to one gratis,
It bore the sad text,—"VANITAS VANITATIS ! "—
And the emblems,—I shudder in writing the tale,—

Were a skull on a looking-glass,—parti per pale :—
The technical term may be wrong :—of Sir Harris
Exactness in matters heraldic the care is ;
But the objects were plac'd,—as your forefathers saw, Sir,—
The skull like a teacup,—the glass like a saucer.—

Such a blazon announc'd to the prosy and dull,
Not a crack in the glass, but a crack in the skull,—
Till the terrible legend was told to its ending.   ·
But a moment for breath, if you please ! 'Twere like
    blending
Ash-Wednesday in sackcloth with loose *Mardi Gras*, if
We touch'd on such horrors without a new paragraph !—

     By the Frith of Forth
     In the canny North
       Once dwelt a noble man ;—
     Brave, braw, and spruce
     Was young Lord Bruce,
       A farthing of Queen Anne !—
     The gamesome and the gay among,
      He bore away the belle ;
     But belles, alas ! can wag a tongue
      Their right to rings to tell ;
     And when some blustering brother talks
      Of Mantons, and eight paces,
       Even fighting Smith, or doughty Dan,
       Or Lady Sale, or Cardigan,
       Or valiant Jack, the Cornish man,
     Might wish he dar'd to walk his chalks
      And ne'er had seen their faces !—

However, Lord Bruce was so general a favourite,
 That, do what he would, 'twas the vote of the Lords,
'Twould be their *own* loss were he sent to the grave for it,
 So they sheathed their toledos, and swallow'd their
  words.

'Twas the time when from Scotland King Jamie the First
 Brought his naked and hungry, our treasure to bone
  here,
And a cat-and-dog sort of affection was nurst
 'Twixt the courtiers of England and stout Caledonia !—
  Mid the proudest at court
   Young Sackville was seen,—
  A champion for England
  A knight for a queen ;—
Like Bayard the Spotless,—of chivalrous France a star,
Or the *preux* of our *own* time, to whom he was ancestor,
Cantilupe,—last of the Dorsets, whose bays
Crown'd heroes and bards in Elizabeth's days.—

Now Sackville detested the Scotch, and protested
 That Bruce, who just then with his sister was flirting,
 If he show'd but his nose in the house, for proposing,
 Should be seiz'd by his vassals, and tumbled the dirt in,
Wherever they jostled,—no matter the spot,—
He muttered the insult of—"beggarly Scot !"—
And Bruce, though 'twas hard his emotions to smother,
Had not e'en the resource to retort—"you're another !"

A Scotman's devotion *pro aris et focis*
As the love of the Swiss for their fatherland, close is.

So that Bruce, thus revil'd, though averse to the action,
Was *forc'd* in the end to demand satisfaction.

But as luck will'd, King Jamie, "their gossip and dad,"
  Got a hint of the business, and swore with an oath,
"If he heard of a meeting between 'em, egad !
  He'd settle in Newgate the hash of them both."—
     To the London police
       He gave them in charge,
     Rehearsing the piece
       Of the "Prisoners at large,"—
     But they turn'd on their heel, and
     Set sail straight for Zealand,
     With seconds and surgeons
     To act in emergence ;
And landing at Antwerp, upon the Escaut, sir,
Agreed they would fight the next day,. at Tergosa.—

     'Tis unpleasant to draw
     On one's brother-in-law :
     And that night, when in bed
     Lord Bruce laid his head,
     And thought of the sorrow
     Might chance on the morrow ;
     Having supp'd on sauer-kraut
     Pumpernickel and stout,
     In which Dutchmen delight,—
     He was tortur'd all night
By a nightmare, just such as one dreams in one's flurry
After seeing Macbeth done to rags at the Surrey !—
And awaking at daybreak, "used up" and affrighted,
Beheld what was worse than ten nightmares united !—

In that province, where webb'd in the foot man and beast
    are,
A mirror is placed in the beds for a tester ;
Like a looking-glass stuck in a comfit-box lid,
Multiplying by two what must else have been hid,—
And making the snoozer snooze double,—too bad O,
My Wordsworth,—to jest on thy Swan and its Shadow !

    Therein of course Lord Bruce expected
    To see his night-capp'd face reflected ;
      But lifting up his eyes,—(the wind
    With hideous moanings howl'd the while,—)
      Behold a human skull thence grinn'd
    Most horribly a ghastly smile !—
    Oh omen dire,— Oh omen dread,—
    His face transform'd to a death's head !—

    He fainted not, nor call'd for aid
    From waiter, or from chambermaid :—
    But softly to himself he said,
    " I'm a ' gone ' coon !—All's up with *me !*—
    My doom is settled—Q. E. D."—
    As though by Babbage prov'd or Whewell,
    A victim pre-ordain'd he knew well
    That adverse fate, with purpose cruel,
    Had sworn to pink him in the duel !—
    So having wash'd and said his prayers
    He took his sword and walk'd down stairs.

In the record George Sackville has left of their fight,
    To prove to all England he was not a scamp,—

He .tells us distinctly it rain'd in the night,
   And the meadow they fought in was wretchedly damp.
He felt but the damp to his feet from the grass,—
But the damper of Bruce was the skull in the glass !
And dazzled and desperate, he rush'd like a fool on
His foe,—in a style that would shock Monsieur Coulon.

From the right breast of Sackville the blood flow'd in
      torrents,
But though pale as a portrait of Canning by Lawrence,
He rallied his strength with a wrench and a start,
And ran his antagonist straight through the heart,
The surgeons drew near,—'twas no manner of use !—
As the omen foretold, all was up with Lord Bruce !

The great Earl of Clarendon tells us this story,
And Steele in the Guardian has placed it before ye ;
But both pass in silence the ghost of the skull,
As an old woman's tale of a cock and a bull.—
Though, when to Culross in procession forlorn
The heart of the dead, cased in silver was borne,
By his mother those emblems were placed on his tomb
Beside the high altar of Bergen-op-Zoom !

MORAL.

   The moral of this dread event
      Should be inscrib'd on brass ;
   Refrain, young lords, on conquest bent,
      From looking in the glass !

THE sun, with his face all ruddy red,
Had made up his mind to go to bed;
For he'd had enough, as he very well knew,
Of the sweetest potation, the mountain dew;

And fearing, like drunkards, an unpleasant dream,
He slaked his thirst with a neighbouring stream,
And shook his cloud-bed in the cosy West.
The shadows stretch'd long as he sank to rest ;
His bed-curtains waved with a ruddy glow,
As they blush'd at the red of his face below ;
And, dreading the night-dews might give him a cold,
He popp'd his nose under the sheets of gold ;
A mountain extinguisher put out his light,
And he quietly tuck'd himself in for the night.
A convent there stood, all embower'd in trees,
Where holy men ate, drank, and slept at their ease.
The vesper bell swell'd on the evening air,
Calling the good and the bad to prayer ;
    There a lone man sat,
    Without any hat,
At an oriel window, with dark troubled face ;
His form it was noble, his beard it was black,
And, to cool his bold forehead, his cowl was thrown back,
And the sun's last rays fell on a very bald place.
    'Twas the Prior who sat
    Without any hat,
Thinking of love, and such nonsense as that.
A castle stood on a hill just by,
Upon which he constantly turn'd his eye ;
    For there dwelt she,
    The Lady that he
Loved to such an immoderate degree,
    Though the wife of another,
    That didn't bother
A man of such eminent piety.

A wife she was, and that's the truth,
The playmate of his early youth,
But married to his *frère* Sir Hugh,
Who'd been her constant playmate too,
Who first into this world of sin
Had come, although the Prior's twin ;
Therefore the castle and the land
Had influenced the lady's hand ;
For the one was poor, the other rich,
Or else it wouldn't have matter'd which;
As daily more alike they grew,
Their mother even hardly knew
  The difference between them ;
For, as they did each other pass,
'Twas like reflection in a glass,
  As all had said who'd seen them.
And, when to manhood they had grown,
Sir Hugh had call'd Amile his own.
The younger brother turn'd devout,
And coolly kick'd his passion's out.

Years roll'd on, and the lady fair
Had fail'd to give the lands an heir.
Sir Hugh got glum, and moped about,
And in the habit of staying out ;
But his lady was mild as unskimm'd milk,
And she quietly sorted her worsted and silk,
As she sat with her maidens round a frame ;
Her grandma and mother had done the same.
Indeed, the family had much fame
For working grim murders in tapestrie,

And handing them down to posteritic.
Sir Hugh walk'd up, and Sir Hugh walk'd down,
And ever was seen on his brow a frown ;
He bit his lip, and his cheek grew pale,
As his eye wander'd over his coat of mail,
And he thought it rather a comic affair
That they should hang rusting and unused there ;
He thought of the blood that was shed galore,
In the golden time call'd the days of yore,
How he long'd, like a true knight, to spill much more !
As he stamp'd his heel on the oaken floor,
I am not quite certain, I think he swore !

Morning breathes forth her sweetest breath,
Shaming all thoughts of blood and death ;
The fleecy mist now upward curls,
Shedding on earth its brightest pearls ;
There's music in the air, which tells
Of fairy blast on wreathed shells,
To summon home to mossy cells
The truant crew, who love to sing
Their matins in the fairy ring,
When, galloping up the deep ravine
In fiery haste, a man was seen.
The pale light shone on his helm afar,
Like Friar Rush with his dancing star,
As he rode in haste through briar and brake,
Hoping to find the warder awake,
And ready to ask him what he'd take,
He bore a letter as big as a plate ;

So, stopping his horse at the castle-gate,
>> He gave a loud ring
>> In the name of the King.
The warder sprang up at the sonorous call,
First taking a peep through a slit in the wall.
Sir Hugh took the letter with trembling hand :
'Twas summoning him to the Holy Land,
>> Where nobles and knights
>> Were flocking in flights,
And leaving their wives and their lares like fools.
>> The cry was Jerusalem,
>> Where, to bamboozle 'em,
The Lion King took them to use them as tools.
>> He quickly repairs
>> To his lady up-stairs,
To talk about all the domestic affairs.
>> The folly of linen
>> Was just then beginning,
And soap was a thing hardly known in the land :
>> So a shirt of mail,
>> With a very short tail,
Was much more convenient, and made to stand .
>> The wear and the tear
>> Of a serious affair
Like that which he'd got in hand.
>> Ere set of sun
>> Everything was done ;
His waistcoat and breeches were polish'd and bright,
And his beaver of steel was screw'd up tight.
A wail arose from the valley below,
For many unwilling were doom'd to go.

Each vassal was summon'd to follow his lord,
The vassal that kept the watch and the ward,
The villeins appendant who stuck to the land,
Or pass'd, like old fixtures, from hand to hand,—
The villeins " en gros," who'd labour and toil,
Yet were sold like sheep from their native soil.
They stood like dark statues before the tall knight,
In the castle court-yard, in the falling twilight—
  Their green hills saw them no more.
The lady stood on the tower so high,
To wish them good luck as they trotted by,
She waivȩd her scarf with a tender sigh, .
  Then went to work as before.

Five long years have come, five long years have gone,
The castle shines bright on an April morn—
  All this time,
  In a foreign clime,
The knight has been fighting like anything,
By the side of his brave, but thick-headed King.
His wife has gone on with her tapestrie
As calm as a duck-pond, and happilie
" No news was good news," and so thought she ;
For hearing at all was uncertainty,
  As no penny stamp
  Was known in the camp
In the golden days of the good Sir Hugh ;
  And if there had,
  It would have been just as bad,
 For there was no post to put it into.

But the Prior, the brother,
Behaved like a mother,
And to comfort her daily he never did fail ;
He came unawares,
Ran up and down stairs,
And was just like a tin kettle tied to her tail.
He his brethren deserted,
And he sat there and flirted,
While the Lady look'd on him with her cold blue eyes,
And her face was so stolid,
Her look was so solid,
That knock'd on the head all his looks and his sighs.
Things were in this situation,
Needing some slight alteration,
When the Prior, who sat on a fallen tree
On the side of the road, (he was going to tea,
At least 'twas a meal at the very same time,
Only made up of things more solid and prime,)
Beheld a tall man in a very black jack,
That cover'd his stomach as well as his back,
Bending his way
Where the castle lay.
His visage was dark, he'd a scar on his brow,
Both speaking of danger and some foreign row ;
The bridge of his nose
Had sunk in repose,
As if to get out of the way of more blows.
'Twas his brother's bold henchman,
He knew at a look ;
So he jump'd up at once,
And three strides he took.

The man turn'd round his sinister eyes
As coolly as if he'd been used to surprise,

And, without a start,
Said, "Lor! bless my heart,
You are my Lord's brother, as sure as eggs.
He's very near here,
And, feeling but queer,

He stopp'd at an hostel to rest his legs."
The Prior he thought for a moment or two
What, under such a chance, he best should do.
He bade him haste to the lady's bower,
  And tell his tidings there,
Then steal from out the castle gate,
  And to his cell repair.

The henchman sat in the Prior's cell,
 He shiver'd as if with cold,
And in his horny palm he held
 A heap of shining gold.
The Prior's eyes were fix'd and bright,
 Like the snake's prepared to spring ;
His cheek was pale as sheeted ghost—
 He look'd a guilty thing !
A dagger sharp and keen now pass'd
 From out the Prior's vest ;
The henchman wink'd his knowing eye,
 As if he knew the rest.
Another whisper pass'd, and then
 This precious pair arose,
The Prior looking solemnly,
 With his finger on his nose.

His heart it flutter'd like a bird,
 As he changed his robe for blue,
As a Palmer fresh from Holy Land,
 With scrip, and a cross'd wand too.

 Then he took out a hat
 Both broad and flat,
With a terrible width of brim :
 It shaded his eyes,
 It shaded his nose,
And had cockle-shells round the rim.

The Lady sat fidgetting in her bower,
Each minute appearing to her like an hour.
 And she constantly stirr'd the fire,
A step is heard upon the stair—
Ah ! is her Palmer Knight, then, there !
(Between ourselves, 'twas the Prior,)
Then the door flew wide, and there appear'd
The palmer dark, with frizzled beard ;
He rush'd to her arms, but he started back ;
As he did so, of course, he look'd over her back ;
And, looking, beheld, 'tis surprising as true,
His own very counterpart standing in blue ;
The very same hat, with the very large brim,
And cockle-shells sticking all out round the rim.
 His ecstasy stopp'd,
 His under jaw dropp'd,
As he looked on the figure, and saw its dull frown ;
 Its hand raised in air,
 As if saying, forbear,
And the large spots of blood on the gown ;
The lady turned to see the cause
 Of such a pause,
But seem'd to look on air ;

And as he stared,
She still declared
She could see nothing there.
He breathed again, for, though a monk
Was game as any bantum,
And did not fear a rush, not he,
Since it was but a phantom :
The supper was brought ; still the figure stood by,
Attracting no notice, attracting no eye.

The lady smiled,
And the meal began ;
But who could eat
When the murdered man,
Looked on with a fishy eye ;
And, pleading fatigue, and heaving a sigh,
He thought it was time to go to by-bye,
And said, as he felt no desire to sup,
He begged that her ladyship wouldn't sit up ;
Then, beckoning a servitor who stood near,
He ordered a rushlight, and finished his beer.

Then, turning his head,
With a feeling of dread,
Beheld there no phantom at all !
But, though as a priest he no courage did lack,
Yet he ordered the vassal to keep to his back,
And he held the rushlight high
As he stalked o'er the floor
Of the long corridor,
He constantly turned his eye ;
When, chancing to see on the neighbouring wall
A shadow not like the vassal at all ;

But there, with eyes as big as a crown,
With the very same hat, and the very same gown,
 Stood the phantom with a light;
It glided on first to the castle gate,

The Prior stalked after, compelled by fate,
 In a pretty tarnation fright;
  He tried to be
  At his *conjuro-te*,
But his tongue quite failed him, it felt so thick,

As dry as a parrot's, or Flanders brick ;
They came to the portal, the gates were wide,
Not a soul was on watch either out or inside.
The phantom pointed down the vale,
    And smiled as if in scoff,
And nodded its head with a mournful nod,
    As if to say, " Be off !"
The priest he turned his head away
    To think of some trick
    To circumvent Nick,
For he knew he'd the devil to pay,
When suddenly he received such a kick
On his holy gown behind,
    That, to believe
    Such a ghost could achieve
He must have been out of his mind ;
    The toe was like steel
    That made him feel.
    He fell with the blows
    On his reverend nose,
But he picked himself up in a trice ;
    Yet still that great toe
    Kept on kicking him so
In the whereabouts not over nice,
    That over and over
    He rolled in the clover,
And the rocks tapped his shaven crown.
    He prayed and implored,
    He shouted and roared,
'Till he'd rolled about halfway down ;
    Then he got on his feet

In case a repeat
Might finish the job quite brown ;
He turned, and beheld the henchman grim,
And many more standing along with him,

And amidst was his brother seen.
He fled in affright,
And well he might,
And the portcullis grinned at the luckless wight
As he bolted down the ravine ;
He heard the abbey vesper-bell,

And loud laughs mingling quite as well.
　　In the morning he starts,
　　And leaves those parts,
　　And goes to Canterburie,
　　And hides his shame
　　With another name,
　　With a like fraternitie.
　　His brother so stout,
　　Who had kicked him out,
　　With his needlework wife,
　　Lived a happy life,
Till they died in the natural course,
　　When he lied by her side,
　　In sculptured pride,
With his valiant legs across.

THE MANXMAN AND HIS VISITOR.

Who are you ?
Thoughtless saying.

A MANXMAN old, in the wintry cold,
   Was seated before his hearth,
And he thought of the past, as the wint'ry blast
   Roll'd fearful o'er the earth.

He had no child, and his home was wild,
   Amid the mountains lone ;
His wife was in bed, but he wish'd her dead,
   For she was a crabbed old bone.

Straight as a beam did the Manxman seem,
   And an awful look had he ;
I speak of his youth, when he in truth
   Did revel upon the sea.

But now was he bent, and his vigour spent,
   And his eye was cold as clay,
And a wicked pain, again and again,
   Did plague him every day.

He once was bold, but now was old,—
   He once was very proud ;
He knew no fear, nor had shed a tear,
   But now he wail'd aloud.

And why did he wail, and why turn pale,
   And his flesh begin to creep,
As from his seat he piled the peat,
   And folded his arms to sleep ?

" For what now here have I to fear,
   With a drop to keep me warm ?
What haunts my head ?" the Manxman said,
   " Since I have done no harm.

" The devil may be upon the sea,
   Or walking o'er the earth ;
Can he molest, when I've done my best,
   E'en from my very birth ?

" I'll stake a penny there's sinners full many,
   Without his need of me ;
Come when he may, give me fair play,
   And vanquish'd he shall be !"

With this speech so bold, the Manxman cold
   Grew calmer than before,
And his blood did flow with a warmer glow
   Right out from his heart's core.

Upon his breast his chin did rest,
   His limbs were gently cross'd,
He did not care the breadth of a hair
   For the world and all its cost.

And slumber now did sweetly throw
   Her gentle mist around,
And the Manxman's eye at her lullably
   Was in silken fetters bound.

Ah, cruel taunt ! ah, idle vaunt !
   The slumberer is deceived,
And hence his mind, more unconfined,
   Is not one whit relieved.

For, soon as sleep did o'er him creep,
   The fearful sights begun,
And now he roll'd, and next he growl'd,
   In sooth it was no fun.

His wife a-bed right over head,
   Came softly down the stairs ;
But he took no heed, so she with speed
   Went back to say her prayers.

And soon she wept, and soon she slept ;
   But first she cried in scorn,
"Through many a night, till morning light,
   I have been left forlorn."

Now the Manxman bold, in spite of his scold
   Had oft done so before ;
For he loved his life, and he loved his wife,
   But he loved his pig the more.

And now for awhile a lurid smile
   Would o'er his features play,
And quickly again he writhed in pain,
   And something strove to say.

What man alive can ever strive
   To guide the brain in sleep,
When dreams will come of ills at home,
   Of terrors o'er the deep ?

HIS DREAMS.

Soon as the Manxman fell asleep,
   A little robin came,
His gentle breast did redden deep
   Before the cottage flame.

Where'er the Manxman's dream did rove,
   That robin chirp'd in song
O'er flood or field, o'er plain or grove,
   The robin roved along.

But oh ! that song was not of earth,—
   'Twas one of wrath and pain,
So reft of all its common mirth,
   It pierced the Manxman's brain.

He dream'd it was a day of youth,
   When he essay'd to play
With other boys (I tell the truth)
   In Ramsay's beauteous bay.

Some builded houses on the sand,
   And some would races run ;
In short, it was a happy band,
   Bent eagerly on fun.

A fair-hair'd boy, of gentle heart,
   And manners sweetly mild,
Did build upon the shore apart,
   And thus his time beguiled.

That boy in music and in song
   Did afterwards excel,
And men would round the minstrel throng,
   They loved his lay so well.

But now a youth with envious eye
   Observed his lonely way,
And more than rudely ask'd him why
   He would not come and play ?

And soon, before he could reply,
   Had passion dealt the wound ;
All gather'd round with pitying eye,—
   The gentle boy had swoon'd !

And now the Manxman saw the blood
  Stream down the fair boy's face ;
He mark'd the other's hellish mood,
  And felt the foul disgrace.

Ay, wide his arms did the Manxman fling,
  And heavily did he sigh ;
But he felt far more the robin's sting,
  As it peck'd beneath his eye.

ANOTHER DREAM.

Again—a dark youth loved a girl,
  They walk'd alone at eve ;
He call'd her oft his fairest pearl.
  He never could deceive.

But men are false, as most maids know,
  And vows are rashly given ;
And, though he swore by all below,
  And all his hope of heaven,

Time soon saw the maid forsaken,
  And mark'd her glazed eye,
And then she ne'er again did waken,
  For she did grieve and die.

They bore her to her grave with song *
  Upon a fine May day ;

* A custom in the Isle of Man.

A multitude did walk along,—
  'Twas ill to keep away.

Above Kirk Manghold church she lies,
  And softly shall she rest,
Until she soars with sweet surprise
  To Him who loved her best.

The Manxman's dream was of her fate
  Her pale corpse seem'd full nigh;
And the robin mark'd his wretched state,
  As it peck'd beneath his eye.

ANOTHER DREAM.

Again—upon a summer's sea
  A seaman sail'd away,
He saw the moon most merrily
  Gleam on the midnight spray.

He watch'd the sun o'er the sapphire wave
  Rise beautiful and grand;
It such a joyous feeling gave,
  He could not wish for land.

Ere long a ruthless wind did blow,
  The sea roll'd mountains mad,
Scarce could they steer that wayward prow—
  Our sailor he grew sad.

At midnight on this wilderness
　A lonely bark did near,
They raised a cry of deep distress,
　And all that cry did hear.

The captain with an oath sail'd on,
　Our sailor cheer'd his word,
And right they steer'd their course along,
　As men that never heard.

They saw the shivering wretches fling
　Their feeble arms on high;
And our Manxman groan'd at the robin's sting,
　As it peck'd beneath his eye.

A FOURTH DREAM.

Again—away from the northern seas
　Our seaman blithely sail'd,
Where the cold his very breath did freeze,
　And like a child he wail'd.

Huge hills of ice as granite stone
　Encompass'd them around,
A floating rock so vast and lone,
　An island when aground.

And now like mountains would they meet,
　With noise as loudest thunder,
As solemnly as friends might meet,
　Then proudly break asunder.

Each moment then might be the last,
    Not one without its fear;
Our sailor mused upon the past,
    When all around grew drear.

Alas! 'twas not a gentle thought
    That stole upon his brain;
He vow'd, or he was good for nought,
    Their captain he'd arraign.

" My boys," he spake unto the crew,
    " We all shall perish here;
Why darkly wait with light in view?
    Away, then, let us steer.

" Our captain is a harden'd man,
    But our stout hands are free;
Come, follow up my glorious plan—
    Hurrah for liberty!"

A missionary, who sail'd along
    For any heathen land,
Who never did a mortal wrong
    Upon the deck did stand.

One word he spake, a word of peace,
    With eye and accent mild,
The angry bursts of passion cease,
    The crew are reconciled.

Our sailor awful oaths did lift
   To God in heaven above,
He would have cast the man adrift
   Upon the waste to rove.

The Manxman saw the anger lurk,
   And the bosom swelling high ;
But he felt the robin more at work,
   As it peck'd beneath his eye.

THE DREAMS ENDED.

The Manxman awoke, and look'd around,
   No robin could he see ;
He saw no sight, he heard no sound,—
   What could the vision be ?

An old grey hare sat on her rump,*
   And coolly wiped her face ;
The Manxman scream'd, and with a jump
   She bounded from the place.

He turn'd, and, seated on a chair,
   Beheld a lady grand.
He could not think what she did there,
   Until, in speech so bland,

She spake :—" I enter here, kind friend,
   For shelter for the night ;

---

* The popular belief that witches enter hares.

I trust you will my cause defend,
    And help the poor to right."

The false Manxman, the false Manxman,
    Says he, "I never will
Drive out the poor from before my door,—
    Myself I'd sooner kill!"

And thus he spake, for wide awake
    He view'd the lady fine,
And many a ring, like a glittering thing,
    Upon her hand did shine.

She talk'd apace, as her wrinkled face
    Was shadow'd by the night,
Save when a gleam from the fire did beam
    Upon her eye so bright.

This ancient dame seem'd to be lame,
    And the hare had limp'd aside;
But glances stole like a burning coal
    From out her eye of pride.

And, though she was old, to the Manxman cold
    She spake so free and tender,
That loudly he swore he'd die before
    He ever could offend her.

"You never gave," said the lady grave,
    "The least offence to me;
And now your speech doth warmly preach
    You'll ever kindly be."

To the Manxman's view the flames burn'd blue ;
   But he cared not for it now ;
For the lady's word was all he heard,
   And it caused a wondrous glow.

" Madam, indeed," said he with speed,
   " You seem to know me well ;
But never before within this door,
   Or in this lonely dell,

" Have I ever seen so gracious a queen
   To talk with one so poor.
And, pray, may I dare to question where
   You have seen me before ?"

" Your parents dear, who lived long here,
   Were right well known to me ;
They loved me well, as I needs must tell,
   And will remember'd be.

" And from your birth, upon this earth,
   Oh ! I have watch'd you long ;
For many an hour, with hearty power,
   You 've named me in your song."

" Your name, indeed," again with speed
   The modest Manxman cried,
" I do not know,—and surely now
   My memory hath denied."

" How can that be," said she, with glee,
  " When you have been my care ?
I saw you play in Ramsay bay
  With the boy of the golden hair."

The Manxman's eyes with quick surprise
  I ween were open'd wide,
And he did stare with an awful glare
  On the lady by his side.

" I saw you walk in loving talk,
  With the girl so young and fair ;
On the very eve you did deceive
  I communed with you there.

" In the funeral hour I saw them lower
  Her pale face in the grave.
And you were as gay as that May-day
  Upon the distant wave.

" Ere the nettle grew, another with you
  Did rove unheeding there—
She is now in bed right over head,
  One broken down with care."

The Manxman groan'd, and glared around
  As wild as a bird of prey ;
All in his fright he cursed the night,
  And long'd for break of day.

But the lady still would have her will,
   Nor could she be denied;
As his blood ran cold, she grew more bold,
   Still closer at his side.

"I could not fail, when you set sail,
   To guide you on the sea,
And when that storm did heaven deform,
   I bade you cling to me.

"I fear'd, indeed, lest your heart should bleed
   When you saw the lonely wreck;
But your captain's voice was all your choice,
   As you swore upon the deck.

"Those seamen brave met a watery grave;
   Most pious souls were they;
And from Paradise they all shall rise
   Upon the judgment day."

The woman scowl'd, and the thunders roll'd
   As she spoke that very word;
He would have pray'd, but was sore afraid
   For all that he had heard.

"I sail'd with you and a jovial crew,
   'Mid the icebergs floating by;
And, when your hand did spurn command,
   I mark'd your blood-red eye.

"The churchman so pale, who did prevail,
  Is still my greatest foe ;
He baffled me then, and will again,
  For the Gospel is to grow."

" And be it so," cried the Manxman now,
  As ne'er he had spake before ;
And the lady frown'd, and stamp'd the ground—
  In truth he said no more.

" I may not yield, for in your field
  I saw you dig last morn ;
You could not find things to your mind,
  As you look'd around in scorn.

" A robin sweet in the snowy sleet
  Did hop within your view,
That little bird by man preferr'd,
  Was basely kill'd by you."

The Manxman's ire burn'd like fire,
  Aloud he cursed and swore ;
The lady fair seem'd in peril there,
  As he flung wide the door.

But oh ! his wrath was like the froth
  Upon a heaving sea ;
The lady was gone, but not alone
  A rescued man stood he.

Full nine feet high to the Manxman's eye
  A hideous form appear'd,
And down he fell as under a spell,
  So soon that form he fear'd.

Of bone and skin, with flame within,
  Of a sulphureous smell,
His awful tone, in an hour so lone,
  Did sound as a funeral-knell.

A lifted hand, that waved command,
  Did slowly beckon thrice,
And the Manxman, pale, for his life did quail,
  As he answer'd in a trice.

" Why come to me, why come to me,
  To fill me with alarm ?
Why seek not him who is steep'd in sin ?
  For I have done no harm.

" Did I destroy the tender boy ?
  Or did I kill the maid ?
Did I pass by the shipwreck'd cry,
  Or draw the rebel blade ?

" On high Barrule, when the nights are cool,
  I never roam'd to steal.
It is too true the bird I slew,—
  And that I do reveal."

He would beguile,—but 'twas plain the while
 He was an unkind man ;
He mock'd at school, and a reckless fool
 He lived as he began.

Next morn on the ground was the Manxman found
 As dead as a man could be ;
And how he was slain will ever remain
 A hidden mystery !

The above describes a Manxman (and a Manxman means an inhabitant of the Isle of Man,) who was of a cruel disposition when a boy, cruel when a young man, and cruel to the last. In this manner the devil had power over him all his life, and comes to claim him before he dies. It will be seen that in his dream he is permitted to look back upon his past errors, and the fact of his having on that very day killed so innocent a bird as a robin is a sore sting to his conscience. His evil spirit comes at first, in the shape of an ancient dame, and then appears as a more hideous figure. The devil is made to assume a form,—that is, the evil conscience incarnates its awful guilt.

The Manx people believe in apparitions, or *second sight*, and are forewarned of the death of others. From a letter of Dr. Sacheverell's to the celebrated Addison, it appears that the wise and learned have given credit to this belief.

An elegant writer, who travelled in the island, says, "Without being guilty of presumption, we may impute these superstitions of the Manx to a native melancholy, cherished by indolence, and heightened by the wild, solitary, and romantic scenes to which they are habitually accustomed. A Manxman, amid his lonely mountains, reclines by some romantic stream, the murmurings of which lull him into a pleasing torpor. Half slumbering, he sees a variety of imaginary beings, which he believes to be real. Sometimes they resemble his traditionary idea of fairies, and sometimes they assume the appearance of his friends and neighbours. Presuming on these dreams, the Manx enthusiast predicts some future event, and, should anything similar occur, he fancies himself endowed with the gift of prescience, and thus disturbs his own happiness and that of others."

"I make no doubt," continues this author afterwards, "but, amid hideous solitudes, a man of a melancholy or superstitious mind may insensibly form visions of some dreadful calamity he is about to suffer, and which may not only receive strength, but even completion, from a sombrous imagination, heightened by traditionary terrors. With the world of spirits we are little acquainted ; but I can never reconcile it to our ideas of the majesty, wisdom, and benevolence of the Deity, that he should communicate to a few indolent recluses such revelations of the unknown world as could only flatter vanity, or accelerate human misery."

Thus speaks our author ; but we must remember that all nations, in all ages, have believed in supernatural agencies. Whoever has read the delightful letters of the younger Pliny, will remember not only the account of the haunted house at Athens, but the firm impression made on Pliny himself, and the best orators and others of that learned age, by the circumstance of dreams. Brutus and Buonaparte, Cæsar and Lord Clarendon, with a host of others, all attest remarkable things ; but the subject is one which requires no mean investigation ; and, at present, it may be best consistent with good sense to observe, that there seems to be as much temerity in never giving credit to dreams, as there is superstition in always doing so. "It appears to me," says an eminent critic, "that the true medium between the two extremes is to treat them as we would a known liar : we are sure he most usually relates falsehoods ; however, nothing hinders but he may sometimes speak the truth."

The Isle of Man has a population of fifty thousand, and the literary acquirements of the inhabitants have greatly increased of late years. Much commercial activity and bustle prevail, and far too much litigation also ; but still her noble hills and secluded glens may be silently and deeply enjoyed. The fame of Bishop Wilson has made the island renowned in many lands, and caused her to be called the "sacred isle." The Manx clergy are liberal and gentle in their views, far more so than the sectaries, and would do honour to a more polished and learned country than Manx-land will be for a while.

THE CORYPHEE.

I AM one of the twelve who come six from each side,
With gauze wings and scarfs, and dance round the bride,
And then in a line to the front we all bound,
Smile at the orchestra, and all twelve turn round !
Retreat to the wing, joyous, buoyant, and fleet, oh !
To make way for the fairy of earth,—Miss Cerito.

I am one of the twelve, (when Cerito's pas's ended,)
Who's supplied at the wing with an active intended.
Sometimes we've twelve sailors, sometimes twelve marines,
Or a dozen gay rustics, with twelve tambourines ;
Then all twenty-four form a ring in the centre,
And waltz till 'tis time for Guy Stephan to enter.

I am one of the twelve, with a long wreath of flowers,
(Made up from the last night's floriferous showers,)
Arranged as a frame for our twelve smiling faces,
And next in four frames, form four sets of graces,
M. Perrot, till now was conceal'd by the trees—he
Completes the tableau with sweet Carlotta Grisi.

The intendeds once more on the stage take their stations,
And the audience begin to show signs of impatience, ·
For the pittites and stalls are vacating whole rows,
Which flattering hint brings the dance to a close.
On one toe, 'midst blue fire, our joy we express,
With our hands to O. P., and our feet to P. S.

MENANDER.

LINES ON THE CARNIVAL AT ROME.

—◆—

The Carnival is o'er, with its strange and wild delight ;
Now my heart is sad and heavy, like a tired child at night;
And my dream of girlish forms is gone, and hands so
　　small to see,
And wavy hair, and bodice tight, and necks of ivory,
And eyes that tremulously glanced from balcony and car,
And the beauteous lady bending near, and the fair girl
　　beck'ning far :
Like faded flowers trodden late in the City's gorgeous
　　street,*
In few short hours Time's chariot-wheels have crush'd my
　　fancies sweet.

The mask'd *festini*† all are o'er, with liquid orbs half seen,
Like glimpses round of crystal wells through dark um-
　　brageous green,

---

* The chief amusement of the Carnival consists in throwing flowers
at the beautiful women in the carriages and balconies, and exchanging
bouquets and *confetti*. The profusion of flowers on these occasions is
incredible.

† These *festini* are the masked balls at the theatres, which take
place every night of the Carnival. Some of them begin at midnight.
By the "shrill accost" is meant the peculiar, disguised, and somewhat
alto tone, which the Italians adopt with much facility.

And shrill accost and jest are hush'd, and playful, saucy
 feet
No longer now, at dead of night, the round fantastic beat.
The visor black, that lately hid both passion's deadly
 frown
And joyous stare of innocence, a thing of nought is grown;
And robes of mystery, that wrapp'd around each working
 breast,
Mere shapeless things of silk, are cast into the silent
 chest ;
All revelry is dead ; whilst the gaunt and shaven priest
In the cold and stately church proclaims the moral of the
 feast. *

But moments of intenser life my soul still cling around,
As I wake from dreams of fairy bliss, or tired sleep
 profound ;
Some pearly sounds are ringing still, that make my chill'd
 heart beat,
Like summer voices heard amidst a calm and green retreat,
When the humming of the fields is o'er, and silence
 ushers eve,
And the very flowers our feet press down their languid
 heads scarce heave—
When, lost in July reverie, with half-closed eyes we see
A dreamy wizard shape assume each Dryad-haunted tree.

 * Immediately after the *abandon* and intoxication of the Carnival
comes the *Quaresima digiúno di quaranta giorni*, during which no
public amusements are allowed. It is dreaded equally by the gay
inhabitant or the gayer stranger, and is the reign and triumph of
priestly mummery, ending with the *Holy Week*.

The equal-feather'd cypress, or the olive's mystic age,*
Laocoon-like, that upward wreathes its limbs, distort with
    rage—
When e'en the shadowy sprite that sighs amid the poplar
    leaves
Is lapp'd in gladness by the hour,—or grieving, silent
    grieves.

The lips which spake those silvery sounds I ne'er again
    may see ;
But oft, like dreams of childish love, they'll haunt my
    memory.
Looks, too, there were, as one had stray'd bright crystal
    gates within,
Where spirits dwell, and met their eyes without reproof
    or sin ;
And hands clasp'd hands unknown before, with strange
    magnetic charm,
Then, all abash'd, their clasp unloosed, with sudden, sweet
    alarm.
Oh ! glorious is the *Carnival*, that rayless pride subdues,
Decking the common things of life with rich, unwonted
    hues.

Right glorious is the *Carnival !* that likes not hollow mould
Of hearts from eager sympathies fenced round with
    cautious gold.

---

* The age of the olive-tree is literally unknown. It is pretended to
show an olive near Tivoli which was dear to Horace ! Certainly these
trees have the appearance of extreme age. The fantastic, gnarled, and
distorted trunks of an olive-grove have a very peculiar effect, par-

The poet and the painter then walk forth with step
    unbound,
And gaze abroad with glistening eye, that never seeks the
    ground,
Like the fiction bravely coin'd of the poet devotee,
Nature, that shackled ever was, triumphantly seems free.

But it is past—strange, innocent *Millenium* of a week ;
Next morn their usual pasture dull the sober'd herd will
    seek ;
And I, that raise my midnight dirge, can scarcely longer
    trace
Already aught of those lost hours, that ran so joyous race,
As Rome, beneath me, like some mammoth skeleton of old,
Sleeps silent in the moonbeams, ribb'd with columns wan
    and cold.
Where late they lay, of impulse bright, the myriad hand-
    maid throng,
As swept that fair array the streets red-tapestried along,
Sweet hecatombs of flowers, that were, with unseen pow'r
    alone.*
And tiny fragrant voices, cry from every perfumed stone,
Bidding the night-breeze fan me, as with scent of gardens
    near,
Whilst in the sleeping street I wake chill Echo from her bier.

ticularly when seen at night silvered by the clear moonshine.   Nothing
can be wilder and more bizarre and grotesque than the shapes this tree
assumes.

   * The flowers that have been trodden under foot by day in the *Corso*,
leave at night a faint, sickly, but not unpleasing, odour in the streets,
—a kind of smell of green fields, which lasts for more than one night
after all is over.

Ye early-gather'd innocents, fresh, gladsome, earth-born
    flowers,
Your fate was good, as late ye died, to wreath those
    glorious hours.

As ceased the twinkling fires of the *Moccaletti* quaint,*
So now my song must find an end with accents weak and
    faint.

---

* The custom of the *Moccaletti* is curious enough. It is the funeral
of the Carnival. Each person, at dusk, on the last day, whether in
carriage, balcony, or on foot, lights one or more little wax tapers,
which there is an universal struggle to extinguish on the part of others
with handkerchiefs, &c., with cries of *Senza moccalo*. This childish
amusement, which amongst this goodnatured and frivolous people,
though it is a kind of romp, never proceeds to mischief, presents a
magnificent *coup d'œil* as one gazes down the *Corso*, perhaps a mile
long. It is one tumult of waving, glancing lights, brilliant as
diamonds, borne by the richly-costumed crowd "*lege solutis.*" All
the balconies are hung with scarlet drapery, adding to the splendour of
the scene. On one occasion, some years past, when the Carnival, from
motives of political apprehension, was forbidden, the *moccaletti* alone
were allowed. This caused a serious tumult, the people crying that
they would not be mocked with the funeral of a Carnival that had
never been born.

GANYMEDE.

AMONG the flowers, the many-colour'd flowers,
  Young Ganymede is thoughtless straying ;
  The zephyr with his tresses playing
A fresher tint to his smooth cheek hath given ;
  And his dark eyes so mutely eloquent,
  . Are carelessly upon the blossoms bent :
    Swiftly the golden hours
Move on their noiseless path,—in the blue heaven
    Hangs not a single cloud ;
The birds sit silent in their forest bowers,
    And by the soft breeze bow'd,
The trembling willows kiss yon placid stream,
Where sportive fishes bask in the warm beam.

    Hark ! stooping from the sky
    The noise of clanging wings !
    No coming tempest sings,
    But yet the sound draws nigh.
And now an orb of brilliant light
Slowly descends—dazzling the aching sight.
 A rainbow line of many tints
  Gleams from the crimson'd west,

As when the sun through soft showers glints
  Upon a summer cloud's dissolving breast.
A heavenly fragrance is diffused around ;
  And Ganymede his lovely face upturning,
Startled by the sudden sound,
    Beholds amid that glory lambent burning,
      The immortal messenger of Jove ;
        The thunder-bearer of the skies.
    He hath descended from above
      To bear afar from mortal eyes
The beauteous object of a godhead's love.
Pillow'd on his majestic pinions,
    Lo, the blushing boy ascends !
    But a downward glance still bends
Upon his father's wide dominions ;
    And to his home and mortal friends
A mute farewell, while gush salt tear-drops, sends.
Tears never more those lustrous eyes shall dim.
    Star after star is pass'd—
      At last
Heaven's lofty portals have received him.
  On to the palace of the God,
  Along the broad ethereal road ;
A thousand spacious domes on either side
Lift their heads in glitt'ring pride,
    Spangled all with gorgeous sheen,
    Richer far than aught, I ween,
That the astonish'd youth before hath secn.
    Now the golden gate is enter'd,
      And the journey long is o'er ;
    There is every glory centred
      That heaven keepeth evermore.

Jewell'd roof, and walls, and floor,
Are shedding wide a pure effulgent light
　　Insufferably bright.
　Around the awful conclave see !
　Each enthroned Deity,
With how majestic and celestial mien ;
While on tissued seats between
Sit the fair goddesses, and their imperious queen.

Welcome, young Ganymede ! for thee a place
　　Is vacant here !
No more shall sorrow cloud thy face,
　Or anguish call into those eyes a tear.
Be thine the pleasing task that cup to fill
　Which the Immortals drain,
And listening with rapt soul to the soft strain
That rings through Heaven, forget each trivial ill
Which thou didst meet on earth ; rescued from pain,
Life's troubles shall not shade thy cheek, nor wound thy
　　breast again !

W. G. J. Barker.

CHOICE FRUIT;

OR, THE BALANCED ACCOUNT.

A TALE OF OLDEN TIME.

—◆—

Peccato occultato
E mezzo perdonato.—*Proverb.*

No foot of merry England's earth,
  I think you'll own,
  Is better known
Than that which gave my story birth.

Where Old Thamesis, with his liquid store,
En passant, deigns to bathe the busy shore
  Of suburb Surrey :
Just opposite that far famed spot,
 Where the grave senators of Britain's realm
 Laud and revile the wight who guides the helm ;
And half the year, in contest hot,
  Each other worry
With many a spleen-fraught round of party jangle ;
 Where judges, throned in magisterial ease,
 Breathe, thro' huge hills of hair, their sage decrees ;
And clients bleed, and sleek-faced lawyers wrangle,
  There stands an inn,
Alias a pothouse, where a thirsty swarm

Of watermen their stomachs cool and warm
         With beer and gin :
Where, every sultry summer Sunday's tide,
The cockney beaux and doxies, side by side,
(The flirting milliner and spruce apprentice,)
In giggling groups of dozens and of twenties,
Arrive to hire the funny, barge or cutter,
    And take a trip to Battersea,
    In board-built-bowers to sip their tea,
And romp and toy, and bolt their rolls and butter,
And scrawl their sweethearts' names upon the shutter.
    A motley group of various barks,
Yacht, wherry, steam-boat, skiff, and lighter,
    Its site conspicuously marks,
                Its sign, THE MITRE.
But why this badge episcopalian
             So oft we see,
The type of houses bacchanalian,
             Or if there be
Some mystical affinity
'Twixt drinking and divinity,
So that (like vine or bush of yore
Which symbolized each tavern door,
To show there was a tap behind it,)
The bishop's cap, where'er we find it,
Bespeaks the presence of good wine,
I will not venture to opine.

This was the place, but for the date,
I cannot, with precision, state
Day, month, or year, but trust 'twill be
Sufficient both for you and me,

That we trace back
Old Tempus' track
Five hundred years, or thereabout;
   Thus to obedient fancy giving
   The supposition that we're living,
When, on the scene I've pointed out,
Instead of bustling streets and shops,
The land was clothed with verdant crops;
'Stead of gas-lights and factories blazing,
Oxen, and cows, and sheep were grazing;
'Stead of pedestrian, cart, coach, chaise, and horse,
   Jostling, as is the present mode,
   Over a well-paved turnpike-road
     Athwart the river;
Each anxious passenger who wish'd to cross,
     Might oft'times shiver
     Some hour or more
     Upon the shore,
Shaking his purse, till he could find
Some boatman who would be so kind
As to desert his bed, or prayers, or drink,
And deign to row him to the other brink.
Here, at the early date I quote,
Peaceful, sequester'd, and remote
From the gay city's busy throng,
Embower'd the lofty elms among,
A venerable convent stood,
Full of grave brethren of the hood;
Its gardens, stretching far and wide,
And reaching to the river's side,
Were fenced around with walls so high

That none their treasures could espy.
For treasures, on my word, were there,
Which, seeing, all had wish'd to share.
    Not merely culinary roots,
And herbs, and pulse, to stew, or boil,
        Or roast, or bake,
    To grace their beef and mutton ;
    But all the most delicious fruits
Which then adorn'd the British soil,
        Enough to make
    An anchorite a glutton !
The man to whose especial care
    These precious dainties were confided,
Was one of qualities most rare,
        His name was Roger ;
        A grave old codger,
    Who long had on the spot resided,
    In a snug cot within the boundary wall,
Where he a triple avocation fill'd ;
    For, when the cherish'd trees were fruitless,
    So that his post might not be bootless,
He ran on errands, and the garden till'd.
    The convent's portly prior, Father Paul,
Was jealous of his luscious store
    As any sportsman of his game,
    Or of her gems a courtly dame,
    And, when to Roger he assign'd the charge,
        He straight began,
    In terms the most impressive, to enlarge
On watchfulness, and told him o'er and o'er,
That if by his neglect 'twas wasted,

Or if a single fruit was tasted,
      By any man,
Woman or child, except his reverend self,
      'Twould raise his ire,
And nought should screen the sacrilegious elf
      From vengeance dire!
But his emphatic exhortation
Was perfect supererogation.
Old Roger was both honest and religious:
Nay, on the latter score, somewhat fastidious;
   For, rather than e'er pass
   At work the hours of mass,
Or miss a sermon, or procession,
Or his hebdomadal confession,
He would have pray'd all day, and toil'd all night:
And, rather than have ta'en a single bite
Of the forbidden fruit, I firmly think
He would have fasted to starvation's brink!
In short, had the grave prior thought
For half a dozen years, or sought
   For fifty miles around,
   He never could have found
   A dragon better form'd for these
   Monastic male Hesperides.
Zounds! what am I about? I'm growing prolix!
Indulging in my old discursive frolics!
Well! 'tis a habit of my wayward brain;
      (I don't affect it,)
And, 'pon my credit, were I e'er so fain,
      I can't correct it!
I'm somewhat like my old friend, Peter Pindar;

For, when a story's in my sconce,
   I ne'er can bolt it out at once ;
Nor can I, for my soul and body, hinder
My muse's whim : she's like a pamper'd horse
   When first he's mounted after three days' rest,
Who, 'stead of trotting in a steady course,
   Obedient to his cavalier's behest,
Will kick, and fling, and rear, and prance,
As if he had Saint Vitus' dance !
But now the jade has had her devious caper,
       So cease your fidgets !
   For straight the subject from my mind,
   Shall, like a skein of silk, unwind,
And gradually descend upon my paper
       Along my digits !
Roger, I beg the reader to take note,—
   Albeit, I have said so much about him,—
Is not the hero of my anecdote,
   (Although it could not well proceed without him,)
So 'tis high time I should make known
That Roger did not live alone.
       He had a son ;
A sprightly, wanton, curly-pated boy,
His only child—and hope—and plague—and joy ;
       Just such an one
As oft we find, gracing a country hovel ;
Or figuring in the pages of a novel !
Now, though the ghostly prior's melting treasures
   Had no temptation for the father,
       The sportive youth,
Being more prone to gastronomic pleasures,

It must not be conceal'd, had rather
    A liquorice tooth ;
And, to purloin the dainties with impunity,
Lack'd nothing but a fitting opportunity ;
Which, rigidly as they were hoarded,
Sometimes (though rarely) was afforded.
    At length one day, when left alone,
Dad on an errand being gone,
He cull'd the richest fruit that could be found
Within the teeming garden's spacious bound ;
Spread them upon the cottage table,
And gorged as long as he was able !
But, as the axiom justly states,
      " Post gaudia luctus,"
Anglicè, the capricious Fates
      Deign to conduct us
To some luxurious, bliss-fraught treat,
And let us taste each choicest sweet ;
Then, just in our enjoyment's nick,
Salute us with a jadish kick,
Which mortifies our hearts the more
The greater were our joys before.

The feasting youth was doom'd to prove
This truth ; for luxury, who, like love,
    Oftentimes makes
      His little coteries
      Of giddy votaries
    Commit mistakes,
Ne'er whisper'd that the haunt was insecure
Till the old conservator op'd the door !

The father's eyes flash'd indignation !
The son's o'erflow'd with tribulation ;
The *first* stretch'd forth his brawny hand to seize
The *latter's* hair, who fell upon his knees !
This storm'd and vow'd he should not live !
That scream'd and pray'd that he'd forgive !
Till, after some few minutes' pother,
Threat'ning the one, and craving t' other,
The suppliant's tears disarmed his rage :
His rigid heart began t' assuage ;
And now his vampire grasp he quitted,
    Demanding, straight, a brief narration
How many times he had committed
    The sin of malappropriation :
        And said that he
        Content would be
If to th' archbishop's palace he'd repair,
And, seeking out the pious chaplain there,
        Make full confession
        Of his transgression ;
          Nor flinch
          An inch
From whatsoever penitence
Might be adjudg'd for the offence.

The urchin, still suffus'd with tears,
Endeavour'd to subdue his fears,
And, rising with angelical serenity,
Thank'd his kind father for his proffer'd lenity.
" THREE TIMES," quoth he, " my craving maw
Has tempted me to break the law ;

But now, obedient to your will,
I'll make confession of the ill,
And patiently endure whatever scourge,
To expiate my crime, the priest shall urge."

He went,—was shriven,—then sought his habitation,
And straight commenced his penal obligation.
Coarse bread and water were his diet,
Pursuant to the chaplain's fiat :
A self-inflicted flagellation
Took place of sleep and recreation :
    While, night and day,
    His debt to pay,
With Ave-Marias and Paternosters
    Both said and sung,
    The cottage rung
As loudly as the convent's cloisters !
Just when the youngster's penitence had ceased,
The honest gard'ner met the absolving priest,
And straight deplored, in terms of piteous grief
That his poor boy had THREE TIMES been a thief.
" THREE !" cried the priest.   " Hold, friend ! 'twas more !
He, at his shrift, acknowledged FOUR :
And I enjoin'd six days and nights
Of austere penitential rites,
To counterbalance the transgression,
And purchase saintly intercession."
Off at a tangent flew th' astonish'd sire,
And hasten'd homeward, almost choked with ire :
    At length, arriving at the cottage-door,
For vengeance on his offspring thirsting,

He found the criminal, his penance o'er,
  Coolly regaling, with remorseless air,
  On a fresh stock of the forbidden fare,
And, with repletion almost bursting.

" Thou worthless wretch !" the man exclaim'd,
" Art not of such base guile asham'd ?
FOUR crimes thou own'st at shriving ; but to me
Falsely declar'd thy errors were but THREE !
Nay, more : e'en now, thou gormandizing brute,
Thou'rt feeding on our master's choicest fruit ;
What canst thou say that I should not
Flay thee alive upon the spot ?"
" Hear !" cried the boy, " good father, I implore you,
While candidly I lay the truth before you.
Th' avowal which I made to you
Was, as I hope for mercy, true :
THREE were my sins,—nor more nor less,—
But, when you sent me to confess,
Such was my flurry, grief, and terror,
I call'd the number FOUR in error ;
And duly suffer'd, for that number,
Fasting, and stripes, and loss of slumber.
At length I hasten'd to reflect
How I my blunder might correct.
What could I do ?   I could not shun
Part of the penance, for 'twas done,
And for a wrong amount,
  Beyond the compass of my ill ;
  So I've just ta'en *a farewell fill*,
And BALANC'D THE ACCOUNT !

HILARY HYPBANE.

CREATION.

A FRAGMENT.

Ere first was form'd this universe and world.
  This sun, this moon, these circumambient stars,
No meteors fell, through constellations hurled ;
  No earthquakes shook with elemental jars ;
No craters rose, sear'd by volcanic scars ;
  No bursting thunders flash'd, with forked light ;
But a vast void's impenetrable bars
  Shut out each sense of hearing, feeling, sight ;
Yet there reign'd one sole will—one everlasting might !

That will went forth, and that Almighty word,
  Creative, pierced the depths of the abyss,
(Which Solitude and Desolation heard,)
  And fill'd the mystic bounds of emptiness ;
Then atoms upon atoms 'gan to press,
  Attracted through infinity of space,
And, concentrating, form'd a nucleus,
  Which gave this world solidity and place,
And then was pre-ordain'd in Heaven the human race.

Firstfruit of matter yet, this infant earth,
   Wrapp'd in the shadows of primeval night,
Offspring of darkness from its earliest birth,
   Invisible and wasted as a blight,
Proportionless in length, and breadth, and height,
   Hung shapeless, lifeless, motionless, and lone ;
God said, " Let there be light, and there was light,"
   Which on its rim opaque obliquely shone,
. Then in the absorbing gulf threw its reflected cone.

Now was this world an undigested mass,
   Confounding all things in its outward mould ;
Containing neither fields, nor trees, nor grass,
   Nor varied landscapes, beauteous to behold,
And though but just existing, it seem'd old.
   The Spirit moved and a new change came o'er,
And that which was ungenial, crude and cold,
   Was warm'd and quicken'd to its inmost core,
And the progressive marks of the Creator bore.

Condensed in clouds now gathering vapours rise,
   Subliming from the surface of the earth,
And float amidst a firmament of skies,
   To fertilize with showers the plains of dearth ;
Now cumulating waters, as a girth,
   Encircle half this globe with sparkling seas,
Giving to isles and promontories birth,
   And spread their wide dominion by degrees,
As yet unswollen by tides, or ruffled by a breeze.

In rugged majesty next mountains frown
    O'er shelving rocks and lessening lands below,
Projecting their bare sides of black, or brown,
    Ere vegetation had commenced to grow ;
Down yawning chasms now rushing torrents flow,
    Scooping their hollow channels to the deep,
And, as in scorn, their spray wide upwards throw,
    Or, murmuring at obstructions, onwards leap,
Then, strangled in the waste of ocean, silent sleep.

The Spirit moved again, and then was seen,
    Extending o'er each earth-bare hill and vale,
A springing vestiture of living green,
    And herbage universal to prevail ;
Now nodding flowers their various sweets exhale,
    And stately trees, and humbler trees of fruit
Bend their broad boughs, whose seed can never fail ;
    And bulbous plants strike their expanding root,
As yet uncull'd by man, or batten'd on by brute.

First glowing in the east, then 'gan the sun
    To tinge the fields of ether with his rays,
And round him self-revolving earth to run
    Her double course of seasons, nights, and days.
Then time commenced successive, which displays
    The rise, duration, and the end of things ;
Which, as a mother, with endearing ways,
    He rears from infancy with fostering wings,
Then, blasting them with age, to dust capricious flings.

Now o'er one half this globe the shades of night
    Impervious hung till the approach of morn,
And slow evolving to the realms of light,
    The earth, as from oblivion, seem'd new born ;
When, from some solitary cape forlorn,
    The moon shed forth her new incipient beam,
Full and as yet unchanged with shallow horn,
    Peering o'er sea, and moor, and rippling stream,
Whilst, flooding in her wake, the tides, attracted, gleam.

Scatter'd around her, as in magic trance,
    Myriads of stars her influence obey,
In her soft shade reposing, twinkling glance
    Their lustre mild, but shun the glare of day.
Now, sown with pearls, appears the milky-way ;
    And streaming comets heaven's vast concave span ;
And northern lights in coruscations play ;
    Whose brilliant rays, which strike the planets wan,
Shall awe the future mind of uninstructed man.

The great creative Spirit moved again,
    Breathing the breath of animated life ;
Prolific from each mountain, lake, and fen,
    Struggling with rival being as in strife,
When Nature labour'd with existence rife ;
    The sea cast up her fry, whose tawny fins
Cut the clear waves as with a golden knife,
    Basking from where the coast outstretch'd begins,
Till round some hollow bay its sinuous course it wins.

The forests, once so still, save when the breeze
    Brush'd them with fitful gale, are still no more ;
Now caverns, rocks, and savage wilds, and trees,
    Re-echo to the lordly lion's roar.
Poised in the air, now screaming vultures soar ;
    From some sequester'd dell the ring-dove coos ;
The massy mammoth seeks his morning store,
    Crushing the matted foliage hung with dews ;
Whilst insects through the air their busy hum diffuse.

Perfection each, imperfect yet the plan,
    Though splendour upon splendour should arise,
Without the presence and the praise of man,
    Wafted in adoration to the skies.
Blind instinct breathes, and vegetates, and dies,
    Nourish'd and mingled with its native soil,
But man's aspiring spirit upward flies,
    Scorning the grosser bonds of earthly toil,
And bounding in his rise, to heaven seeks to recoil.

The noble task was done : when forth appear'd,
    Youthful, majestic, energetic, strong,
The sire of man, by all creation fear'd,
    Of those that fly, or creep, or gathering, throng.
In his right hand he gently led along
    Woman, the mother of the human race,
God's fairest works the loveliest among ;
    Angelic sweetness beaming in her face,
And in her mien and gesture dignity and grace.

                                  W. B.

THE POST-MORTEM EXAMINATION;

OR, LIKE MASTER LIKE MAN.

AN INFERNAL STORY.

——•——

Che tu mi segni, ed io saro tua guida,
E trarrotti di qui per luogo eterno,
O'v udirai le disperate strida.
DANTE, *Inferno*, Canto I.

AMONGST the musty sentences oracular
　　(Famed for their truth and laconism)
Which decorate our tough old tongue vernacular,
　　There is a certain aphorism
Which tells us that " A mendicant,
　　When raised from the pedestrian level,"
(As if resolved to fly from want,)
　　" Will spur his palfrey to the devil : "
An adage which, from dearth of skill,
I'm now preparing to fulfil :
For, finding, spite of all my pains,
Just at this juncture, that my brains
Of mundane themes for doggerel strains
　　　　Are somewhat scanty ;
Urged by a potent, self-wrought spell,
I bid terrestrial scenes farewell ;

Mount Pegasus, and post to—(well,
I'll spare the rhyme, lest it should shock the ladies,
And Grecify the *low* expression)—Hades,
    Like Father Dante.

    Nor will the world, I trust, refuse
    Implicit credence to my muse ;
    For, when the witty Florentine
    Described, in poesy " divine,"
    His journey to th' infernal regions ;
    His gossip with Abaddon's legions ;
    The varied miseries which whelm
    Poor wretches in the gloomy realm,
        And whom he met there ;
    His downward trip was ta'en for granted ;
    No *route* or *carte du pays* was wanted :
    And not a human being cared
    Whether, in real truth, the bard
        Contrived to get there.
    If, then, the tales which Alighieri
        Brought from th' abyss
    Excite in readers' minds no query,
        Wherefore should this ?

    I hope this little introduction
    Will not produce unkind construction :
    For, *entre nous*, I shrewdly thought
    That, as my anecdote is brought
    From so profound and dark a source,
    The reader would expect, of course,
    Some explanation prefatory,

To claim his sufferance, before I
Could venture to relate the story.

But, to begin.—There lived of late
  A certain wight
  John Dubson hight :
A yeoman, who, from mean estate,
Dame Fortune's slippery hill had scaled,
Nor e'er had in his footing fail'd :
In fact, the wheel-borne, sand-blind elf,
Had bless'd him with such store of pelf,
  That not a squire
  In all the shire,
When aught was to be sold, could hope,
In bargaining, with him to cope :
And many a mother, when she press'd
Her daughter to her anxious breast,
And view'd his petted, *only son,*
Whose boyhood's race was nearly run,
Breathed a fond, fervent wish that she might catch
For her dear offspring such a splendid match.

At length, just when his hopeful heir
The name of minor ceased to bear ;
And, to *his sire's* delight, had grown
A brawny boor of thirteen stone :
When, chuckling in his sleeve, he found
His wealth on every side abound ;
His wide-spread lands, well fenced and till'd ;
His coffers nigh to bursting fill'd ;
His cellars cramm'd with choicest wine ;

His meadows stock'd with sheep and kine ;
His mews with every breed of horse
Known on the road, or field, or course,
And deck'd with carriages so gay,
They might have graced a Lord Mayor's day ;
His warm conservatories lined
With flowers and fruits of every kind,
And shrubs, and trees of choicest mark ;
His thick preserves and spacious park,
With game and ven'son well supplied ;
Swoln with repletion, gout, and pride,
   He died !

Scarce had his vital spirit flitted
To confines for its nature fitted,
When Roger Thong, his lusty charioteer,
Dropp'd, like a sacrifice, to grace his bier.
Full thirty years he'd held his driving station
   Without reproach,
And merely changed his whip by elevation
   From plough to coach ;
Ne'er envying his master's growing treasures ;
But sharing all his griefs and *all his pleasures.*

Not only during life, with firm attachment,
 He clung to him, and *those he held most dear ;*
  But, at the moment of his dissolution,
  Proved that his love had known no diminution ;
Not even tarrying to behold his hatchment,
 Or o'er his corpse to drop a pitying tear ;
But, when the farmer from the world retired,
   He, too, expired !

What caused the portly coachman's death
None knew ; for so it chanced, his breath,
Without a moment's warning, fail'd him ;
Nor gave him time to tell what ail'd him.
'Tis true, the neighbours all supposed
That when his patron's eyes were closed,
His sorrow would admit no cure ;
His gentle heart could not endure
  Such dire disasters.
Be this, however, as it may,
When disencumber'd of its clay,
His soul was book'd for Charon's wherry,
And wafted o'er the Stygian ferry,
  To join his master's.

Soon as, within the realms of night,
The coachman's met the yeoman's sprite,
Each guilty elf with conscious shame was stung,
And on each faltering, incorporeal tongue
A half-supprest inquiry trembling hung ;
So anxious each to know by what event
The other was to Pandemonium sent.

At length the master-spirit broke
The ice, and gravely thus bespoke,
  With quiv'ring lip,
  The spectred whip :—
" Roger, attend, while I relate
What doom'd me to this hopeless fate !
But first your memory I must task,
  With me to trace

Act, time, and place,
Ere we were stript of the corporeal mask.

" Doubtless you recollect full well
When first my wealth began to swell,
What festive transports fill'd my house
When first I graced it with a spouse.
You also know that many a bitter sigh
Escaped my breast, and many a tear my eye,
When Fortune, deaf to every prayer,
Refused to bless me with an heir :
        But, above all,
        You must recal
That happiest moment of my life,
        When, after years
        Of doubts and fears,
Blest by indulgent Heaven, my wife
Fulfill'd the views which made us one,
And crown'd my wishes with *a son !*
        Not even yet
        Can I forget
With what ecstatic glee and pride
The bouncing urchin first I eyed ;
        Yet this same boy,
        My earthly joy,
Became the innocent occasion
Of his poor father's condemnation.
To hoard up wealth, for *his* enjoyment,
I fondly cherish'd the employment
Of every base, dishonest wile,
Each wight less crafty to beguile :

Nay, when no other means were left,
Unblushingly I've stoop'd to theft :
In short, to tell each several way
    In which I've sinn'd,
    To raise the wind,
Would occupy a summer day.
    Let it suffice
    That in a trice,
Whilst I was heaping plum on plum,
Unconscious that my time was come,
Omniscient Heaven, enraged at my career,
Gave that voracious cormorant, Death,
A draft, at sight, upon my breath,
And, to requite my vices, sent me here !

" But, honest Hodge, it much amazes
My soul to find *you* midst these blazes :
You, who, in all our mortal time,
I ne'er knew guilty of a crime !
    Pray, what might be
    Th' iniquity
Which, at your earthly sojourn's close,
Makes you companion of my woes ? "

" Oh, sir," quoth Roger, " if a ghost could blush,
Shame and remorse my conscious cheek would flush ;
    For *my* transgressions, like your own,
    Were vastly numerous, though unknown :
Yet, 'tween ourselves, *my* peccadilloes,
    Placed 'gainst *your* faults, were mere abortions,—
    Less, in their relative proportions,

Than osier-wands to full-grown willows.
    It must, however, be confest
        That *one offence*
    By far exceeded all the rest ;
        And, only thence,
    With rueful certainty, I date
    My present miserable fate.
    Oh listen, sir, to the relation,
    And grant me your commiseration ! "

DUBSON.

Proceed, then, shade of my ex-faithful Roger,
        And you shall find
        Your master's mind
As friendly now as when on earth a lodger.

ROGER.

    The sin with which my soul is tainted
        I almost shudder at revealing ;
    Yet you so glowingly have painted
        The fondness of parental feeling,
That, to a spirit of your tender bearing,
Haply my guilt may not appear so glaring.
Know, then, that, ere my thread of life had run
Full thirty years, *I* had an ONLY SON.
    'Tis true, I used nor craft nor stealth,
        Nor neighbours of their goods beguiled,
    Like you, to gain him store of wealth ;
    Nor was such kindness of me needed,
    For *he* to great estates succeeded ;
        Yet 'twas my bane ; for that same child

Owed his existence to the heinous crime
Which doom'd his parent to this horrid clime.

DUBSON.

You!—you possess'd a son !   Alas, poor groom !
Sincerely I compassionate your doom ;
For well I know what 'tis to be removed
From the dear offspring whom we long have loved :
   And yet 'tis strange that, while on earth
     Together in the flesh we tarried,
   I heard not of this urchin's birth,
     Nor ever knew you had been married ;
Then, further still your confidence to share,
Pray tell me, Hodge, *who was your son ?*

ROGER.

YOUR HEIR !

FITZMORTE;

OR, THE SON OF THE DEAD WOMAN.

A STORY OF THE SAXON TIMES.

———◆———

The groundwork of this legend is taken from "The Treatise of Walter de Mapes, de Nugis Curialium," written in the reign of Henry II., preparing for publication, from a unique MS., by Thomas Wright, Esq., M.A. The name of "Fitzmorte" occurs in several early documents.

"NAY, Cummer, nay," said the aged crone,
    "It will surely die—it will surely die !
Though twenty were born, the first born alone
    Doth live in this fatal family :
But one, as the ancient saying tells,
Doth live to hear his marriage-bells.
Coo, my baby, coo, and smile ;
Death is near thee, and laughs the while.
Nay, Cummer, nay, though he's likely and strong,
He is not the first-born—he dies ere long.
Slumber, my baby, long and deep ;
Soon comes a longer and deeper sleep.
There—he is sleeping—now I will tell
How on this house the curse befel.
When the Bat's Tower, so old and grey,—
Where no ivy clings to the crumbling walls,

Or daisy grows, or wallflower gay,
Or nettle, or dock, or rank grass tall,
Doth ever on its dry walls wave,—
That ruin which hath not the life of a grave,
Where the lichen scarce forms ere it peels away,—
When that old tower so old and grey,
Was the keep of a castle strong and proud,
The voice of mirth in the hall was loud ;
While in ladye's bower there nestled a dove,
Gentle and meet for a Baron's love ;
Ay, long before the Norman day
Was the prime of that tower so old and grey.
Well, there lived in the castle a Baron bold,
Lord of broad lands, and of beeves, and gold ;
And when his horn blew, for right or for wrong,
His vassals mustered a thousand strong ;
And 'tis said that he led but a so-so life
While his blood was young, till he took a wife,
And oh ! that wife was a dainty thing,
Gentle, and fair as a blossom of spring.
Mind me to-morrow, Cummer, and we
Will steal up to the western gallery,
And I'll show thee her picture, that few may see.
It does not flaunt on the wainscot wall,
Amid stately dames and Barons tall—
Ay, ever of a noble port
Are those who live of the house Fitzmorte ;—
But 'tis hidden away, and deeply set,
And hath doors like an oaken cabinet.
They say no luck comes of even a peep
At this picture the family secret keep ;

But I've often thought, could I only get
Thee to go with me, I'd see it yet.
But where was I?   Oh! the Baron was wed,
And a happy life for some years he led.
If deer was hunted, or hawk was flown,
The Baron now never went forth alone ;
My ladye's palfrey, my ladye fair,
Fearless and smiling, still was there ;
And when at the feast proud guests did meet,
The dame there filled an honoured seat ;
Or, sweeping her lyre at sunset hour,
She sang to her lord in her own fair bower,
And the Baron loved her well, then why
Did the Baron frown, and the lady sigh ?
It was that a childless wife was she,—
This made them look so gloomily.
' I would I might die, and pass away,
   Could my death give an heir to my noble lord,'
Cried the dame as she roved in the woods one day,
   And the silent woods answer'd not a word ;
But when her handmaids, fear distraught,
Their mistress in the wild woods sought,
In the glade where she, by sorrow led,
Had wandered forth, lay the lady—dead !
The death-bell toll'd for the parted soul,
And the Baron wept for his ladye fair,
And when to her grave her body he gave,
He cried, ' I would fain her cold bed share ! '
        But, a hunting he did go !
        A hunting he did go !
     For the hunter gay of the olden day

Did not give way to woe.
Now once, 'twas at evening's close,
   And his merry men all outrode,
He had got—where ? why, nobody knows,—
   Neither he nor the horse he bestrode ;
And he came, as he chased a mighty boar,
To a part of his woods he'd ne'er seen before,
Where wych elms formed a mystic ring,
And there was an awful gathering.
For not a dame that in picture-frame
Did on the walls of his castle hang,
      But a measure trod
      On that woodland sod,
To the song the night-winds sang.
And not a sire of his ancestry,
Who, he thought, in the abbey hard by did lie,
Whether pictured or not,—for the story goes,
That he knew them all by their length of nose,
      But there joined the dance,
      With a solemn prance,
Like a camel's trot when the simoom blows."
Here came a note that the Saxon crone
Confessed this simile was not her own.
" Well, the Baron looked on most curiously,
While the night-winds sang right furiously ;
      And the bright moon shone,
      And the dance went on,
Like sport enjoyed luxuriously.
      Till the Baron perceived—
      He could not be deceived—
That each dame had a partner, all but one ;

And, as she pirouetted,
And solus pousetted,
That she was his darling, the bone of his bone,
The dear defunct, the gentle departed :
Like a hawk on his quarry the bold Baron darted !
Dead or alive,—a spirit or corse,—
In a moment more she was up on his horse,
The Baron behind her, away and away
Went the steed and its riders, and catch them who may ?
Whether the dance that moment broke up,
Or whether his ancestors staid to sup,
The Baron, it seemed, never thought to inquire :
He asked no questions ; he'd got his desire,
His wife back, and hearty ;—and now, Cummer, now
Comes the best of the story,—she bore him an heir ;
And when to his christening all the folks came,
She very much scandalised every one there
By vanishing—ay ! in a brimstone flame !
She was never more seen—she was never more found,
A warning it was to the country round,
For every man of family
        Of the knights of Kent
        To rest content ;
If their wives should die just to let them be.
And thus, to cut a long story short,
Came the curse on this family now called Fitzmorte.

'Twas early dawn in the midst of summer,
  When, leaving the nursery all on the sly,

The gossips twain, the crone and her Cummer,
   Stole up to the western gallery.
They'd hardly been gone half an hour from the nursery,
When a housemaid looked in, with a glance somewhat
   . cursory,
She, thinking,—as she's never tired of declaring,—
That the nurse and the child had gone out for an airing,
"Just to tidy the room," as that housemaid said,
Turned up the child in a press-bedstead,
And baby Fitzmorte was found smothered and dead.
But now, to record what the butler declares :—
Mr. Jinkins deposeth, about six o'clock
The old hags came tumbling down the back stairs—
'Twas a wonder their necks did not break by the shock ;—
That, as to the picture, 'twas all " a flam ;"
   The frame " deeply set,"
   The " oak cabinet,"
Was the cupboard in which he kept his Schiedam !
And those wicked women had broken the lock.

                      CAPTAIN JOHNS, R.M.

GENIUS;

OR, THE DOG'S-MEAT DOG.

BEING A "TAILED SONNET," IN THE ITALIAN MANNER.

———◆———

"Hal, thou hast the most unsavoury similes."
Falstaff.

SINCE Genius hath the immortal faculty
 Of bringing grist to other people's mills,
 While for itself no office it fulfils,
And cannot choose but starve amazingly,
Methinks 'tis very like the dog's-meat dog,
 That 'twixt Black Friars and White sometimes I've
  seen,—
 Afflicted quadruped, jejune and lean,
Whom none do feed, but all do burn to flog.

For why? He draws the dog's-meat cart, you see,—
 Himself a dog. All dogs his coming hail,
 Long dogs and short, and dogs of various tail,
Yea, truly, every sort of dogs that be.
 Where'er he cometh him his cousins greet,
 Yet not for love, but only for the meat,—
  In Little Tower Street,

Or opposite the pump on Fish-street Hill,
Or where the Green Man is the Green Man still,
   Or where you will :—
It is not he, but, ah ! it is the cart
With which his cousins are so loth to part ;
   (That's nature, bless your heart !)
And you'll observe his neck is almost stiff
With turning round to try and get a sniff,
   As now and then a whiff,
Charged from behind, a transient savour throws,
That curls with hope the corners of his nose,
   Then all too quickly goes,
And leaves him buried in conjectures dark,
Developed in a sort of muffled bark.
   For I need scarce remark
That that sagacious dog hath often guess'd
There's something going on of interest
   Behind him, not confest ;
And I have seen him whisk with sudden start
Entirely round, as he would face the cart,
   Which could he by no art,
Because of cunning mechanism.   Lord !
But how a proper notion to afford ?
   How possibly record,
With any sort of mental satisfaction,
The look of anguish—the immense distraction—
   Pictured in face and action,
When, whisking round, he hath discovered there
Five dogs—all jolly dogs,—besides a pair
   Of cats, most debonair,
In high assembly met, sublimely lunching,

Best horse's flesh in breathless silence munching,
  While he, poor beast ! is crunching
His unavailing teeth ?—You must be sensible
'Tis aggravating—cruel—indefensible—
  Incomprehensible.
And to his grave I do believe he'll go,
Sad dog's-meat dog, nor ever know
  Whence all those riches flow
Which seem to spring about him where he is,
Finding their way to every mouth but his.—
  I know such similes
By some are censured as not being savoury ;
But still it's better than to talk of "knavery,"
  And "wretched authors' slavery,"
With other words of ominous import.
I much prefer a figure of this sort.
  And so, to cut it short,
(For I abhor all poor rhetoric fuss,)
Ask what it is I mean—I answer thus,
  THAT DOG'S A GENIUS.

                    EGERTON WEBBE.

AD MOLLISSIMAM PUELLAM Ê GETICÂ CARUARUM FAMILIÂ

OVIDIUS NASO LAMENTATUR.

— · —

I.

Heu ! heu !
   Me tædet, me piget o !
Cor mihi riget o !
Ut flos sub frigido . . .
   Et nox ipsa mî, tum
Cum vado dormitùm,
Infausta, insomnis,
Transcurritur omnis . . .
Hoc culpâ fit tuâ
Mi, mollis Carùa,
Sic mihi illudens,
Nec pudens.—
   Prodigium tu, re
Es, verâ, naturæ,
Candidior lacte ;—
Plus fronte cum hâc te,
Cum istis ocellis,
Plus omnibus stellis
Mehercule vellem.—
Sed heu, me imbellem !
A me, qui sum fidus,
Vel ultimum sidus

TO THE HARD-HEARTED MOLLY CAREW,

THE LAMENT OF HER IRISH LOVER.

OCH hone !
  Oh ! what will I do ?
Sure my love is all crost,
Like a bud in the frost . . .
  And there's no use at all
In my going to bed ;
For 'tis dhrames, and not sleep,
That comes into my head . . .
  And 'tis all about you,
My sweet Molly Carew,
And indeed 'tis a sin
And a shame.—
  You're complater than nature
In every feature ;
The snow can't compare
With your forehead so fair :
And I rather would spy
Just one blink of your eye
Than the purtiest star
That shines out of the sky ;
Tho'—by this and by that !
For the matter o' that—

Non distat to magis . . .
Quid agis !
   Heu ! heu ! nisi tu
Me ames,
Pereo ! pillaleu !

          II.

Heu ! heu !
   Sed cur sequar laude
Ocellos aut frontem
Si NASI, cum fraude,
Prætereo pontem ? . . .
   Ast hic ego minùs
Quàm ipse LONGINUS
In verbis exprimem
Hunc nasum sublimem . . .
   De floridâ genâ
Vulgaris camœna
Cantaret in vanum
Per annum.—
   Tum, tibi puella !
Sic tument labella
Ut nil plus jucundum
Sit, aut rubicundum ;
Si primitùs homo
Collapsus est pomo,
Si dolor et luctus
Venerunt per fructus,
   Proh ! ætas nunc serior
Ne cadat, vereor,
   Icta tam bello

You're more distant by far
Than that same.
   Och hone, wierasthrew !
I am alone
In this world without you !

II.

Och hone !
   But why should I speak
Of your forehead and eyes,
When your nose it defies
Paddy Blake the schoolmaster
   To put it in rhyme ?—
Though there's one BURKE,
He says,
Who would call it *Snub*lime . . .
   And then for your cheek,
Throth 'twould take him a week
Its beauties to tell
As he'd rather :—
   Then your lips, O machree !
In their beautiful glow
They a pattern might be
For the cherries to grow.—
'Twas an apple that tempted
Our mother, we know ;
For apples were scarce
I suppose long ago :
But at this time o' day,
'Pon my conscience I'll say,
Such cherries might tempt

Labello :
   Heu ! heu ! nisi tu
Me ames,
Pereo ! pillaleu !

III.

Heu ! Heu !
   Per cornua lunæ
Perpetuò tu ne
Me vexes impunè ? . . .
   I nunc choro salta
(Mac-ghìus nam tecúm)
Plantâ magis altâ
Quàm sueveris mecùm ! . . .
   Tibicinem quando
Cogo fustigando
Ne falsum det melus,
Anhelus.—
   A te in sacello
Vix mentem revello,
Heu ! miserè scissam
Te inter et Missam ;
Tu latitas vero
Tam stricto galero
Ut cernere vultum
Desiderem multùm.
Et dubites jam, nùm
(Ob animæ damnum)
Sit fas hunc deberi
Auferri ?
   Heu ! heu ! nisi tu

A man's father !
  Och hone, wierasthrew !
I'm alone
In this world without you !

III.

Och hone !
  By the man in the moon !
You teaze me all ways
That a woman can plaze ;
  For you dance twice as high
With that thief Pat Maghee
As when you take share
In a jig, dear, with me ;
  Though the piper I bate,
For fear the ould chate
Wouldn't play you your
Favourite tune.
  And when you're at Mass
My devotion you crass,
For 'tis thinking of you
I am, Molly Carew ;
While you wear on purpose
A bonnet so deep,
That I can't at your sweet
Pretty face get a peep.
Oh ! lave off that bonnet,
Or else I'll lave on it
The loss of my wandering
Sowl !
  Och hone ! like an owl,

Coràm sis,
Cæcus sim : elcleu !

IV.

Heu ! heu !
  Non me provocato,
Nam virginum sat, o !
Stant mihi amato . . .
  Et stuperes planè
Si aliquo manè
Me sponsum videres ;
Hoc quomodo ferres ?
  Quid diceres, si cum
Triumpho per vicum,
Maritus it ibi,
Non tibi !
  Et pol ! Catherinæ
Cui vacca, (tu, sine)
Si proferem hymen
Grande esset discrimen ;
Tu quamvis, hìc aio,
Sis blandior Maio,
Et hæc calet rariùs
Quam Januarius ;
Si non mutas brevi,
Hanc mihi decrevi
(Ut sic ultus forem)
Uxorem ;
  Tum posthâc diù
Me spectrum
Verebere tu . . . elcleu !

FATHER PROUT.

·Day is night,
Dear, to me without you !

IV.

Och hone !
    Don't provoke me to do it ;
For there's girls by the score
That loves me, and more.
    And you'd look very queer,
If some morning you'd meet
My wedding all marching
In pride down the street.
    Throth you'd open your eyes,
And you'd die of surprise
To think 'twasn't you
Was come to it.
    And 'faith ! Katty Naile
And her cow, I go bail,
Would jump if I'd say,
"Katty Naile, name the day."
And though you're fair and fresh
As the blossoms in May,
And she's short and dark
Like a cold winter's day,
Yet if *you* don't repent
Before Easter,—when Lent
Is over—I'll marry
For spite.
    Och hone ! and when I
Die for you,
'Tis my ghost that you'll see every night !

S. Lover.

THE SON TO HIS MOTHER.

—•—

THERE was a place in childhood that I remember well,
And there, a voice of sweetest tone bright fairy tales did
tell ;
And gentle words and fond embrace were given with joy
to me,
When I was in that happy place, upon my mother's knee.

When fairy tales were ended, "Good night !" she softly
said,
And kiss'd and laid me down to sleep within my tiny
bed ;
And holy words she taught me there,—methinks I yet
can see
Her angel eyes, as close I knelt beside my mother's knee.

In the sickness of my childhood, the perils of my prime,
The sorrows of my riper years, the cares of ev'ry time ;
When doubt or danger weigh'd me down, then pleading,
all for me,
It was a fervent pray'r to Heaven that bent my mother's
knee !

And can I this remember, and e'er forget to prove
The glow of holy gratitude—the fulness of my love?
When thou art feeble, mother, come rest thy arm on me,
And let thy cherish'd child support the aged mother's
    knee!

SAMUEL LOVER.

SONGS AMONG THE WINE-CUPS.

—•—

I.—THE OLD TIME IN CYMRI.

FOR titles, let others go wrangle and grieve,
    For their rights let plebeians shout,
For office, the statesman our joys here may leave,
    We care not who's in or who's out.
Save the *in* and the *out* of our own merry flask,
    On nought else we rejoice or complain ;
And when the wine's out we but then simply ask,
    That it soon may be in, boys, again.

As for titles and office and dignities fair,
    I have never yet heard of a clime,
Which, in its arrangements for these, could compare
    With sweet Wales in the good olden time ;
When the maker of mead was a chief in the land,*
    And rank'd before parson and proctor,
Quaff'd his cup with the King, kiss'd the court-maidens,
      and
    Was a twice better man than the doctor.

* The mead-maker was the eleventh person in dignity in the Courts
of the ancient Princes of Wales ; and he took place according to the
degree of precedence noted above.

And even for monarchs, like him was there one
   Who ever o'er mortals held sway,
And could boast that his own jolly brother, the sun,
   Beheld him light-hearted each day ?
Of Excise he had none, and of Customs no need,
   All his tribute, throughout the year long,
Was the right first to broach every fresh cask of mead,
   And have sung to him every new song.*

Ah ! those were the measures, and those too the men,
   That were worth, if aught were worth, dispute ;
For wine ran in streams, like full rivulets, then,
   And the spirit of song was not mute.
Yet, still we'll despair not, since we too have laugh'd,—
   Though a few of those blessings we've miss'd,—
We have ruby wine left that remains to be quaff'd,
   And still rubier lips to be kiss'd.

II.—THE TULIP-CUP.

Praise they who will the saucy vine,
  With her thousand rings and her curls so fine ;
      But I fill up
      To the Tulip-cup,
All looking as though it were bathed in wine.

---

* "There are three things in the Court which must be communi-
cated to the King before they are made known to any other person :
1st, every sentence of the judge ; 2nd, every new song ; 3rd, every
cask of mead."—*Welsh Triads.*

Ah, show me the flower,
In hall or bower,
That looks half so well as this bowl of mine !
Oh, who this night will fail to fill up
To this goblet so gay—the Tulip-cup ?

Praise they who will the willow-tree,
With her drooping neck and her tresses free,
That bend to the brink
Of the brook and drink
Of a draught that never will do for me ;
While the Tulip-cup
Is for ever held up,—
As though it could drink for eternity.
And that is the very best bowl for me,
Who like not the sickly willow tree.

The water-lily praise who will,
Of water we know that she loves her fill.
But what, pray, is she
To the Tulip we see,
Erect and steady and tippling still ?
The lily !—I think her
A mere water-drinker,
That stoops to the draught she can draw from the rill.
Then fill up to-night to the Tulip tall,
Who holds forth her cups and can drain them all.

III.—TIRADE OF THE TEUTONIC TIPPLER.

Do you ask what now glows
In this goblet of mine ?
    Wine ! wine ! wine ! wine !
To the stream, do you ask,
Shall my cup-bearer go ?
    No ! no ! no ! no !
Let water its own frigid nature retain.
As water it is, let it water remain.
Let it ripple and run in meandering rills,
And set the wheels going in brook-sided mills.
In the desert, where streams do but scantily run,
If so much they're allow'd by the thirsty old sun,
There water may be, as it's quaff'd by each man,
Productive of fun to a whole caravan.
    But ask what now glows
    In this goblet of mine.
      Wine ! wine ! wine ! wine !
    To the stream, do you ask,
    Shall my cup-bearer go ?
      No ! no ! no ! no !
Yes, water, and welcome !—in billows may rise
Till it shiver its feathery crest 'gainst the skies ;
Or in dashing cascades it may joyously leap,
Or in silvery lakes lie entranced and asleep ;
Or, e'en better still, in full showers of hope,
Let it gaily descend on some rich vineyard's slope,

That its sides may bear clusters of ripening bliss,
Which in Autumn shall melt into Nectar like this—
    Like this which now glows
    In this goblet of mine ;—
        Wine ! wine ! wine ! wine !
    No attendant for me
    To the river shall go,—
        No ! no ! no ! no !
Let it bear up the vessel that bringeth us o'er
Its freight of glad wine from some happier shore ;
Let it run through each land that in ignorance lies,
It the heathen will do very well to baptize.
Yes, water shall have every due praise of mine,
Whether salt like the ocean, or fresh like the Rhine.
Yes, praised to the echo pure water shall be,—
But wine ! wine alone, is the nectar for me.
    It is that which now glows
    In this goblet of mine,—
        Wine ! wine ! wine ! wine !
    No attendant for me
    To the river need go,—
        No ! no ! no ! no !

J. D.

THE END.

JAN   1918

BRADBURY AND EVANS, PRINTERS, WHITEFRIARS.